WITHDRAWN
University of
Illinois Library
at Urbana-Champaign

GENERAL
WORLD ATLASES
IN PRINT
1972–1973

GENERAL
WORLD ATLASES
IN PRINT
1972–1973

A COMPARATIVE
ANALYSIS

Compiled by
S. Padraig Walsh
Author of *General Encyclopedias in Print*

R. R. BOWKER COMPANY
New York & London
A Xerox Education Company

XEROX

Published by R. R. Bowker Co. (A Xerox Education Company)
1180 Avenue of the Americas, New York, N.Y. 10036
Copyright © 1973 by Xerox Corporation
All rights reserved. Reproduction of this work,
in whole or in part, without written permission
of the publisher is prohibited.
Printed and bound in the United States of America

Library of Congress Cataloging in Publication Data

Walsh, James Patrick, comp.
  General world atlases in print.

  Includes bibliographies.
  1. Atlases—Bibliography—Catalogs. I. Title.
Z6028.W27   1973   016.912   72–13053
ISBN 0-8352-0562-2

ISSN 0000-0337

016.912
W16g
1973
cop 3

REFER

CONTENTS

PREFACE

General World Atlases in Print was first published in 1966 to meet the need for a concise yet comprehensive guide to all available general world atlases in the English language. Prior to 1966 there existed no one source of full and up-to-date information on every title in print, although separate reviews of many, especially the larger and more important works, could be found in a variety of review media, the major examples of which are the American Library Association's *Booklist and Subscription Books Bulletin,* the *Wilson Library Bulletin,* the *Library Journal,* and a number of other professional journals. No one publication was available, however, which brought all this essential data together in one convenient and updated format.

General World Atlases in Print was created expressly to meet this need, by gathering together all the scattered information, critical reviews, and general articles; maintaining the material up-to-date; and presenting it in a comparative format by analyzing each atlas within a carefully developed set of standard and uniform evaluative criteria. In the first edition of 1966, the survey dealt with 28 major atlases and 21 minor atlases (i.e., works retailing at less than $9.00). In the second edition, published in 1969, the survey again covered 28 major atlases but increased its coverage of smaller works to 34. Many changes have taken place since then, with several new titles appearing on the market while, at the same time, a substantial number of titles have also been discontinued. Compounding the problem a little more is the fact that a considerable number of atlases are now appearing under two or more titles, sometimes at a wide variation in cost.

In this new and substantially enlarged fourth edition, *General World Atlases in Print* has greatly extended its coverage to deal with 40 major atlases and almost 100 smaller atlases which retail at less than $7.50 in the United States or at £2.50 or less in the United Kingdom and other English-speaking countries.

During this same period, *General World Atlases in Print* has grown from a modest paperbound booklet of 61 pages to more than 200 pages packed with vital information about almost every general world atlas in print which is (a) published in the United States or the United Kingdom, and this includes foreign-made atlases which have been imported and adapted or translated to meet the map reference needs of English-speaking users, and (b) in the category of general world atlases as distinct from special-purpose atlases.

The purpose of *General World Atlases in Print* has been, and will continue to be, the provision of a practical guide in the choice of a general-reference world atlas. As such, it is directed mainly to the average or non-specialist user, but it is hoped that it will serve equally well librarians, educators, professional cartographers, and specialist geographers.

The information presented, together with the statistical data for each title, is as accurate and as current as it has been possible to compile, and has been assembled from the information provided by all the major map-making firms in the United States and the United Kingdom, and by the publishers, where these differ from the actual manufacturer. In a number of instances, especially for new titles, detailed questionnaires were submitted to the publishers to ensure complete accuracy. Without exception, answers were provided in detail with courtesy and promptness. Again, almost without exception, review copies were made available for a detailed physical examination. This commendable and greatly appreciated co-operation, assistance, and advice has enabled a number of improvements to be implemented in this edition, and the end result is a much improved and enlarged survey of all current world atlases.

Although *General World Atlases in Print* is, in the main, restricted to the more expensive world atlases of a nonspecialized nature, we have also included a considerable number of smaller atlases of a relatively inexpensive nature, and these are described briefly in Appendix A. Additionally, in Appendix B, the compiler has listed several large or medium-sized atlases which have discontinued publication within the past 20 years. Technically, these are not atlases in print, but they may still be encountered in discount and secondhand bookstores, and there is always the possibility that these may be revised and reissued at some future date, or the titles may be used for different works.

The prices quoted herein are the lowest at which the various atlases can be purchased through normal retail outlets and have been verified as correct at the time of going to press. Inevitably, due to the ever-increasing costs of production, these are subject to change by the publishers at any time and it is always wise to check these before actual purchase, especially if the difference is considerable. Note, however, that some atlases are available in a variety of better quality bindings at higher prices although the actual contents may be identical. Some atlases are also published under more than one title and there may again be a wide margin in price in such instances. Further complicating the price range is the fact that some atlases can be purchased at a considerable discount when acquired in a package or combination deal with encyclopedias, dictionaries, and other reference works or sets of books. All such variations, where known, are clearly specified with the pertinent titles, with or without qualifying comments. Not given in this survey, however, are the costs of special text editions which are normally available only to libraries, schools, and other educational institutions at special rates or liberal discounts.

Part I: GENERAL INFORMATION

CHOOSING AND USING
AN ATLAS

1. DEFINITION AND PURPOSE OF AN ATLAS

Basically, an atlas is a collection of maps representing different regions of the world on a fairly uniform scale, preferably preceded by an adequately detailed table of contents (including the scales for each map), and followed by an equally adequate index which should facilitate the location of every place or feature contained on the maps. It is a combination of graphic and verbal geographic information: the collection of maps representing the graphic medium, and the table of contents and the index the verbal medium. Most of today's atlases, and certainly all of the best ones, adhere to this basic format, but the majority now also contain varying amounts of additional information, some of which is useful, but some of which is best described as padding for sales purposes. Examples of the more useful additional material are thematic and special-purpose maps, studies in map projection methods, explanation of the scales used, and instructions on how to read and use maps. Less useful although perhaps interesting are such items as historical maps; guidebook and tourist information; tables of social, economic, and political data; forms of government; major products; population statistics; illustrations and text on places of interest; material on space activities; and business forecasts. In this latter category of material, probably the most useful is that on the new science of space exploration and on the use of artificial satellites, which have opened up whole new avenues of geographic information by revealing former inaccuracies in the mapping of the earth.

There are, of course, different types of atlases. The most important is the so-called general-reference atlas, which is the only type dealt with in this survey. Many atlases, however, do not fall into this category, but are designed to deal with a special topic such as history or economics, or with one particular part of the world. At the same time, most general-reference atlases do contain additional maps which are specialized in content, and these vary widely from atlas to atlas. The selection of such additional maps is the responsibility of the atlas editor and is made in keeping with his ideas as to what is most important in understanding the surface of the earth. There is no standard formula for the selection of such specialized maps, but the most often encountered and therefore probably the most useful are those showing soils, natural vegetation, climate, population distribution, languages, religions, standards of living, energy production, major products, and land use. The choice is wide, however, and an atlas editor has to take great care not to overload a general-reference atlas with specialized maps which would be better dealt with in a thematic or special-purpose collection of maps. For these and other reasons an atlas is a very special tool. It will look like a conventional book but is much more than that. A well-made atlas can be, and often is, a creative achievement, a work of art.

Modern living requires almost everyone, young and old, to use atlases to find places, to follow news events, or simply to learn about the world in general. This has been particularly noticeable in the past decade or so, during which there has been a measurable and significant increase in the audience of nonspecialists who are eager to use maps in a variety of ways, be it for business, for administrative reasons, for travel, for school and college use, or simply for enjoyment. The beauty of a well-made atlas can indeed bring a great deal of pleasure to its users. In any event, the use of an atlas is essential to a thorough understanding of the world in which we live, but before it can be used, it must be understood. Providing a basis for that understanding is the purpose of this publication.

2. WHAT AN ATLAS SHOULD COST

There are literally hundreds of general-reference world atlases now available, ranging in price from a few cents up to one hundred dollars or more. Some of the very low-cost atlases do, of course, provide some quite useful information but, as with almost everything else in modern society, the less the cost, the less the atlas will provide really adequate data. Most of these smaller atlases, it should be noted, are abridged from much larger works by the same publisher or cartographic manufacturer. These abridgments usually follow one of two courses: (a) an actual reduction in the physical size is implemented although all or most of the original material will be retained; or (b) more commonly there will be a reduction in the number of pages or maps by either omitting or abbreviating some maps, reducing the number of index entries, or omitting or reducing tables of information or illustrative material. More rarely a combination of both methods will be encountered. Occasionally, the remaining material may be rearranged to create the impression that it is an entirely different work, and frequently the abridged or reduced versions will be printed on lower quality stock or bound in flimsier covers. Irrespective of the method of abridgment, however, the original quality of the atlas is inevitably affected detrimentally in varying degrees. Very rarely, and this applies only to padded premium atlases containing a great deal of nonatlas material, is an improvement effected.

How much, then, should be paid for an atlas? Bear in mind that an atlas is a very special kind of work which is enormously expensive to produce and that for a very small expenditure you will not get much. At the present time you can be sure that very little indeed can be purchased for less than $2.00 (or 50p) and not much more for less than $5.00 (£2.00). Quality and quantity improve from there, but based on the works analyzed in this survey, the price one must expect to pay is a minimum of $7.50 (or £ 2.50) for a worthwhile general-reference atlas. Although the best purchase is, or should be, the largest and most expensive atlas which can be afforded, such an atlas is not necessarily the best or the most suitable for the purchaser's individual map reference needs. It should also be borne in mind that atlases in the same price range are sometimes poles apart in quality or they may serve quite different audiences. Keep in mind also that some otherwise good, moderately priced atlases are too frequently available in a variety of expensive bindings which greatly inflate the cost of the work. This gimmick does not enhance the basic value of the atlas as a source of geographic reference, although its physical appearance may be much improved. Atlases which are offered at a discount in combination with encyclopedias, dictionaries, or similar subscription book items can sometimes be a real bargain, however, especially if the accompanying works are of a useful nature and are of acceptable quality. To sum up, the best atlas to buy is the one you can best afford, providing that it is a work of high quality and suitable to your needs. Guidance in this respect is provided in the statistical table Atlases in Order of Cost, which includes individual ratings to clearly differentiate quality.

3. PURPOSE AND AGE SUITABILITY

As with most reference books, atlases are usually geared to a specific age group or designed for a specific purpose. This automatically limits their usefulness outside their intended audience. Of course, it must be borne in mind that age-group categories are necessarily very general; an individual's needs may well cross the boundaries of a book in his suggested age group. However, in broad terms, atlases can be broken down into four arbitrary categories or age groups as follows:

1. Advanced reference atlases. Almost invariably the largest and most detailed, these are the atlases for the specialist or the more advanced user, and those always found in library reference collections. Younger students would begin using them from about the age of 15.

2. Intermediate school and college atlases. These, although quite comprehensive, will not be as detailed as those in the first category and should be easier to use. For this reason, younger students will be able to use them from the age of about 12, and they will also be more common as home atlases.

3. General-purpose home and desk atlases. As with those in category two, they will be suitable for use by students from the age of 12 through college. As a general rule these are also likely to be more encyclopedic in character than the purer atlases of the first two categories. As such they will be more popular and thus more favored for all-round family use.

4. Atlases for children and elementary schools. By far the greater majority of these will be quite small and inexpensive works with a minimum of detail and relatively simple maps which will be readily comprehended by children between the ages of 7 and 12.

In the case of an atlas for general family use the most appropriate choice will be one which caters to the widest possible range of interests, but the serious student, the advanced user, and libraries will be better served by the more comprehensive and specialized atlases which require more than an elementary grasp of map-reading skills. Elementary school students should, of course, confine themselves to those atlases which fall within their range of comprehension and move on to the more advanced works as their understanding increases. As a general rule of thumb, atlases for younger children should be confined to relatively simple maps with a minimum of detail, political boundaries, and physical features, but with as much explanatory text as is appropriate to the understanding of maps without turning the atlas into a geography textbook. Desirable features at this level would be a description of map projections and scale, an explanation of the most important map symbols, and instructions on how to read maps and use atlases, all written in simple terms. At the other end of the scale are the highly detailed large-scale atlases which cover the entire world in meticulous detail. In these, explanatory material will be reduced to a minimum on the premise that the user is already well versed in the reading and use of maps.

In between the two extremes are what may be loosely termed the general-purpose or popular atlases, the works most likely to be acquired by the average user. They can be divided into two distinct categories: the intermediate-sized, medium-priced atlas which bridges the gap between the elementary and advanced works; and the encylopedic-type atlas, which is usually an atlas in the intermediate range but augmented by varying quantities of general subject matter which will appeal to a wider family audience—the "all things for all ages" type of atlas. Several atlases will, of course, overlap in terms of purpose or age suitability, especially at the intermediate level. For this reason a Suggested Age Suitability Chart (Part III: Statistical Tables) has been compiled, which lists atlases retailing at $7.50 (or £2.50) or more in one of these categories. At best, however, this is an arbitrary listing and is provided as a guide rather than a definitive categorization of the individual works.

4. AUTHORITY

Perhaps the most important criteria in determining the worth of an atlas or, for that matter, any type of reference book, are the qualifications, competence, and reputation of the editors, compilers, cartographers, contributing specialists, and last, but by no means least, the publishers. In most instances a good atlas will be only too ready to indicate the competence of its editors, cartographers, and others primarily responsible for the work, by listing these in detail together with their special and/or unique qualifications. The absence of any such list, however, does not necessarily denote a lack of authority or a lowering of standard, as most of the best-known and most well established firms such as Rand McNally, Hammond, and the National Geographic Society in the United States, and John Bartholomew, George Philip, and the Oxford University Press in the United Kingdom, have their own permanent and often unnamed special staffs of expert cartographers. Even in the most outstanding atlases, such as the *Times Atlas*, these are not listed. Where the cartographic firm is not known, however, it is certainly advisable to check on their reputation and integrity through a public library, but care must be taken at the same time not to confuse the publisher per se with the actual map makers. It is by no means uncommon, for example, for trade publishers, whether they be well known, long established, and reputable concerns, or relative unknowns, to arrive at an arrangement with the actual map makers to publish a collection of maps under their own imprint, and sometimes even under a quite different title from the original. The reputation of the publishers is thus sometimes only a relative rather than a positive check, and even the most reputable publishers often offer a range of atlases which can vary quite widely in terms of quality as well as cost. Overall, however, caution should be exercised when either the actual publisher or the map makers, or both, are not immediately recognized as reputable concerns of long standing. No publisher or map maker worthy of the name is likely to object.

5. ACCURACY AND UP-TO-DATENESS

It seems superfluous to state that an atlas must be accurate and up-to-date, but it is an astonishing fact that a considerable number of atlases over twenty years old are still in common use, presumably on the false premise that there has been little change in the world since the political upheaval following the end of the Second World War. In fact, however, although physical changes per se may be minimal, there have in the past decade alone been, according to Caleb Hammond, more than 5,000 geographic alterations or political changes, all of which necessitated page changes. This ever-fluctuating political, social, cultural, and economic pattern of the world requires that atlases be revised and updated at frequent intervals. It has been estimated that, on the average, an atlas can well decline in up-to-dateness at a rate of from 4 percent to 5 percent per annum. Atlases, however, are unique works of reference with unique problems, and constant revision is by no means an easy or inexpensive task. The better atlases, certainly, do keep abreast of current geographic developments by maintaining a policy of either continuous (usually annual) revision or the issuance of new editions at frequent intervals. Such a policy is particularly necessary when the atlas provides supplementary material such as population statistics, economic, political, and social data, and other material which is subject to a considerable degree of change. Always a good guide to the up-to-dateness of an atlas is the copyright date on the verso of the title page (sometimes on the maps also) which indicates that there has been sufficient change in the contents to warrant a new copyright. Note, however, that an atlas may also be reprinted with or without corrections, and this reprinting date may also appear on the verso of the title page. This does not constitute either a completely revised new edition or a substantial change in the contents. Such reprintings may also be accompanied by a new and different format which will further the illusion that it is a new or different work. A sound and well-tried check on currency which can be self-applied is to look up the entry for a country or place which has recently changed its name or political status. There are many more of these each year than is commonly realized.

6. TYPES OF MAPS

A considerable number of atlases, including those of relatively modest size, provide a wide variety of maps. However, unless it is a special-purpose atlas, with which this survey is not concerned, an atlas will be comprised of one basic series of maps which will be either physical or political or, as is becoming more common, a blend of the two with one subordinate to the other. In the larger atlases certainly, and frequently in quite small atlases, these will be supplemented by thematic, special-purpose, distribution, resource, relief, and historical maps. Political maps, as such, are restricted to the delineation of state, province, and country boundaries, and smaller administrative divisions. They do not show physical features such as mountains, but may or may not map man-made features such as roads and railroads. Physical or topographic maps, on the other hand, are primarily concerned with the representation of the natural physical features of the earth, and political boundaries and divisions are relegated to a secondary role or even omitted completely. Frequently, however, and this is becoming more and more the practice, the two basic types of maps are skillfully welded together to represent mainly the physical features with as much detail of a political nature as possible, or alternatively, the maps are basically political with only the most important physical features represented in detail. It requires a high degree of cartographic skill to blend the two basic series of maps into a composite whole. Badly done, they can be cluttered with too much detail, but well done, they can be quite beautiful. Special-purpose or thematic maps are now an integral but secondary part of all larger atlases, and of smaller school and college atlases. These special maps, which are usually drawn on a small scale, are designed to illustrate, in a cartographic format, such useful information as population distribution, industries and manufactures, climate and rainfall, natural vegetation, livestock distribution, religions, and languages. Historical maps are yet another example of special-purpose maps found in some atlases, designed to depict the historical development of the world, or parts of it, from the earliest times to the present day. In recent years there has also arisen an increasing interest in'the activities of man in space, and many atlases now include sections on the universe, the solar system, the moon, etc., and maps or charts on these related subjects are rapidly gaining acceptance as a part of general world atlases. Many atlases, especially those on a large scale, also provide special inset maps. Usually these are special maps of conurbations, major cities, and industrial regions of major importance, but the insets are also used on occasion to indicate economic activity or other special interests.

7. BALANCE, SCOPE, CONTENTS, AND ARRANGEMENT

The true measure of the worth of an atlas lies in the fullness and uniformity of its geographic information. Ideally it should present information without allocating disproportionate attention to the country of origin. Rarely, however, is this the case. Most American-originated atlases, for example, will devote more attention and space to North America and to the Western Hemisphere than they will to other parts of the world. Conversely, atlases which originate in Europe will tend to deal with European countries in greater detail than the Americas. This bias, although barely noticeable in some instances, applies to even the best and relatively well-balanced atlases. Based on an examination of the five leading world atlases, the following table indicates the approximate average amount of space which has been allocated to the main regions of the world:

AREA	APPROX. % OF TOTAL PAGES
North America	20 to 25
Europe	16 to 21
(or about 41% between the two, depending on the country of origin)	
Asia	18
Africa	10
U.S.S.R.	7
South America	6
Australasia	5
Central America	3
Other areas of the world	10

The order of arrangement will, inevitably, vary from atlas to atlas according to the policy of the editors and publishers, but the presentation should be logical and orderly and certainly, no matter what the arrangement in between, it should be prefaced by a well-detailed list of contents and concluded with as comprehensive an index as possible. As a general rule, although this is by no means inflexible, the arrangement follows the pattern of dealing first with the universe, then the world as a whole, proceeding from the country of origin, continent by continent, to the point farthest away. Atlases, however, are especially susceptible to the whims of the editors and publishers, and will vary so much in both content and arrangement that almost any order, be it logical or seemingly haphazard, may be encountered. Ideally, but rarely achieved, an atlas should consist of: (a) a well-detailed list of contents, preferably in an easily understood arrangement, and certainly showing the scale at which each map is drawn; (b) a relatively brief preface explaining the purpose of the atlas and how best to utilize it; (c) an explanation of map projections and scale; (d) a well-detailed list of map symbols; (e) an adequate representation of the earth on as large a scale as the page size permits and of a uniform and well-balanced nature; (f) a glossary of geographic terms and abbreviations; and (g) a comprehensive index of all the places and features on the maps, preferably with their latitude and longitude.

8. SUPPLEMENTARY MATERIAL

Several of the larger atlases contained in this survey contain special additional material in various forms, such as illustrations; guidebook or tourist material; tables of comparative geographic data; road, rail, and air distance tables; steamship and airlines routes and distances; star charts; space activity supplements; forecasts of economic conditions; political, social, and economic data; historical and Bible atlases; environmental supplements, and in at least one instance, a list of American colleges and universities. Some of this supplementary material is useful and even desirable in a general world atlas, especially one designed for home use, but unfortunately, there are quite a number of atlases at the present time which tend more and more to pad the volume by the inclusion of material which is nonessential or even, in rarer instances, of an ephemeral or nonatlas character that is of little or no real practical value. Not only is such information better sought in other and more specialized sources, but the inclusion of such material will, inevitably, inflate the cost of the basic atlas, sometimes to an absurd and unjustifiable extent. Occasionally, but this is the exception rather than the rule, an atlas will be enhanced by its marriage to another work, especially one which is designed for all-round family use. Purchasers should, however, carefully study and assess the worth of such additional material in the light of their own requirements.

9. METHODS OF PROJECTION

The curved surface of the earth cannot be shown on a flat surface without some degree of distortion. Obviously, the smaller the scale at which a map is drawn, the greater this degree of distortion, and conversely, the larger the scale, the less the map will be distorted. This serves to reemphasize the desirability of acquiring an atlas which maps the entire earth on as large a scale as is feasible within its physical limits. This is clearly illustrated in even the largest atlases which, at one stage or another, map large areas of the world in which, inevitably, the distortion is considerable. There is no simple answer to this cartographic problem and although there are literally hundreds of ingeniously designed methods of projection in everyday use, no single one shows the mapped area truthfully. For this reason the user will find in most atlases that a wide variety of projections has been employed, the most common of which is the so-called equal area projection, but each of which is considered to be the most suitable for a particular map. The serious atlas user needs to make himself conversant with these methods of projection if he is to make full use of the maps, and a good atlas will cater to this need by providing an adequate explanation of the methods of projection used. Moreover, the projection used should be clearly stated on each map. There are atlases which do not do so.

10. FORMAT AND SCALE

Obviously, the larger the atlas, the easier it should be to use, although this in itself is not synonymous with quality. The page sizes given in this survey are the actual single page sizes but, as some atlases spread their maps over two facing pages, these sizes are not necessarily indicative of the true span of an atlas, and can be misleading. In most atlases, additionally, a margin is left between the map border and the actual page edge, which further reduces the actual size of the map. In other atlases, maps are bled to the edge of the page, utilizing the available space to its maximum, although this is a disadvantage if the atlas needs to be rebound at a later stage or if it gets heavy use and page wear.

Scale is very important, but the average user is probably apt to pay little attention to this or even to ignore it entirely as an incomprehensible mathematical equation, although it is in fact a relatively simple part of a map. In simple terms, the scale of a map is its size in relation to the actual area of the world which it represents. Putting it even more simply, if the scale given on a map page is 1:3,000,000 (sometimes written 1:3M), this means that the map on the page is one three millionth the real size of the area covered. A perhaps better-appreciated explanation is that if the map user were about 500 miles out in space, he or she would be viewing the earth at a scale of 1:3,000,000. The larger the scale, i.e., the lower the fractional representation, the more accurate the map should be and the more detail it should provide. Thus, if the user were to zoom down from space to a point 50 miles above the surface of the earth, he would then be viewing it on a scale of 1:300,000 and he would be able to pick up details which were invisible at the scale of 1:3,000,000, ten times smaller or farther away. Scale, however, even in those relatively simple fractions, may still be confusing to some users.

What is usually readily understood and often makes more sense is the scale equivalent in miles per inch. Now take again the example given above of a map at the scale of 1:3,000,000. Converted into its equivalent terms of miles per inch, it means that this scale is approximately 47 miles to the inch, and a map which is drawn at the ten-times-larger scale of 1:300,000 will represent the mapped area at approximately 4¾ miles to the inch, naturally enabling a great many additional features to be included. For ease of use, a scale conversion chart has been included as an appendix in this survey, relating the various fractional scales to their equivalent in miles per inch. Usually, but not invariably, the larger the page size of an atlas, the larger the scale and the more detailed the map, but this, for a number of reasons, does not always hold true. The pages, for example, may include more than one map or provide text matter or other material in addition to the map. In such instances there can be a large page format but small-scale maps in relation thereto. Other atlases, an outstanding example of which is the *National Geographic Atlas of the World*, use large pages to their fullest extent and are thus able to show large regions at a quite large scale. Small-format atlases can, of course, map the world on a quite large scale, but to do so they must break the surface of the earth down into very small units (road atlases are a prime example), which results in an unwieldy number of separate maps.

Irrespective of whether an atlas is mapped on a large or a small scale, it is essential that every map page should clearly indicate the natural (or fractional) scale on which each map is drawn, represented by numerals. This has been a worldwide specification since 1913 and allows for comparing the scales on various maps. Preferably it should also give the equivalent (or approximate equivalent) in miles per inch (or kilometers per centimeter). This is frequently implemented in American atlases, but is less common in atlases originating elsewhere. Clearly visible also should be the bar scale, a bar divided in terms of both inches and kilometers to represent distances, the only accurate method of determining distance when a map has been enlarged or reduced. Ideally the entire earth should be mapped on as large and as equal a scale as possible. This, however, is an impractical proposition as it would take literally dozens of volumes to implement. For this reason map scales within an atlas will vary considerably. Most map makers follow the practice of mapping the most important areas of the world at as large a scale as possible and allocate smaller scales progressively to the less important regions. For example, a large-scale map of the British Isles is desirable because of its detail and density of population, whereas a map of the Sahara Desert at the same scale would be almost meaningless. Nationalistic tendencies are another important factor in determining scales, and both American and European atlases can be faulted on these grounds. American atlases seem especially prone to this as several of them allocate an entire page to each of the fifty states of the United States, while at the same time limiting other equally important but larger areas of the world to the same page limit. Texas, for example, is likely to be allocated a full page, but so may Ohio, which is much smaller in area. Again, the state of Delaware may be given a full-page coverage, but if the whole of France is contained on a page of identical size, then the scale is greatly distorted in favor of Delaware. However, if the eastern seaboard of the United States were mapped instead of just Delaware, then the scales would be relatively uniform.

11. METHODS OF INDICATING RELIEF

Various methods are used by map makers to simulate natural features on physical maps and these are frequently used in various permutations. In most atlases, especially those with basically physical maps, the most common method is by layer tinting in from six to twelve colors or by merged shading, sometimes in combination with contour lines and hill shading. Well executed, this can result in a striking three-dimensional effect. A scale of the colors used should always be provided in the page margins of each map to clearly key the elevation meanings of each color. The usual range is from green at sea level, through shades of brown for the elevations, to white for permanently snow-capped peaks. In recent years, however, attempts have been made to introduce new color ranges to break the traditional greens and browns. None of these have been successful to date, primarily because the methods of showing relief in color should always be in pleasing shades as near as possible to the natural shades of the earth, neither too light nor too dark, presenting a clear and accurate picture of the terrain. Sometimes, fortunately now the exception, the color effects are overdone, the end result being a gaudy display of garish colors. However, the tremendous advances in color printing processes during the past decade have greatly improved cartographic techniques, and the best atlases of the present time can well be regarded as works of art as well as accurate representations of the surface of the earth. These same advances in printing techniques have also seen the decline of purely political maps, although even these, when encountered, represent elevations by hachures and hill shading.

12. INDEXING

Apart from the actual maps in an atlas, the most important feature is the index, and the merit of an atlas is often weighed by the comprehensiveness of the index, or gazetteer as it is sometimes called.

Not all atlases, even some expensive works, are so equipped. This is an omission which, professionally at least, rules them out as reference works of real value, putting them at a considerable disadvantage because they cannot be properly utilized. When an index is provided it should be in one complete alphabet at the end of the maps to which it relates, but this again is not uniform practice, and there are a number of atlases available which, although they provide indexes of a sort, do so in an inconveniently broken arrangement which is confusing to the user. The top-rated atlases in this survey, without exception, provide responsibly compiled indexes comprehensive enough to locate all but the very smallest or most insignificant places or features. Indexes in some of the lesser-rated works will not only be lacking in comprehensiveness, but may also be divided into segments or sections which may or may not be found near to the countries, continents, or regions to which they relate. Too frequently, and this is especially true of American atlases, each individual state (and Canadian province) has its own separate and specific index. This requires the user to know the state or province a particular place or feature is located in before he can pinpoint its exact location. This is sometimes overcome by consolidating the separate indexes into one master index at the end of the atlas, but this, naturally, necessitates duplication of the entries, increases the size of the atlas unnecessarily, and adds to its final cost. Broken arrangements such as these do not make for ease of use, they are inconvenient, unsatisfactory, irritating, and may also be unnecessarily expensive. Indexes may also vary in that some will provide brief gazetteer information, population statistics, and other data. Others will employ different methods of place location, some by the simple letter-number grid system which locates a place or feature within a grid square of varying size, others by the much more exact specification of latitude and longitude. Some indexes include physical features, others do not. Some use the Anglicized form of spelling only, others use the official local spellings with cross-references from the more familiar Anglicized forms. Indexes do, therefore, vary quite considerably from atlas to atlas in quantity and quality, not only in the number of entries but also in the manner in which each place or feature is located, and whether additional information is or is not supplied. Ideally, an atlas index should (a) be in one complete alphabetical sequence; (b) use the official forms of spelling as used in the different countries of the world as specified by the Permanent Committee on Geographical Names (United Kingdom) and the U.S. Board on Geographic Names, with cross references from the alternative spellings; (c) include physical features as well as places with, wherever necessary, identifying abbreviations or symbols; (d) accurately refer the user to the most appropriate map page (if more than one page pertains) and, by one method or the other, the specific part of the page where the information is located; (e) preferably, although this is not quite so essential, specify the latitude and longitude. It should also be as comprehensive as possible, and obviously, the bigger the index, the better the atlas itself is likely to be. The index of the atlas, *The Times Atlas of the World,* has some 200,000 entries. Several others have well in excess of 100,000 entries, and these can be regarded as quite comprehensive. For most practical purposes, however, it is generally accepted that the most important places and features of the world will be included in an index of approximately 60,000 entries. Indexes totalling less than this become progressively less useful, but no matter how small, there should be an index, a key to the contents of the atlas. Where no index at all is provided an atlas is virtually worthless, regardless of the quality of its maps.

SUMMARY

1. What type of atlas do you need? Is it to be for casual use or brief reference use? If so, then one of the smaller intermediate atlases will probably suffice. But if yours is a growing family, then you may find that one of the smaller or intermediate atlases which includes a variety of encyclopedic information will provide a wider range of interests. Students and serious users, however, will need to acquire one of the large scholarly atlases or one of the better intermediate atlases, which include a variety of thematic or special-purpose maps.

2. How much should you spend? The simple answer is to spend as much as you can afford, but ensuring at the same time that you are purchasing quality as well as quantity. Cost alone is not a decisive factor; it must be qualified by several other criteria. You are unlikely to be able to purchase a really worthwhile atlas for less than $7.50 (or £2.50), and you should be prepared to pay as much as $20.00 and more, depending on your atlas needs.

3. Is your choice acceptable in terms of age suitability? Your selection may well be the best atlas available, but some of those analyzed herein require more than a passing knowledge of map reading and use. It would be a discouraging experience for a younger student, for example, to have an atlas thrust upon him which is beyond his present comprehension.

4. Are the atlas makers, editors, and/or publishers well known? Atlases emanating from long and well-established cartographic firms are much less prone to error, especially individual works which have been in existence for some time. New atlases from newly established concerns are more susceptible to error, and a really outstanding atlas is quite a rarity, occurring maybe only once in a decade.

5. Have you checked for accuracy and up-to-dateness? This is something anyone can do for himself. Look up a couple of remote places on the maps. Are they in the index? Reverse the process by looking up a couple of places in the index. Are they where they are supposed to be on the maps? Look up some country or place which has recently changed its name or its territorial boundaries. Is this recorded in the atlas? Is there a copyright date on the verso of the atlas's title page? If so, how recent is it?

6. What sort of maps are provided? Are they basically physical with political and cultural features, or political with some physical features? Are they reasonably well detailed, showing at the very least rivers, elevations, railroads, highways, and political boundaries? Are there any special-purpose or thematic maps? If so, how useful are they?

7. Is the atlas well balanced? Does it cover the entire world at an acceptable scale of uniformity, or does it place too much emphasis on the country of origin? Is it logically arranged? Is there a prefatory list of contents? Is there an index? Is there an explanation of the map symbols and abbreviations employed?

8. Is there supplementary material of an encyclopedic nature? If so, how useful is it? Does it add greatly to the cost of the atlas as such? Would that additional information be better sought in more up-to-date sources such as the *Statesman's Year Book*, the *New York Times Encyclopedic Almanac*, or similar inexpensive annuals?

9. Are the projections used identified on every map? Is there, elsewhere in the atlas, an explanation of map projections?

10. How big is the atlas? Do the maps cover the entire page or only utilize part of a page, together with text and/or illustrative material? Are the maps spread over two facing pages for maximum coverage? Is the scale shown on every map? If so, is it clear and easily understood? Are the scales constant throughout or a confusing mixture which defies easy comparison of different parts of the world? Does the list of contents specify the scale for each map? Is there an explanation of scale?

11. If the atlas is comprised primarily of physical maps, is the method of showing relief clear and comprehensible? Is there a color key in the map margins to the layer tints used? Are the colors used pleasing and natural to look at or are they too vivid and disconcerting? Are they too dark, obscuring detail, or too light, emphasizing secondary features?

12. Is there an index? If so, how comprehensive is it? Does it include all the places on the maps or only a selection from them? Is the latitude and longitude of each place or feature given? Are the standard forms of official spelling employed, as recommended by the U.K. Permanent Committee on Geographical Names and the U.S. Board on Geographic Names?

EVALUATIVE AIDS

Prospective purchasers are strongly advised to take the time and trouble to determine the merits or demerits of atlases under consideration by reading the careful evaluations of those titles which have appeared in such unimpeachable publications as *The Booklist and Subscription Books Bulletin*, published by the American Library Association on the first and fifteenth of each month; the *Library Journal*, also published on the first and fifteenth of each month (monthly during July and August); the *Wilson Library Bulletin* (monthly); *Choice* (monthly); *College and Research Libraries* (bimonthly); *Reference Quarterly*, and a number of other professional periodicals. Other valuable sources of information are the atlas listings in the Catalog series issued by the H. W. Wilson Company, which are compiled by authoritative panels of professional librarians, and such useful bibliographies of reference books as Winchell's *Guide to Reference Books* and Walford's *Guide to Reference Material*, all of which are accompanied by frequent updating supplements. Do not, however, look for very recent titles in these latter sources as it may take several months before they are included. It can safely be assumed, however, that except for the very newest atlases or completely new editions of older atlases, all of the top quality works have been reviewed and evaluated in most or all of the periodical media. Such reviews as have appeared, together with other relevant sources of information, are listed at the end of each analytical entry. Above all, be sure to visit your local library. Here you will find a wide variety of atlases available for use, a variety which will certainly include the best atlases currently available.

TODAY'S ATLASES: AN OVERVIEW

This overview surveys briefly the 40 major atlases presently available. It is broken down into four groups of atlases of different quality, but for a detailed evaluation and full analysis of any single work, it is essential that reference be made to the full entry in Part II. It will be seen quickly that except for the very good *The International Atlas*, produced by Rand McNally in 1969, and the good *National Geographic Atlas of the World*, all the better-quality atlases emanate from the United Kingdom and other countries in Europe. This has been reflected in the surveys by other evaluators and professional cartographers who have tended to view European-originated atlases more favorably than those produced in the United States. This has been wrongly attributed to a deficiency of skills in the United States. There is no valid reason why a super-quality atlas should not be produced in the Western Hemisphere, and this has now been proven by the publication of *The International Atlas*, which certainly ranks with the best produced anywhere. Apart from this isolated instance, and to a lesser extent, the long-established and well-thought-of *Goode's World Atlas*, the range of Rand McNally atlases is surprisingly mediocre. Both these and the atlases emanating from the New Jersey-based cartographic firm of Hammond Incorporated are noticeably imbalanced in that they all emphasize coverage of the United States and Canada. In these atlases, small states such as Delaware may occupy the same page space as, for example, the gigantic state of Texas. This policy results not only in an imbalance of coverage, but also a multiplicity of scales, rendering comparison of like areas difficult. This policy is undoubtedly due to a popular but relatively unsophisticated demand on the part of the general public and is therefore geared to sales. Now that the fine *The International Atlas* has broken with this tradition, it may well be that there will henceforth be a swing in the contents of American atlases to a more uniform treatment of the surface of the earth, with better and more detailed maps. British and European atlases also, give preferential treatment to the United Kingdom and Europe, but to a much lesser extent, certainly not on the scale of atlases produced in the United States, where as many as 50 percent of the maps may be devoted to coverage of the United States alone.

ATLASES RATED IN THE TOP QUALITY GROUP

Only four titles were considered worthy of a top quality rating in this survey, which must surely prompt the map-making firms of both the United States and the United Kingdom to reassess their atlas-making policies. Although there are four or, to be more exact, six titles in this category, there are in fact only three separate atlases, and even from these, two are closely related. Easily heading the list is the magnificent *Times Atlas of the World,* with a maximum rating of 25. This is by far the best atlas produced in the English-speaking countries and, in all probability, is the best atlas in the world in any language, despite the excellence of such great atlases as the Russian *Atlas Mira* and the Italian *Atlante Internazionale. The Times Atlas* is, of course, expensive at $65.00 (£20.00) but, where it can be afforded, is an automatic first choice for its detailed coverage of the world, the superbly detailed maps, and the massive index of 200,000 entries.

Following in second place, with a near top quality rating of 23, is the best atlas ever to be produced in the United States, *The International Atlas*, first published in 1969. International in fact as well as in name, it is the result of a unique and splendid cooperation between Rand McNally in the United States and their subsidiary in Stuttgart, Cartographic of Budapest, the Esselte Map Service of Stockholm, George Philip and Son Limited of London, and the Teikoku-Shoin Company of Tokyo. One hundred and fifteen cartographers from 14 countries are reputed to have been concerned in its compilation, and it is printed in four languages: English, German, Spanish, and French. The maps are well detailed and accurate but perhaps not as pleasing in color as those in *The Times Atlas*, and it has a fine index of 160,000 entries. At $35.00 (£13.95), it is certainly a very acceptable alternative to the top-rated work. Practically identical to *The International Atlas* is the *Britannica Atlas*, equally rated at 23 and retailing at the same price of $35.00. The only difference between the two works is the substitution of 40 pages of World Scene thematic maps in the *Britannica Atlas* in place of the 16,000-word essay "Patterns and Imprints of Mankind" in the *International Atlas*. The *Britannica* version will also be encountered as the *Compton Atlas*, which is identical in every respect except for the cover. Both the *Britannica Atlas* and the *Compton Atlas* are usually sold only in combination with the *Encyclopedia Britannica* and *Compton's Encyclopedia and Fact Index* respectively. *The International Atlas* is, of course, available through regular trade outlets.

The only other atlas judged worthy of a top quality classification is an exciting newcomer, first published in the fall of 1972. In the United States this is to be known as the *New York Times Atlas of the World*, but it will be sold simultaneously in the United Kingdom as *The Times Concise Atlas of the World*. The two editions will be otherwise identical in content. It is smaller than the other atlases in this group, with fewer maps and a smaller index of just under 100,000 entries, but it is somewhat cheaper at $35.00 in the United States and at only £7.75 in the United Kingdom. The majority of the superb maps are drawn and adapted from the magnificent *Times Atlas of the World* and, although reduced in size by about 20 percent contain the same wealth of detail and the beauty of the parent set. There are, additionally, several completely new maps, especially notable being the 15 pages of new conurbation maps of 33 cities of the world and a fine series of 40 pages of thematic maps.

ATLASES RATED ABOVE AVERAGE QUALITY

Some of the atlases in this group might well have been considered for inclusion in the top-rated group but for inadequacies of one sort or another. *The National Geographic Atlas of the World*, for example, rated 19 and a good buy at $24.50, contains a wealth of detail and has a fine index of 139,000 entries, but the maps are of a political nature only, and the scales used are far from uniform. It also contains a wealth of encyclopedic text, but this is marred by excessively flowery language. An atlas which would certainly have been included in the top quality group were it not for the fact that it is becoming badly dated in parts, is the excellent *Pergamon World Atlas*, now rated at 18. Polish in origin, it has excellent maps with great detail and a fine index of 140,000 names, but unfortunately, there are no plans for a new edition or a revised and updated reprint. It is now expensive at $49.50 (£20.00). However, there is now on the drawing board a smaller atlas based on the *Pergamon*. To be published in late 1973, it is expected to retail at about $25.00 (£7.00) and should be a useful work. It has been tentatively entitled the *Universal Reference Atlas*. Another fine atlas in its time was the *McGraw-Hill International Atlas*, now at a rating of 17. German in origin, it contains excellent physical maps and a fine index of 175,000 entries, although this was divided into two sections: the world and Central Europe. There was some emphasis on Europe in its coverage, but its biggest defect now is that the last publication date was

1964, which places it far behind the times, and it is now very expensive at $59.50.

Apart from the two *Times* atlases, the two best atlases produced in Britain are the *Oxford Atlas* and the *Atlas of the Earth* (in its subscription edition, called the *Caxton Atlas of the Earth*). Both are rated at 15, but the *Oxford Atlas*, which is a "pure" atlas with no supplementary material, is considerably cheaper at $16.50 (£4.50) than the *Atlas of the Earth* at about $35.00 (£13.95). The latter, however, is combined with a 144-page well-illustrated and well-written encyclopedia of the environment. Both atlases have a fine series of physical–political maps on a reasonably large scale, but both place some emphasis on the British Isles. The *Atlas of the Earth* has rather greater coverage than the *Oxford Atlas*, with some 40 more pages, and also a slightly more comprehensive index of 65,000 entries, compared with 50,000 in the *Oxford Atlas*. A really fine college and school atlas is the *Aldine University Atlas*, rated at 14. This is a well-executed adaptation of the British *Library* and *University* atlases published by George Philip. Rather smaller in format than the atlases described above, it measures only 11½ by 9½ in., but packs into a relatively small space a fine series of well-balanced maps of the world, an exceptionally well selected series of thematic maps, and a good index of 50,000 entries. At $8.50 (£3.75) it is an excellent value, especially for college and university courses. It is considered superior to *Goode's World Atlas*, which costs $10.95 and is rated slightly lower at 13. *Goode's* is a basic school atlas on all approved lists and has a really fine series of physical-political maps and a judicious selection of thematic maps. It is similar in several respects to the *Aldine University Atlas*, but has a few less maps, is more expensive, and has a shorter index of 35,000 entries.

The *Panoramic World Atlas*, rated 12, is published under the imprint of Hammond Inc., but is, in fact, produced in Britain. It is relatively inexpensive at $8.95 and is a very attractive work with excellent three-dimensional maps, but a somewhat limited index of 25,000 entries. *The University Atlas*, published by George Philip in London, is another very good medium-sized atlas from Britain. This has been adapted for American use and published in the United States as the *Aldine University Atlas*. Rated 12, it is a good value at about $7.50 (£3.00). It is derived directly from and is almost identical to the *Library Atlas*, also rated 12, except for the omission of 32 pages of special thematic maps. Both atlases are inclined to emphasize coverage of the British Isles and both have the same reasonably comprehensive index of 50,000 entries. For the additional 32 pages the *Library Atlas* retails at about $8.50 (£3.75). The *World Book At-*

las and the *Cosmopolitan World Atlas* can be considered together, although the *World Book Atlas* has a slightly higher rating at 11 than the *Cosmpolitan* at 10. Both are made by Rand McNally and Company, and the series of maps are practically identical. The *World Book Atlas*, however, has an excellent series of thematic maps and well-written instructions on how to use an atlas and develop atlas skills. These works have identical indexes of 82,000 entries, but both are marred by their exceptionally heavy coverage of the United States and Canada, with each state or province allocated a full page. This has resulted in an imbalance of world coverage and a bewildering mixture of scales. The maps are also less detailed than those in other atlases in this group. Highways, for example, are not shown. The *World Book Atlas* is usually sold in combination with the *World Book Encyclopedia* and is considerably more expensive at $31.20 than the *Cosmopolitan* at $19.95. Similar in some respects but very different in others is the *Ambassador World Atlas*, rated at 9. This is the third largest in the Hammond range, but represents a better value at $14.95 than its larger companion atlases, the *Hallmark* and *Medallion* world atlases (see next group). The arrangement of the Hammond atlases is exceptionally good in that it brings together all the information, map, text, and statistical tables, on any given country or state. With each map is provided an index of the country or state in question, together with such additional information as flags, area, population, etc. The maps, however, are relatively small, sometimes much smaller than the page sizes and, moreover, are divided into two separate series of political and physical maps, but the detail on each is limited, lacking, for example, lines of communication. As with the two preceding atlases there is a heavy imbalance in favor of the United States and Canada, which again results in a confusing mixture of scales which makes comparison difficult. A redeeming feature, however, is the consolidated general index of 110,000 entries.

ATLASES RATED AVERAGE IN QUALITY

The majority of the atlases in this category are of a mediocre quality. The best is considered to be the *Odyssey World Atlas*, rated 8. In fact this was one of the best atlases ever to be produced in the United States, with a good series of maps and a fine index of 105,000 entries. Originally it was available in two editions, one in a large format of 16½ by 12¼ in., the other in a *Universal* edition measuring 13¼ by 10 in. The larger work retailed at $24.95 and the smaller at $9.95, although the contents were identical. The past tense is employed in describing this atlas because the larger edition is no longer available. The smaller *Universal* edition is still being retailed, but when stocks are exhausted will be phased out of existence. A good but small British atlas is the *Concise Oxford Atlas*, which is a 20 percent reduction in page size, with some different material, from the *Oxford Atlas*. It has good but relatively small-scale maps and a reasonably comprehensive index of 40,000 entries. Rated at 7 and retailing at $8.00 (£2.50), it is a useful desk atlas for quick reference, although very British in emphasis and coverage. The *Physical World Atlas* or, in other editions, the *Advanced Atlas of Modern Geography* and the *Edinburgh World Atlas*, is rated at 8. The American edition is fairly highly priced at $14.95. It is considerably cheaper in the United Kingdom at £2.50. It comes from the famous firm of John Bartholomew of Edinburgh, which also compiles the great *Times Atlas of the World* and part of the smaller *Times Concise Atlas of the World*. It is a good medium to large school atlas in a fairly large format with clear, well-detailed physical maps, but a rather limited index of 26,000 entries divided into two sections: 24,000 world entries and 2,000 entries for the United States. The *Reader's Digest Great World Atlas*, rated at 7, retails at $17.00 (£4.50). It has some good maps and is colorful, interesting, and encyclopedic in character. The indexes, however, although totalling some 80,000 entries, are in three parts: (a) the world, (b) the United States, and (c) text. Of its 232 pages, only 90 are allocated to maps. The *Medallion and Hallmark World Atlases* are the largest and most expensive in the Hammond range. In content the works are absolutely identical, but whereas the *Medallion* is in one volume, with padded covers, the *Hallmark* is in two volumes, again with padded covers, and in a slip case. There is a wide variation in cost, with the *Medallion* (rated 6) at $24.95, and the *Hallmark* (rated 3) at $39.95. A much better value than either is the *Ambassador World Atlas*, which retains all the better features of the two more expensive works, including a good index of 110,000 entries, but omits such nonessential material as an atlas of the Bible lands and a 32-page section on the environment. Cartographically speaking, the *Soviet World Atlas* is a superb atlas, nearly equal to the *Times Atlas of the World*, with beautifully drawn maps and a comprehensive coverage of the world in a well-balanced format at a large scale. Its cartographic excellence, however, is marred by its confusing use of nonwestern place names, the wrong location of places in the U.S.S.R., which appears to be deliberate, according to a *New York Times* article (Jan. 18, 1970, 1:6). Despite the 250 pages of excellent maps, it is exceedingly expensive at $76.50 ($85.00 with index) and for these reasons is rated at 6 only. The *Premier World Atlas*, rated 5 and retailing at $14.95, is a shortened version of the popular *Cosmopolitan World Atlas,* omitting 88 pages of text and 19 pages of city plans. Otherwise, including the good index of 82,000 entries, it is identical to the larger parent volume, with the same relative lack of detail on the maps and the heavy imbalance in favor of the United States and Canada. Smaller in format, measuring 12½ by 10 in., is another Rand McNally atlas, the *Family Edition World Atlas,* which is about 20 percent reduced from the larger works. Rated at 4, it comes in two editions, a regular trade edition at $9.95 and a luxury at $12.95. Again, as with the larger works, the coverage emphasizes the United States and Canada, the maps lack detail, and are at a confusing mixture of scales. The index in this edition, of 30,000 entries, is also very much shorter. The Rand McNally *Worldmaster Atlas,* also rated at 4, retails at $6.95. This is an exact duplication of the *Family Edition World Atlas* from pages 1–247, with exactly the same faults. Completing this group are two very similar works, the *Citation World Atlas* and the *Cram Modern World Atlas,* with ratings of 4 and 3 respectively. The *Citation* retails at $10.95, and the *Cram Modern World Atlas* at $12.50. The map content of both is identical to that in the Hammond *Ambassador World Atlas,* but there is less prefatory material and a much reduced index of 25,000 entries. The *Cram Modern World Atlas* is virtually identical to the *Citation,* but adds some additional material and maps from older Cram atlases. Both are badly scaled and needlessly overemphasize coverage of the United States and Canada.

LOW QUALITY ATLASES

For one reason or another the atlases in this group are not recommended for purchase as general-reference world atlases. For example, the *Faber Atlas* is a small British atlas with a heavy emphasis on Europe. Rated 1, it retails at $8.50 (£3.50). The maps are of fair quality but the index is limited to 20,000 entries. The *Hammond Contemporary World Atlas,* also rated 1, is published by Doubleday at $12.50. In a small format it supplies 250 pages of Hammond political maps, poorly detailed, and heavily imbalanced in favor of the United States. What little merit it possesses is dissipated by the lack of a consolidated index. The *Hammond International Atlas* is a makeshift sort of atlas. It is comprised of the first 200 pages only of the *Citation* world atlas, and omits the individual maps of the United States and Canada. Except for the indexes on the map pages there is no index as such. Designed for overseas use, it retails at $6.95. The *Advanced Reference Atlas,* another Hammond publication, is a compilation of four different works. The maps in the atlas section are poorly scaled, lack detail, and are further limited by the nonavailability of an index. For the retail price of $7.50 it represents poor value. The *Illustrated Encyclopedia Library World Atlas* (or *Hammond Illustrated Family World Atlas*) is a subscription item in two volumes, issued under the imprint of the Bobley Publishing Corporation. As with similar publications, the maps are political only, lack detail, and are not indexed. Priced at $11.20, it is usually sold as part of the *Illustrated World Encyclopedia* package deal. The *Hammond World Atlas: Classics Edition* is practically identical to the *Citation World Atlas* but is much more expensive at $25.00. Designed for the premium and subscription markets, it offers too little for too much. The *Standard World Atlas* is identical to the first 332 pages of the *Classics Edition* but, although this also is designed for the premium and subscription markets, it is considerably cheaper at $12.50. Neither work is provided with an overall index. The *School and Library Atlas of the World* is physically a gigantic work, measuring 22 by 16 in., and contains 350 pages of heavily calendered paper. It provides a wealth of statistical detail and text but the maps themselves are crude, poorly colored, awkwardly arranged, and heavily imbalanced in favor of the United States. It has no general index and is a poor value at $39.50. In appearance it resembles the *Rand McNally Commercial Atlas and Marketing Guide*, but is quite different in content.

MAGAZINE ARTICLES 1960–1971

"Great Gift is the Question-Answerer: A Good Atlas," *Sunset,* December 1971, p. 46.

"Published Sources of Information About Maps and Atlases," *Special Libraries*, February 1970, pp. 87–98, 110–112.

"World Atlases for General Reference," Daniel A. Gomez-Ibanez, *Choice*, July–August 1969, pp. 625–630.

"Map Publishers Learn to Live with Crisis," *New York Times*, July 22, 1967, p. 28.

"Utility of Atlases," A. C. Gerlach, *The Journal of Geography*, May 1967, pp. 204–205.

"Atlases Revisited," D. S. Melvin, *Ontario Library Review*, February 1966, pp. 29–30.

"Atlases and Maps," *British Book News*, July 1964.

"Atlases in the School Library," J. A. Morris, *School Librarian*, July 1964, p. 132ff.

"Maps, Globes and Atlases," S. Marsh and J. Pottle, *Grade Teacher*, November 1964, p. 90.

"Atlases Revisited," Richard Edes Harrison, *Saturday Review*, March 24, 1962, pp. 37–40.

"World Atlases," W. W. Ristow, *Library Journal*, April 15, 1962, pp. 1553–1554.

"New Atlas Available," R. M. Northway, *Instructor*, December 1961, p. 10.

"How to Select an Atlas," R. E. Porter, *Library Journal*, November 1, 1961, pp. 3747–3750.

"Atlases Today," *Geographical Magazine*, April 1960.

OTHER SOURCES OF INFORMATION

Alexander, Gerard L. *Guide to Atlases*. Metuchen, N.J.: Scarecrow Press, 1972.

Association for Childhood Education International. *Bibliography of Books for Children*. 1968.

Bagrow, Leo. *History of Cartography*. Cambridge, Mass.: Harvard University Press, 1964.

Barton, Mary, and Bell, Marian V. *Reference Books*. 7th ed. Baltimore: Enoch Pratt Free Library, 1970.

Bonk, Wallace J. *The Use of Basic Reference Sources in Libraries*. Ann Arbor, Michigan: Campus Publishers, 1964.

Cheney, Frances Neel. *Fundamental Reference Sources*. Chicago: American Library Association, 1971.

Church, M. et al. *A Basic Geographical Library*. Washington, D.C.: Assn. of American Geographers, 1966.

Deason, Hilary J. *AAAS Science Book List*. 3rd ed. Washington, D.C.: American Academy for the Advancement of Science, 1970.

Galin, Saul, and Spielberg, Peter. *Reference Books; How to Select and Use Them*. New York: Random House, 1969.

Gaver, Mary C. *Elementary School Library Collection*. 5th ed. Newark, N.J.: Bro-Dart Foundation, 1970.

Hammond Incorporated. *Your Atlas; Its selection and use*. Maplewood, N.J.: Hammond Inc., 1966.

Harris, Chauncy D. *Bibliographies and Reference Works for Research in Geography*. Chicago: University of Chicago, 1967.

Hodges, Elizabeth D. *Books for Elementary School Libraries*. Chicago: American Library Association, 1969.

Katz, William. *Introduction to Reference Work*. 2 vols. New York: McGraw-Hill, 1969.

Lock, Muriel C. B. *Geography; A Reference Handbook*. Hamden, Conn.: Archon Books, 1968.

Lock, Muriel C. B. *Modern Maps and Atlases*. Hamden, Conn.: Archon Books, 1969.

Matkin, Robert B. *Your Book of Maps and Map Reading*. New York: Transatlantic Arts, 1970.

Minto, C. S. *How to Find Out in Geography.* Elmsford, N.Y.: Pergamon Press, 1966.

Murphey, Robert W. *How and Where to Look it Up.* New York: McGraw-Hill, 1958.

National Association for Independent Schools: Library Committee. *Books for Secondary School Libraries.* New York: R. R. Bowker Co., 1971.

Naomi, Sister M. *Basic Reference Books for Catholic High Schools.* Haverford, Pa.: Catholic Library Association, 1963.

Neal, Harry Edward. *Of Maps and Men.* New York: Funk and Wagnalls, 1970.

Noonan, Eileen F., ed. *Basic Book Collections for High Schools.* Chicago: American Library Association, 7th ed. 1963.

Oliver, John E. *What We Find When We Look at Maps.* New York: McGraw-Hill, 1970.

Peterson, Carolyn S. *Reference Books for Elementary and Junior High School Libraries.* Metuchen, N.J.: Scarecrow Press, 1970.

Reference Services Division: Basic Reference Books Committee. *Reference Books for Small and Medium Sized Libraries.* Chicago: American Library Association, 1969.

Shores, Louis. *Basic Reference Sources.* Chicago: American Library Association, 1954.

Shores, Louis. *Instructional Materials.* New York: Ronald Press, 1960.

Spengler, Margaret V., ed. *Basic Book Collections for Junior High Schools.* Chicago: American Library Association, 3rd ed. 1960.

Stanek, Muriel Novella. *How to Use Maps and Globes.* Chicago: Benefic Press, 1968.

Voight, Melvin J., and Treyz, Joseph H. *Books for College Libraries.* Chicago: American Library Association, 1967.

Walford, Arthur J. *Guide to Reference Material.* New York: R. R. Bowker Co., 2nd ed. 1966–1970.

Whyte, Frederica H. *Whyte's Atlas Guide.* Metuchen, N.J.: Scarecrow Press, 1962.

H. W. Wilson Company. *Children's Catalog.* New York: H. W. Wilson, 12th ed. 1971 and supplements.

H. W. Wilson Company. *Junior High School Library Catalog.* New York: H. W. Wilson Co., 2nd ed. 1970 and supplements.

H. W. Wilson Company. *Senior High School Library Catalog.* New York: H. W. Wilson Co., 9th ed. 1967 and supplements.

H. W. Wilson Company. *Public Library Catalog.* New York: H. W. Wilson Co., 5th ed. 1968 and supplements.

Winchell, Constance W. *Guide to Reference Books.* Chicago: American Library Association, 8th ed. 1967 and supplements.

Wright, J. K., and Platt, E. T. *Aids to Geographical Research.* New York: Columbia University Press, 2nd ed. 1947.

Wynar, Bohdan S., ed. *American Reference Books Annual 1970–* Littleton, Colo.: Libraries Unlimited, 1970– .

Wynar, Bohdan S. *Introduction to Bibliography and Reference Work.* Littleton, Colo.: Libraries Unlimited, 4th ed. 1967.

Ziskind, Sylvia. *Reference Readiness.* Hamden, Conn.: Shoe String Press, 1971.

Part II: ATLAS ANALYSES

Group One:
TOP QUALITY ATLASES

THE TIMES ATLAS OF THE WORLD: COMPREHENSIVE EDITION

Merit Rating Rating: 25 (Maximum Rating)
Group One—Top Quality: *VERY HIGHLY RECOMMENDED*

PUBLISHER
Times Newspapers Limited, Printing House Square, London EC4P 4DE, England. Distributed in the United States under the imprint of the Houghton Mifflin Co., 2 Park St., Boston, Mass. 02107.

PUBLISHING HISTORY AND REVISION PROGRAM
The Times Atlas of the World was first published in five volumes between 1955 and 1960 and was then known as the *Mid Century Edition* to distinguish it from two earlier *Times* atlases, one published in 1921, which was also produced by John Bartholomew and Sons, and one in 1895 which was of German origin. The present one-volume *Comprehensive* edition, which contains all and even more than the original five-volume atlas, was first published in 1967, when it was also completely updated. A second revised edition was published in 1968, and a third in 1971, although this was for the United States only. The present edition, the fourth, was published in early 1972. Politically and geographically it is as up-to-date as was possible at the time of printing. There is no stated program of revision, but clearly there are to be new editions at frequent intervals which will incorporate corrections, additions, and other forms of updating.

EDITORS, CARTOGRAPHERS, AND CONTRIBUTORS
No editors as such are named, but the maps were created by John Bartholomew and Sons Limited, Edinburgh. With a few exceptions, the entire atlas is the result of collaboration between the Bartholomew cartographic staff and the staff of Times Newspapers Limited. Named as a Geographic Consultant, however, is H.G. Lewis, O.B.E., Directorate of Military Survey, and immediately following the title page is a detailed list of acknowledgments containing the names of 112 persons and institutions from all over the world (many from the United States). Their impressive qualifications are indicative of the quality and authority of this atlas.

33

HOME SALE AND RETAIL PRICES

Available in the United States at $65.00, and in the United Kingdom at £ 20.00. Now in a *Comprehensive* one-volume edition it was, until the mid-sixties, available only in a massive five-volume edition (now completely out of production) at the prohibitive cost of $125.00. The substantial reduction in cost has been achieved by a reduction in the width of the page margins and by printing the maps on both sides of the pages, without in any way reducing the size of the maps or the contents of the five-volume edition. The newest edition is bound in a dark brown cloth with lettering in gold.

PURPOSE AND AGE SUITABILITY

This is an advanced reference atlas, designed to meet the map reference needs of specialists, scholars, researchers, and serious students. It will be difficult for children in the elementary grades (although it will attract and motivate them), but will come increasingly within the comprehension of junior and senior high school students, and will attain maximum effectiveness from the age of 15. It is essential at college, university, and research level for adult specialists.

SIZE AND NUMBER OF PAGES

The single-page bound size is 18 by 11½ in., and it is one of the biggest atlases available. Every map is spread over two facing pages for an actual map coverage of 22 by 17½ in., after allowing for the relatively narrow margins. The atlas is comprised of 556 pages, made up of 40 pages of prefatory material and thematic maps, 244 pages (122 plates) of maps, and a 272-page index.

TOTAL MAP PAGES AND TYPES OF MAPS

Comprised of 122 plates of physical maps (244 actual pages), augmented by 40 prefatory pages which are part text, part special purpose maps, and part diagrams. Every map is in full color (6 shades) and nearly every map plate carries additional inset maps of even very remote islands and plans of metropolitan areas, those for London and Paris being contained on double page spreads. There are no locator or comparative maps, however, which would have been useful. The main series of maps is physical, but with adequate and clearly delineated political boundaries and divisions, including de facto and disputed boundaries. A color key to the layer shading is provided on every map page and heights and depths are shown on this in both feet and meters. Relief is shown by a beautifully designed series of layer tints and contours. The amount of detail on the maps is tremendous and includes both natural and cultural features such as deserts, salt flats, dunes and blown sand areas, lakes, swamps, reefs, volcanoes, glaciers, arterial and main roads, tracks, railroads, canals, oil pipe lines, and major and secondary airports. A detailed list of map symbols is provided on the plate immediately preceding the main series of maps, and (a very unusual and useful innovation) this is repeated on a loose plastic card which can be inserted into any part of the atlas in the same manner as a book mark. The map projections employed are clearly stated on every map but there is nowhere in the atlas an explanation of map projections, which would have been helpful to younger users if not to specialists. The scale at which every map is drawn is clearly stated as a numerical fraction, but not in its equivalent of miles per inch, which would also be more meaningful to younger users and others not fully conversant with scale. A scale bar in both miles and kilometers is also provided on each map page.

SCALE

There is no explanation of scale anywhere in the atlas, yet another feature which could be considered for inclusion in the next edition. All areas of the earth are mapped at exceptionally large scales, even remote places and islands, and in great detail. The scales vary slightly even within countries, but the overall balance is excellent. The United States and Canada are mapped mostly at 1:2,500,000, except for areas of both major and minor importance, as indicated by a scale of 1:1,000,000 for the Middle Atlantic Seaboard, and 1:5,000,000 for Alaska and Northwest Canada. Especially notable are the inset maps of major American and Canadian cities at scales varying from 1:100,000 for Quebec to 1:250,000 for such cities as New York, Montreal, Toronto, Baltimore, Philadelphia, Washington, Chicago, and Detroit. The British Isles are extensively mapped at 1:850,000, with London at 1:100,000. Europe generally is also well mapped, ranging from 1:515,000 for the Low Countries through 1:1,000,000 for Germany, France, and Italy, to 1:2,500,000 for lesser European nations. The rest of the world is mapped at a uniform scale of 1:5,000,000 except for such important areas as Israel at 1:500,000; the Middle East at 1:2,500,000; Japan at 1:2,500,000; and New Zealand, also at 1:2,500,000. Additionally, there are scores of inset maps of major areas at larger scales.

BALANCE

The Times Atlas of the World is exceptionally well balanced in its coverage, as indicated by the number of pages allocated to the various regions. Thirty-six pages are devoted to North America, of which 26 are allocated to the United States alone. Included as insets are the metropolitan areas of six Canadian and 14 American cities. Europe is given 70 pages, of which 12 are allocated to the British Isles. Included are eight inset maps of metropolitan areas or regions of special importance. Four pages are allocated to Central America, including Mexico, and 13 pages to South America. The rest of the world is divided up as follows: U.S.S.R., 20 pages; Asia, 44 pages; Australasia, 14 pages; Africa, 24 pages. A further 15 pages are concerned with Polar Regions and the oceans of the world. A notable feature is the provision of 60 metropolitan areas as inset maps.

INDEXING

There is a massive 272-page index containing more than 200,000 entries. This is by far the most comprehensive of its kind, 25 percent larger than its nearest competitor. The index includes both geographic features and inhabited places, and it is especially notable for the fullness of its entries, which are given in the following order: name of place or feature, country in which situated, latitude and longitude, map plate number, and cross-key grid reference. Additional aids to the index are the end papers, which identify place locations for the entire world at a glance. The spelling of place names conforms to the rules recommended by the U.S. Board on Geographic Names and the Permanent Committee on Geographical Names (United Kingdom), which use both the local official forms of spelling in current use, and the more familiar Anglicized spellings. The index is pure in that it does not supply extraneous gazetteer information or population statistics, although the size of cities is indicated approximately by the size of the type faces used on the maps.

SCOPE, CONTENTS, AND ARRANGEMENT

A detailed list of contents is provided at the front of the atlas, including text as well as maps. The scale is given for every listed map. There is little in the way of text in the atlas, apart from the material in the prefatory pages which includes such useful material as a Table of States, Territories and Principal Islands; a Table of Geographical Comparisons; an essay on the Resources of the World; thematic maps (spread over two pages) for Minerals, Energy, Food and Climate; the Universe; the Solar System; Star Charts of the Northern and Southern Skies; the Earth and Its Atmosphere; Sunrise and Sunset; Space Flight and Satellites; and the Moon, including a map of the near side of the Moon. The maps are arranged in seven broad groups: the World; the Orient; Eurasia; the U.S.S.R; the Mediterranean and Africa; North America; and South America.

SUMMARY

An atlas should be comprehensive, accurate, up-to-date, legible, on as large a scale as possible, and well indexed, the criteria by which all atlases should be judged. *The Times Atlas of the World* has all these qualities to a greater degree than any other atlas examined. More than that, it is a work of great cartographic skill and a work of great artistic merit, made with loving care. It is probably the best atlas in the world at the present time. It is certainly by far the best and most significant world atlas published during the past 25 years. As such, it is essential to libraries of all types and, where it can be afforded, the best for student and home use. A landmark in geographic publishing, it spans the entire world in tremendous detail, with exceptionally well-balanced coverage of the most important areas. Made and printed in Britain (except for the index), *The Times Atlas* is noted for the beauty and accuracy of its maps, the meticulous attention paid to small islands and remote areas of the world, the highly useful large-scale maps of more than 60 major cities and metropolitan areas of the world, the utilization of various up-to-date methods of map projection, the treatment of place names, the clear detail of arterial and main roads, the maps of the oceans, and the valuable information on such natural physical features as deserts, salt flats, dunes and blown sand areas, lakes, swamps, reefs, volcanoes, and glaciers. Man-made features such as roads, tracks, railroads, canals, oil pipe lines, airports, and other lines of communication are equally well detailed. Of inestimable value also are the series of thematic and special-topic maps dealing with world resources and distribution, physiography, oceanography, climatology, vegetation, population, air routes, etc. The 40 pages of prefatory material have excellent additional material on the universe, extraterrestrial activities, the moon, and the solar system. *The Times Atlas of the World* is everything an atlas should be and a credit to its makers and publishers. There are a number of good, and some very good atlases available, but not one anywhere near the equal of this. It is, of course, expensive, and those who cannot afford it could well take a long hard look at its near relative, *The New York Times World Atlas* or, in Britain, *The Times Concise Atlas of the World*, which retains many of the features of the larger work, but at less than half the cost.

CRITICAL REVIEWS AND INFORMATIVE ARTICLES

Choice, July-August 1969, pp.625-630.
America, November 30, 1968, p.566.
Economist, December 7, 1968, p.57.
Scientific American, August 1968, p.46.
Booklist, July 15, 1968, p.1244.
Choice, July 1968, p.612.
College and Research Libraries, July 1968, p.331.
Wilson Library Bulletin, June 1968, p.1043.
Saturday Review, May 18, 1968, p.46.
Book World, May 5, 1968, p.7.
Atlantic, April 1968, p.136.
New York Times, April 15, 1968.
(Note: All of these reviews refer to the first or second editions of 1967 and 1968, but are equally applicable to the present fourth edition of 1972).

OTHER SOURCES OF INFORMATION

Barton. *Reference Books*. 7th ed. 1970.
Cheney. *Fundamental Reference Sources*. 1971.
Choice. *Opening Day Collection*.
Katz. *Introduction to Reference Work*. 1969.
Lock. *Modern Maps and Atlases*. 1969.
Walford. *Guide to Reference Material*. 2nd ed. 1966-1970.
H. W. Wilson Co. *Public Library Catalog*. 5th ed. 1968.
Winchell. *Guide to Reference Books*. 8th ed. 1967; 2nd supplement 1967-1968.
Ziskind. *Reference Readiness*. 1971.

THE INTERNATIONAL ATLAS

Merit Rating: 23
Group One—Top Quality: *VERY HIGHLY RECOMMENDED*

PUBLISHER

Rand McNally and Co., P.O. Box 7600, Chicago, Ill. 60680. Distributed in the United Kingdom by Geo. Philip and Son Limited, 12–14 Long Acre, London WC2E 9LP, England.

PUBLISHING HISTORY AND REVISION PROGRAM

The International Atlas is the newest atlas on the market at the present time. It was first published in 1969, and is understood to have been more than a decade in preparation. There is no stated policy of revision, but a work of this quality will certainly be revised at frequent intervals. A new second edition is to be published in the fall of 1972, but at the time of going to press no details were available on the amount of revision or change in price, if any.

EDITORS, CARTOGRAPHERS, AND CONTRIBUTORS

An international atlas in the real sense of the word, developed by a team of 115 cartographers and geographers from 14 countries. Listed opposite the title page are an eight-member International Planning Conference, and eight specialist map advisors for Europe, Asia, Australia, Anglo-America, and Latin America. The verso of the title page contains a full list of the *International Atlas* staff, including Andrew McNally III as publisher, and Richard L. Forstall as editor. Also listed are nine members of Rand McNally, Stuttgart; 11 members of Cartographic, Budapest; the Esselte Map Service, Stockholm; the cartographic staff of George Philip and Son Limited, London; and finally, the Teikoku-Shoin Co. Limited, of Tokyo.

HOME SALE AND RETAIL PRICES

Available in two editions: a standard edition in buckram binding at $35.00, and a deluxe edition, in an attractive slipcase, at $40.00. In Britain it is marketed by Geo. Philip and Son Limited, at £17.50. Note, however, that with some minor differences, it is also marketed as the *Britannica Atlas* (q.v.) and as the *Compton Atlas*.

PURPOSE AND AGE SUITABILITY

This is a scholarly, advanced reference atlas designed mainly for the professional cartographer, the researcher, the serious student, and the teacher. It will be difficult, for the most part, for children in the elementary grades, but will become of increasing usefulness to junior and senior high school students. It will be still more useful at college and university level. The suggested beginning age is 15. It is designed for international use, with most of the text in four languages: English, German, French, and Spanish.

SIZE AND NUMBER OF PAGES

The single-page bound size is 14¾ by 11 in. Nearly all the maps, however, are spread over two facing pages for an actual map coverage of approximately 14¾ by 22 in., with the relatively narrow margins utilized for additional information. The work is comprised of a total of 558 pages, of which 195 are allocated to the index.

TOTAL MAP PAGES AND TYPES OF MAPS

Almost half of the atlas is given over to maps, 261 pages in all. The main series of maps consists of physical maps drawn at uniform scales of 1:1,000,000; 1;3,000,000; 1:6,000,000; and 1:12,000,000. These are augmented by a fine series of thematic maps on specific subjects, political maps of the continents, large-scale city maps, and portrait maps of the world. Relief is shown by a series of layer tints in soft and pleasing shades, with well-executed hill shading to provide a three-dimensional effect. A key to the layer colors is provided in the margins of each physical map page, with heights and depths given in both meters and feet. Locator maps in the page margins show the relation of the mapped area to larger areas. The detail on the maps especially the 1:300,000 series, is excellent, showing such man-made features as shopping centers, airport runways, locks on canals, oil wells, and other places of interest. On the smaller-scale maps, highways, railroads, and other cultural and natural features are shown in adequate detail. A full detailed explanation of the various symbols employed is provided at the beginning of the atlas. The projections used are clearly identified on each map, as also are the scales employed, which are given not only as numerical fractions, but also with the equivalent in kilometers per centimeter and miles per inch, a commendable feature. The usual scale bar is also provided, and this also is in both miles and kilometers. Not provided are explanations of scale or map projections, which would have been useful and meaningful to younger users and nonspecialists.

SCALE

Beautifully designed, only six basic scales are used in *The International Atlas* to provide a really comprehensive coverage of any area in the world. The smallest of these (at a scale of 1:24,000,000) deals with the continents, including Antarctica). These are followed, in descending order, by political maps of regions of the world at a scale of 1:12,000,000; then by the main series of physical maps at a scale of either 1:6,000,000 or 1:3,000,000, depending on the importance of the region. Still larger-scale maps are provided for the major geographic areas at a scale of 1:1,000,000 (about 16 miles to the inch), which enables great detail to be recorded, such as three classifications of roads and highways, two classes of railroads, drainage and transportation patterns, airports, canals, ferries, bridges, and tunnels. The largest-scale maps are those for the metropolitan areas of some 60 major world cities, drawn at a scale of 1:300,000 (about 4.7 miles to the inch).

BALANCE

The International Atlas has exceptionally good balance in its treatment of the various regions of the world, with mapping at an even and very adequate scale. Fifty-four pages are allocated to North America, of which 41 are devoted to the United States and 13 to Canada. Europe is contained within 42 pages, of which six are allocated to the British Isles alone. Central America, including Mexico and the Caribbean, are covered in 12 pages, and South America in 17 pages. The Soviet Union is very well covered in 18 pages; Asia (including the Near and Middle East) in 44 pages; Australasia in 16 pages; and Africa in 26 pages. Including European Russia, the three continents of North America, Europe, and Asia are each allocated about one fifth of the total map pages. There is perhaps some bias towards North America in the city and metropolitan area maps. Of the 29 pages of these, 11 are allocated to North America. Fourteen of the 60 cities are also situated in North America. Overall, however, the balance is excellent.

INDEXING

A superbly compiled computer-produced index containing more than 160,000 entries is provided in the index of 195 pages. Places and physical features are exactly located by the provision of latitude and longitude and the map page number. A notable feature is the inclusion of historical names no longer in official use. Another useful and original feature is the employment of special symbols to indicate topographic, hydrographic, and cultural features. A key to these is provided at the foot of each index page and translated into four languages for international understanding. Neither population statistics nor gazetteer information is given in the index, although a population table elsewhere in the atlas provides the most recent figures for all important cities, including every urban center with a population in excess of 50,000. The tables, however, are arranged (a) alphabetically by country, and (b) alphabetically within the country. This necessitates referring first to the index to ascertain the country in which the city or town is located.

SCOPE, CONTENTS, AND ARRANGEMENT

A detailed list of the maps is provided at the front of the atlas. This gives the scale for every listed map, first in English, and then in each of the three other languages. Also provided in the prefatory material is an index to the regional and world maps, and a list of selected map references. Following the 22 pages of prefatory material is a fine 16,000-word essay entitled the "Patterns and Imprints of Mankind," written by Marvin W. Mikesell, Professor of Geography at the University of Chicago. Occupying 22 pages, it includes 18 thematic world maps dealing with population, rainfall, growing seasons, limits of the habitable world, land use, industrial resources, transportation, etc. Augmenting the text and the thematic maps are 25 color photos. The atlas proper is comprised of 280 pages. The maps begin with the world, oceans, and continents. These are followed by the regional maps: Europe, the Soviet Union, Asia, Africa, Australasia, Canada, the United States, Central America, and South America. Following these are the special large-scale maps of 60 of the world's major metropolitan areas. Preceding the index are an additional 23 pages containing a glossary of geographic terms, abbreviations (both in four languages), a world information table as of January 1970, and populations of cities and towns. The 195-page index is preceded by a four-page introduction on how to use the index.

SUMMARY

The publishers claim that this new *International Atlas* is "a masterpiece of cartography, design and production." It is not too extravagant a claim. It is a very good atlas indeed and a superb work of reference which should be in every library, large or small, public, school, or specialized. It is certainly the best atlas ever to be produced in the United States and ranks as one of the best atlases in the world at the present time. This really is an international atlas, created with the collaboration of more than 100 specialists from other countries, although basically the atlas is a product of the Rand McNally Co., Chicago. Nearly all the text, with the exception of the 16,000-word essay "Patterns and Imprints of Mankind," is in four languages: English, French, German, and Spanish. The metric system of measurement is given preference over the Anglo-American measurements of feet, miles, etc., although these are given subordinately. A minor drawback in the use of the four languages is that the repetition of the information takes up a fairly considerable amount of additional space, but this is counteracted by the fact that it can be used by almost everyone anywhere in the world. It is well balanced and comprehensive in coverage, uniformly scaled, exceptionally well detailed, and thoroughly indexed. The coloring of the maps is well done and pleasing to the eye, and although possibly a bit "muddy" and dark in some areas, it is nevertheless vastly superior to the cartography of other Rand McNally atlases. *The International Atlas* has a number of notable features, and especially worth noting is the color coding of the scales used: a gold panel indicating a scale of 1:12,000,000; a wine-colored panel for 1:6,000,000; a green panel for 1:3,000,000; and a blue panel for maps at 1:1,000,000. Other noteworthy features are the highly effective tridimensional shaded relief, and the spectacular fold-out maps. Exceptionally useful is the superb series of large-scale maps of the major metropolitan areas of the world, in which details such as shopping centers, places of interest, canal locks, oil wells, and airport runways are clearly shown. The 16,000-word essay by Professor Marvin Mikesell is excellent, although purists may question its inclusion in a work of reference. It discusses the condition man found the earth in, what he has done to it, and what problems (pollution, waste of resources, etc.) have to be resolved if man is to survive. One reviewer at least has boldly stated that this is the best large single-volume world atlas available for general use. This is too ambitious a claim, but it certainly is very close. Indeed, in some respects, it is probably better than the *Times Atlas of the World*, but overall does not quite match up to that impressive work. Younger students may find it difficult to use, due to the complexity of the material, but they will nevertheless be attracted by its striking format. Specialists, and libraries of all types, will find it invaluable for its comprehensiveness and accuracy. *The International Atlas* is very highly recommended for home and general as well as library, school, and office use, especially where purchasing the more expensive *Times Atlas* would be a strain on the budget.

CRITICAL REVIEWS AND INFORMATIVE ARTICLES

American Reference Books Annual, 1970, p. 97.
College and Research Libraries, March 1970, p. 116.
Wilson Library Bulletin, January 1970, p. 566.
Booklist, October 1, 1970, p. 113.
Economist, January 17, 1970, p. 51.
Life, December 5, 1969, p. 14.
Saturday Review, December 6, 1969, p. 52.
Library Journal, November 15, 1969, p. 4129.
Publishers Weekly, May 5, 1969, pp. 66–72.

OTHER SOURCES OF INFORMATION

Cheney. *Fundamental Reference Sources.* 1971.
H. W. Wilson Co. *Senior High School Library Catalog.* 1971 supplement.
Ziskind. *Reference Readiness.* 1971.

BRITANNICA ATLAS
and
THE COMPTON ATLAS

Merit Rating: 23
Group One—Top Quality: *VERY HIGHLY RECOMMENDED*

PUBLISHER

Encyclopaedia Britannica, Inc., 425 North Michigan Ave., Chicago, Ill. 60611 and the F. E. Compton Co. (a subsidiary of Encyclopaedia Britannica, Inc.), by special arrangement with Rand McNally and Co., Chicago.

PUBLISHING HISTORY AND REVISION PROGRAM

Although this is an entirely new atlas, first published in 1969, it has been preceded by other atlases bearing a similar title and also published by

Encyclopaedia Britannica, Inc. The first was copyrighted in 1942 as the *Encyclopaedia Britannica World Atlas.* This used maps by Hammond, Inc., from 1942 to 1948, and these were then superseded by the series of *Cosmo* maps from Rand McNally, from 1949 to 1964. In 1965 an entirely new series of maps copyrighted by the Istituto Geografico de Agostini, a well-known Italian firm of cartographers, comprised the bulk of the atlas. These continued until 1968, although in 1966 the title was shortened to the *Britannica World Atlas.* The present work is virtually identical to *The International Atlas,* except for the differences already noted. *The Compton Atlas* is identical to the *Britannica Atlas* in every respect but title. There is no stated policy of revision, but new editions will, as with the *International Atlas,* appear from time to time, including revisions to the World Scene section.

EDITORS, CARTOGRAPHERS, AND CONTRIBUTORS

The editors, cartographers, and contributors to the world atlas section and index are exactly as for *The International Atlas.* The *Britannica Atlas* (and the *Compton Atlas*) also include the editors and contributors to the World Scene section, which is not in the *International Atlas.* They exclude Professor Marvin W. Mikesell, the author of the essay "Patterns and Imprints of Mankind," which is replaced in the *Britannica* and *Compton* editions by the World Scene section. For the *Britannica Atlas,* Ruth M. Cole is listed as Geography Editor, together with 22 other staff members. Also listed as contributors to the World Scene section are 13 well-qualified specialists. Ten of these are American, two are Canadian, and one Swedish. Listed as designer of the special maps for the World Scene is David L. Burke.

HOME SALE AND RETAIL PRICES

As far as is known, each is available in one edition only (in cream buckram) at $35.00, plus $.75 for postage and packing.

PURPOSE AND AGE SUITABILITY

The same as for *The International Atlas.* The only difference between these two atlases is in the substitution of a World Scene series of thematic maps for the essay "Patterns and Imprints of Mankind." This does not lessen or increase the suggested age suitability.

SIZE AND NUMBER OF PAGES

Almost exactly as for the *International Atlas,* 14¾ by 11 in., but with a slight difference in the number of pages. The *Britannica* and *Compton* editions are comprised of 575 pages as against 558 in the *International,* the additional 18 pages comprising the World Scene section.

TOTAL MAP PAGES AND TYPES OF MAPS

The atlas proper is identical to the atlas section of *The International Atlas.* Different, however, is the World Scene section, composed of 40 pages of thematic maps of the world on such subjects as Politically Related

Areas; Political and Territorial Changes since 1945; Seaward Claims; The World at 1 January 1914; The World at 1 January 1937; Population; Agricultural Regions; Forests and Fisheries; Minerals; Energy Production and Consumption; Manufacturing; Motor Vehicles; Gross National Products; International Trade; Commodities Traded; Intercontinental Air Connections; Continental Transport Routes; Climate, Temperature, and Precipitation; Surface Configuration; Earth Structure and Tectonics; Natural Vegetation; Soils; and Drainage Regions and Ocean Currents.

SCALE

Exactly as for *The International Atlas.*

BALANCE

Exactly as for *The International Atlas.*

INDEXING

Exactly as for *The International Atlas.*

SCOPE, CONTENTS, AND ARRANGEMENT

Almost exactly as for the *International.* As has already been mentioned, there is only one major difference between the editions, i.e., the substitution in the *Britannica* and *Compton* editions of the World Scene (described in detail above) for the essay contained in the *International* edition.

SUMMARY

The same comments apply here as to *The International Atlas,* and it will be necessary for users to refer to both entries before making a final choice. This boils down to the selection of either the World Scene section of thematic maps in the *Britannica Atlas* or the essay in *The International Atlas.* This becomes a matter of personal choice. It should be mentioned, however, that the *Britannica* and *Compton* atlases are usually sold on a subscription basis only, and usually in a package deal with the *Encyclopaedia Britannica* or the *Compton Encyclopedia and Fact-Index.* All three titles are excellent general-reference world atlases, and all are very highly recommended.

CRITICAL REVIEWS AND INFORMATIVE ARTICLES

American Reference Books Annual, 1971, pp. 172–173.
Booklist, October 1, 1970, pp. 113–116.
Wilson Library Bulletin, January 1970, p. 566.
Library Journal, November 15, 1969, p. 4129.
(See also *The International Atlas.*)

OTHER SOURCES OF INFORMATION

Cheney. *Fundamental Reference Sources.* 1971.
(See also *The International Atlas.*)

THE NEW YORK TIMES WORLD ATLAS
and
THE TIMES CONCISE ATLAS OF THE WORLD

Merit Rating: 21
Group One—Top Quality: *VERY HIGHLY RECOMMENDED*

PUBLISHER

For the United States: Quadrangle Books (a division of the New York Times), 330 Madison Ave., New York, N.Y. 10017. For Great Britain: Times Newspapers Limited, Printing House Square, London EC4P 4DE, England.

PUBLISHING HISTORY AND REVISION PROGRAM

First published in late 1972 and up-to-date as of the summer of 1972. It has been in the planning stage for several years and is a direct descendant of *The Times Atlas of the World*. The publishers state that new editions will be published as necessary, probably at quite frequent intervals. Although derived from the *Times Atlas*, a great deal of the material is entirely new, excepting only those maps which are adaptations from the *Comprehensive* edition.

EDITORS, CARTOGRAPHERS, AND CONTRIBUTORS

No one person is named as editor, but a highly authoritative Editorial Board is comprised of senior editorial executives of (a) the *Times*, London, (b) the *New York Times*, and (c) Senior Professors and Lecturers of the University of London. Among those named are: William Rees-Mogg, Editor of the *Times*; Louis Heren, Deputy Editor of the *Times*; John Oakes, Editorial Page Editor of the *New York Times*; Walter Sullivan, Science Editor of the *New York Times*; Derek Jewell, Publishing Director of the *Times*; Barry L. D. Winkleman, Publishing Manager of the *Times*; Professor J. C. Pugh, and Professor E. M. Rawstron, both of the University of London. The atlas is produced by the *Times* of London and the *New York Times* in collaboration with John Bartholomew and Sons Limited, Edinburgh, who also produce the great *Times Atlas of the World*.

HOME SALE AND RETAIL PRICES

These were not finalized at the time of going to press, but according to information provided, the British edition will retail at £7.75 and the American edition at from $35.00.

PURPOSE AND AGE SUITABILITY

This entirely new atlas has been expressly designed to bring the best features and the cartography of the great *Times Atlas* into a price range within the reach of the average family. The concept behind the atlas is to provide a guide to world affairs for the interested and intelligent layman as well as for younger users. Because of its greater selectivity and the simpler presentation of the maps and index, it can be used by students from the age of 12 through to college. Smaller branch libraries will find this a boon to their reference collections, but larger libraries and advanced users will need the much more comprehensive *Times Atlas.*

SIZE AND NUMBER OF PAGES

The single-page bound size is 14¾ by 10¾ in., which is approximately a 20 percent reduction in size from the larger *Times Atlas of the World.* About half the maps, however, are spread over two facing pages for a map coverage of approximately 14½ by 21 in., after allowing for the relatively narrow margins. There is a total of 272 pages. Forty of these are allocated to the preliminary section, 144 to the maps, and 88 to the index.

TOTAL MAP PAGES AND TYPES OF MAPS

More selective than the larger *Times Atlas*, this *Concise* edition contains 144 pages of six-color physical-political maps. Of these, 15 pages are comprised of entirely new conurbation metropolitan-area maps, published here for the first time. Thirty-three such areas are mapped, of which ten are in the United States. There are several other similar maps of insets. The main series of physical maps is adapted directly from the superb maps in the *Times Atlas of the World: Comprehensive Edition.* Beautifully drawn, they clearly delineate political boundaries and divisions, including de facto and disputed areas. Relief is shown by layer shading, in six shades, and contour lines in exceptionally pleasing yet clear detail. A color key to the shading is provided in the margins of each map, and heights and depths are given in both feet and meters. The amount of detail is tremendous, yet the maps remain uncluttered. Both natural and cultural features such as deserts, salt flats, dunes and blown sand areas, lakes, swamps, reefs, volcanoes, glaciers, arterial and main highways, tracks, railroads, canals, pipe lines, and airports are shown. A detailed list of map symbols is provided on a prefatory page. The map projections employed are clearly identified on each map, as are the scales at which the maps are drawn (given both as numerical fractions and on bar scales, indicating miles and kilometers). The work would have been even more useful, however, especially to the younger student and intelligent family user, if explanations of both map projections and scale were provided. A miles-per-inch scale equivalent would also have been more meaningful to the nonspecialist.

SCALE

The entire world is drawn at a uniform scale and in more than adequate detail. All of the United States, for example, is mapped at a scale of 1:3,000,000, but with the more important metropolitan areas at 1:500,000. Similarly, most of Europe is at a scale of 1:3,000,000, but there are selected areas at an even larger scale of 1:1,000,000. Most other parts of the world are at 1:6,000,000, but again with selected areas of importance at 1:3,000,000 and 1:1,000,000.

BALANCE

A very well balanced coverage of the most important areas of the world. Twenty-nine pages are allocated to the North American continent, of which 24 are allocated to the United States and four to Canada, in addition to which there are ten pages of metropolitan area maps for North American cities. Europe is allocated 46 pages, of which ten are allocated to the British Isles alone. For the rest of the world, four pages are allocated to Central America, six pages to South America, nine pages to the Soviet Union, 24 pages to Asia, eight pages to Australasia, and eight pages to Africa. For the world generally, the oceans, and polar regions, there are ten pages of maps. To these are added 15 pages of the new metropolitan area maps.

INDEXING

There is a quite comprehensive index of 95,000 entries, which is large for an atlas in this category. Unlike the larger *Times Atlas*, degrees of latitude and longitude are not given, the location of places and features being made by the grid system of letters and numbers, which is simpler to use but less exact. The index is pure in the sense that it contains no extraneous material such as population statistics or gazetteer information, although preceding it is a list of the countries of the world, together with the capital city, area, and population.

SCOPE, CONTENTS, AND ARRANGEMENT

A well-detailed list of contents precedes the atlas section, with a full list of the maps, including the scale for each. The atlas is divided into three broad sections: 40 pages of preliminary matter, 144 pages of maps, and the index with some accompanying material. The preliminary section is comprised largely of text, illustrated with diagrams and thematic maps. The subjects covered, all spread over two facing pages, include the Earth and Its Origin; Land and Sea Forms; Atmosphere and Climate; Vegetation and Water Resources; Minerals and Their Uses; Food and Nutrition; Population; Patterns of Human Settlement; Fuel and Energy; Manufacturing Industry; Patterns of World Trade; World Tourism; the Balance of Man's Environment; Techniques of Navigation; the Universe; the Moon; and the Stars. The order in which the maps are listed is as follows: Europe, The Soviet Union, Asia and the Middle East, Africa, The Americas, Central America, South America, and Australasia. Preceding the index are: (a) a list of the countries of the world, and (b) a table of geographic comparisons.

SUMMARY

The New York Times World Atlas or *The Times Concise Atlas of the World* is an important new atlas of great quality. It is claimed to be entirely new, and though this is certainly true of a great part of it, it does stem directly from the huge, scholarly *Times Atlas of the World*. Cognizant of the fact that the larger work, because of its cost and comprehensiveness, was destined more for the specialist and the shelves of larger libraries and universities, the publishers decided some years ago to prepare a new atlas more suited for use by families and by younger students, at a cost within the reach of most. To this end Times Newspapers Limited, London, joined forces with the *New York Times*, and the result is this new work, to be published simultaneously on both sides of the Atlantic under different titles. The maps, with the exception of the new series dealing with the conurbation areas, were printed and compiled by John Bartholomew and Son, Edinburgh, the makers of the great *Times Atlas*. Some of these have been adapted from the *Comprehensive* edition to fit into this smaller format, but they are in no sense simply scaled-down versions and, in fact, some of them are entirely new. Entirely new also is the preliminary section, which, with text, thematic maps, and diagrams, is concerned with the science of geography in the widest sense. These 40 pages first describe the origin and geology of the earth, its physical nature, and its resources of climate, vegetation, and minerals. This is followed by an examination of the major features of the geography of man, stressing in particular his settlements and population patterns, his trade and industry, his use of energy, the development of tourism, and the effect of these activities on the balance of his natural environment. Rounding off this section is a fine description of the present stage of our knowledge of the universe. Entirely new also is the index of more than 95,000 entries, very accurate and up-to-date, which follows the rules of spelling recommended by the U.S. Board on Geographic Names and the Permanent Committee on Geographical Names (United Kingdom). This is a great new atlas of high quality which is very highly recommended for home and general use, for smaller libraries with restricted budgets, and for desk and office use. It is smaller than the two atlases rated above it, but it is also much less expensive and is an ideal alternative to those unable to afford the more comprehensive works.

CRITICAL REVIEWS AND INFORMATIVE ARTICLES

As this analysis was compiled before the actual publication date of this atlas, no reviews have yet appeared.

OTHER SOURCES OF INFORMATION

None yet available.

Group Two:
ABOVE AVERAGE
QUALITY ATLASES

NATIONAL GEOGRAPHIC ATLAS OF THE WORLD

Merit Rating: 19
Group Two—Above Average Quality: *HIGHLY RECOMMENDED*

PUBLISHER
The National Geographic Society, 17th and M Sts., Washington, D.C. 20036.

PUBLISHING HISTORY AND REVISION PROGRAM
The National Geographic Atlas of the World was first published in 1963, and was immediately acclaimed by professional reviewers as one of the best atlases published in the United States up to that time. As such, it was chosen by the Reference Services Division of the American Library Association as one of the best reference books of 1963. A second, improved edition was published in 1966, and the present third edition in 1970. New editions are appearing at intervals of from three to four years, ensuring a high degree of up-to-dateness at all times.

EDITORS, CARTOGRAPHERS, AND CONTRIBUTORS
The title page lists Dr. Melville Bell Grosvenor as editor in chief, with Frederick G. Vosburgh as editor, and Wellman Chamberlin as chief cartographer. Also listed are Dr. Melvin M. Payne, President of the National Geographic Society; Athos D. Grazzini, Associate Chief Cartographer; William T. Peele, Assistant Chief Cartographer; Franc Shor, Atlas Editor; and Jules B. Billard, Atlas Text. A complete list of the members of the atlas staff and the National Geographic Society's Committee for Research and Exploration, and the names of the presidents, vice presidents, and board of trustees of the society is provided on an end page of the atlas.

HOME SALE AND RETAIL PRICES
Available in two editions: a boxed hard-cover deluxe edition at $24.50 and a soft-cover standard edition at $18.75. Because the soft-cover edition will not

withstand hard wear, and also because of the very reasonable cost, the deluxe edition is recommended.

PURPOSE AND AGE SUITABILITY

Designed for high school, college, university, and specialized use as a comprehensive reference atlas of the world. In some areas it can be used by junior high school and even upper elementary school students, but it is suggested that its maximum usefulness will be to those of age 15 and over.

SIZE AND NUMBER OF PAGES

One of the largest general world atlases, if not the largest, available in English, it measures a gigantic 19 by 12½ in., and, as the maps have no margins, this is the actual single-page map size. Additionally, with only a few exceptions, the maps are spread over two facing pages for a tremendous overall span of 19 by 25 in. There are 331 numbered pages. This total is 12 less than in the second edition of 1966, but 31 more than in the original edition of 1963.

TOTAL MAP PAGES AND TYPES OF MAPS

The atlas section is comprised of 170 pages, but of these 139 are actually allocated to maps, the remaining 31 comprising related text. Printed in a full range of 11 pleasant pastel shades, 116 pages contain 58 political maps (with a limited range of physical features); seven world and continental physical maps; a variety of special scenic and historical maps of the United States (showing national parks and Civil War battlefields); and descriptive note maps of the Nile Valley and the Holy Land. The main series of maps is political only. These clearly show political and administrative boundaries and provide a wealth of detail such as roads, highways, railroads, parks, oil pipe lines, toll roads, and trails. The only relief features, however (apart from the continental physical maps), are major elevations, done in a rather dull and ineffectual hill shading in gray. On the physical maps, relief is shown both by hill shading and by layer coloring. The methods of projection employed are shown on each map page, as are the scales used, which are given both in a numerical fraction and in their equivalent in miles per inch, a useful feature. Heights, where shown, are given in both feet and meters. There are no thematic maps as such, but included as inserts on many of the map pages are enlargements of important regions, plans of major world cities, and a number of special maps and tables. All maps show their copyright date, in this case 1970, a very desirable practice which other atlases would do well to emulate. A full explanation of the symbols used on the maps is provided on page 6 of the atlas. Not provided, on the other hand, are explanations of map projections and scale, which would have been useful.

SCALE

The *National Geographic Atlas* differs from all other atlases in that it gives the scale not only as a numerical fraction but also as miles per inch, and all the maps are based on a scale of 1:63,360 (1 mile to the inch). This results in a somewhat bewildering mixture of scales of exact fractions which correspond exactly to a given number of miles to the inch. The National Geographic Society has pioneered in many areas of cartography and this is yet another example of breaking with tradition. The editors probably had in mind that it is easier to visualize a mapped area at, for example, 4¾ miles to the inch than at the approximate numerical scale of 1:300,000, and they are probably right, but because the scales are not uniform, comparison of areas is not easy. The sections of the United States, for example, are mapped at a scale of 45 miles per inch, except for the eastern seaboard, which is at 16 miles to the inch, and Alaska, which is at 65 miles to the inch. The Hawaiian Islands, on the other hand, are shown in great detail at scales of from 3 to 8 miles per inch. Canada, like the United States, is mapped mostly at 45 miles to the inch, except for the western provinces, which are far less detailed at 80 miles to the inch.

Central America, including Mexico and the West Indies, is at the unusual scale of 78 miles to the inch, but South America has to make do with the relatively small scales of 105 and 115 miles to one inch. Europe is mapped at a large but varied scale. The British Isles are well detailed at 19 miles to the inch, and the Low Countries are even better detailed at 17 miles per inch, but the other European countries vary up to as much as 48 miles per inch for Scandinavia. Asia is not adequately dealt with at all, Japan and Korea coming out best at a scale of 60 miles to the inch, but China is at a scale of 105 miles per inch, and India is at 97 miles to the inch. Russia is also harshly dealt with in only two maps, Eastern Russia and Western Russia, the former at only 100 miles to the inch, and the latter at only 180 miles per inch. Africa is mapped in three regions at 125 miles to the inch, and Australasia is virtually dismissed at a scale of 110 miles per inch. The publishers would have made the atlas easier to use if they had listed the maps more fully on the contents page, with the scale shown for each map for easier comparison.

BALANCE

Although the world is covered in fair detail, with parts of it in great detail, there is a decided imbalance in the allocation of space to the various regions. There is definite emphasis on North America, for example, which takes up almost one third of the map pages, with the United States alone being allocated some 20 percent. Broken down, there are 40 pages allocated to North America, with 28 of these devoted to the United States, and eight to Canada. Europe is also allocated 28 pages, with the British Isles covering six of these. Central and South America are contained in 13 pages, Asia in 19, Africa in nine, and Australasia in seven. The U.S.S.R., conversely, is very poorly covered in only four pages of relatively small-scale maps. Additionally, there are nine pages of maps of the world, six pages for the oceans, and four pages of special maps. This is not a good balance at all.

INDEXING

As one of the best features of this work, *The National Geographic Atlas* provides a really comprehensive index with more than 139,000 entries in 148 pages, an increase of more than 1,000 over the 1966 edition. A pure index, it does not provide such additional information as population statistics or gazetteer data, although a great deal of this will be found in the text sections of the atlas. Location of places and features is by the grid system of letters and numbers. Latitude and longitude locations are not provided, information which would have been expected in an atlas of this size and scope.

SCOPE, CONTENTS, AND ARRANGEMENT

The atlas is comprised of 11 major sections or divisions, preceded by nine pages of prefatory and introductory material. The List of Contents itemizes both maps and the pertinent text, but is deficient in that it fails to indicate the scale of each map listed. Beginning with the United States, the maps are then grouped by broad geographic areas. A feature of the atlas is that each map section is preceded by succinct sketches for each country, state, or province within that section. The inside front cover contains a graphic description of "The Earth in Space," which includes a history of astronomy and a description of the universe. The inside back cover provides an interesting history of map making.

SUMMARY

The National Geographic Atlas of the World is a comprehensive, informative, accurate, and attractive atlas, authoritatively regarded as one of the best world atlases ever to be produced in the United States, providing, as it does, many unique maps and a wealth of detail not to be found in other atlases. Most of the maps in the atlas have also been issued singly as folded supplements with the *National Geographic Magazine*, but some are original. All of the maps in this third edition bear a copyright date of 1970, important when checking for recent political changes. All are accurate, clear, and exceptionally easy to read despite the profusion of informative notes on every map page. At first glance the pages have an overcrowded appearance, but the well-chosen and well-edited print makes them exceptionally legible. This is a good atlas—not the best in the world, certainly, but nevertheless an atlas which does provide a great deal of valuable information which will not easily be found elsewhere. The most noteworthy features are: (a) the astonishing quantity of useful and unusual information including location of railroads, highways, air services, missile tracking stations, missile bases, oil pipelines, fathom lines, ocean currents, and many other details; (b) the excellent coverage of obscure and lesser-known areas; (c) the many inset maps of major world cities and metropolitan areas; (d) the special large-scale maps of United States national parks; (e) the fine historical maps of the American Civil War battlefields; (f) the useful temperature and rainfall charts for over 200 cities around the world; and (g) the informative profiles of over 200 countries, states and territories, which also include the national flags (but the reader should watch out for outdated material here). There are, however, factors which detract from this being a really great world atlas, the most notable of which are: (a) its rather weak balance of coverage, with one map in every five allocated to the United States; (b) the bewildering mixture of scales and apparent lack of uniformity, and (c) the inclusion of encyclopedic text which although useful is not properly within the function of an atlas. Purists will be still more offended by this latter provision because of the rather disconcerting lush or flowery text employed. Overall, however, the *National Geographic Atlas* has both merit and quality, which has been professionally recognized by its inclusion in most standard lists of reference books. It is designed to interest laymen as well as scholars, specialists, and students. It does so at a remarkably low cost. It is highly recommended as an atlas for home use as well as for libraries of all types.

CRITICAL REVIEWS AND INFORMATIVE ARTICLES
Saturday Review, April 17, 1971, p. 40.
Choice, July-August 1969, p. 628.
National Geographic Magazine, June 1966, pp. 818-821.
Booklist, July 15, 1964.

OTHER SOURCES OF INFORMATION
American Reference Books Annual. 1972. p. 196.
Barton. *Reference Books.* 1970.
Cheney. *Fundamental Reference Sources.* 1971
Deason. *AAAS Science Book List.* 3rd ed. 1970.
Katz. *Introduction to Reference Work.* 1969.
Lock. *Modern Maps and Atlases.* 1969.
Reference Services Division. *Reference Books for Small and Medium Sized Libraries.* 1969.
Walford. *Guide to Reference Material.* 2nd ed. 1966-1970.
H. W. Wilson Co. *Children's Catalog.* 12th ed. 1971.
H. W. Wilson Co. *Junior High School Library Catalog.* 2nd ed. 1970.
H. W. Wilson Co. *Senior High School Library Catalog.* 9th ed. 1967.
H. W. Wilson Co. *Public Library Catalog.* 5th ed. 1968.
Winchell. *Guide to Reference Books.* 8th ed. 1967, Supplement 1965-1966.
Ziskind. *Reference Readiness.* 1971.

PERGAMON WORLD ATLAS

Merit Rating: 18
Group Two—Above Average Quality: *HIGHLY RECOMMENDED*

PUBLISHER

Pergamon Press Limited, Headington Hill Hall, Oxford OX3 OBW, England, and the Pergamon Press, Inc., Maxwell House, Fairview Park, Elmsford, N.Y. 10523.

PUBLISHING HISTORY AND REVISION PROGRAM

First copyrighted by the Pergamon Press in 1967 (several map pages have the copyright date on them), and first published in this English adaptation in May 1968, but actually first published in Poland between the years 1962 and 1965 as the *Atlas Swiata.* As the atlas is now more than five years old, some of the information is becoming dated, which detracts from its otherwise considerable merit. Although the work was designed in a loose-leaf bound format which in theory permitted the insertion of updated or additional maps without the necessity of reprinting the entire work, no such supplements have been published. The publishers state that there is little likelihood of a new edition before 1977 or 1978. They have also advised, however, that an entirely new concise and updated atlas, based on the *Pergamon,* is to be made available in mid- or late 1973 at less than half the cost of the larger work. This is provisionally entitled the *Universal Reference Atlas.* Further information on this new work will be found under the pertinent entry.

EDITORS, CARTOGRAPHERS, AND CONTRIBUTORS

This atlas was prepared and printed in Poland by the Polish Army Topographical Service under the direction of a general committee of 16 Polish professors and cartographic specialists and three high-ranking officers of the Polish Army, assisted by an editorial committee (under the same chairman) of nine other Polish specialists, nearly all of whom are ranking officers in the Polish Army. Named as the editor in chief of the original Polish edition is Brigadier General Teodor Naumienko. The *Pergamon World Atlas* is a special edition of the original, translated into English and adapted for English-speaking users. This was prepared by nine well-qualified specialists, six of whom were British (including the principal editor, Stanley Knight, F.R.G.S., Head of the Cartographic Department of the Pergamon Press), one American, one Canadian, and one Australian. A full and imposing list of all the committees, the editors, and advisors, is printed on pages ii–iv of the atlas.

HOME SALE AND RETAIL PRICES

Available in one edition only, in a handsome green plastic loose-leaf binder, embossed in bronze. It retails in the United States at $49.50, and in the United Kingdom at £20.00.

PURPOSE AND AGE SUITABILITY

Designed mainly for the specialist and the advanced user, the *Pergamon World Atlas* is a large, comprehensive, and well-detailed reference atlas for cartographers, geographers, lecturers, students, and business executives. Because of its advanced nature, it will not be suitable for use by students below 15 years of age, nor for general home use when there is no special interest in or need for such detailed information. Smaller libraries can certainly manage without it, but it is a must for large reference collections and business libraries.

SIZE AND NUMBER OF PAGES

The single-page bound size is 16 by 12 in., but note that the majority of the maps fold out to make double and treble page spreads of 16 by 24 in. and 16 by 36 in. respectively, for exceptionally wide coverage. The whole work is made up of 524 pages, including four pages of introductory material and a 150-page index.

TOTAL MAP PAGES AND TYPES OF MAPS

The atlas section itself consists of 370 pages containing 200 multicolored topographic maps, frequently using double and treble page spreads to provide an extensive coverage of the more important regions of the world. Included in the atlas section are ten pages of text, tables, statistics, etc. The main series of maps is physical, but is clearly overlaid with political boundaries and administrative divisions, and a wealth of detail, particularly on communications networks of roads, railways, canals, and shipping routes, is provided. Relief features are shown on the maps by an excellently executed series of layer tints in ten delicate shades. Contours, incidentally, as well as spot heights, are given in meters, not feet. A color key to the layer tints is provided on each map page, but this is given in both meters and feet. In addition to the main series of physical maps there are political maps for the world as a whole, for the continents, and for some important larger areas. A notable feature of the atlas is its provision of some 450 small thematic and special-purpose maps dealing with a wide and often unusual range of topics of political, social, and economic importance. These are in three series: global, continental, and individual countries and territories. The various projections employed are clearly stated on each map but, as with most advanced atlases, there is no explanation of projection or scale. The scale is shown on each map in its correct numerical fraction and a scale bar is provided in both miles and kilometers. A legend of the symbols employed is provided on a prefatory page.

SCALE

Every map is well drawn on a large and even series of scales, carefully designed to comply with the geometrical progression of 1:1,250,000; 1:2,500,000; 1:5,000,000 and 1:10,000,000. Europe, not unnaturally, gets preferential treatment, being mapped overall at a scale of 1:5,000,000 as opposed to 1:10,000,000 for North America, South America, Africa, Asia, and Australasia. The larger-scale maps are sensibly provided on a formula of population density. Where this exceeds one person per square kilometer, the region is mapped at 1:5,000,000. When it exceeds ten persons per square kilometer in Europe, or 50 persons per square kilometer in America, or 200 persons per square kilometer in other areas, these regions are mapped at the large scale of 1:2,500,000. For the still more densely populated areas, and for areas of special geographic, political, and economic interest, the scale is still larger at 1:1,250,000. This policy ensures that all the vital areas of the world are adequately dealt with. Additionally, plans of all the world's major cities are provided at the exceptionally good scale of 1:250,000.

BALANCE

Although the *Pergamon World Atlas* is a comprehensive atlas, with coverage of the entire world in fine detail, it does have a decided leaning in favor of European countries, the maps for which are generally more detailed than are those for the western hemisphere. Poland alone, for example, is allocated nine pages. This bias is even more pronounced in the page breakdown by regions, in which North America is allocated 40 pages (including 26 for the United States and eight for Canada), whereas Europe is allocated 110 pages (including ten for the British Isles). Soviet Russia is very well treated with a high ratio of 40 pages, a remark which can be applied to other countries behind the Iron Curtain. Asia is also well detailed in 54 pages, with exceptionally good coverage of China. Africa is allocated 28 pages, Australasia 16, Central America 7, and South America 23.

INDEXING

Very well indexed indeed. The 150-page index contains approximately 140,000 entries for places and physical features. The official (Romanized) spellings have been used for each country, with cross-references from the standard Anglicized spellings, e.g., Cairo (El Qahira). Places are located by the page number and the letter-number system of grid reference but not, surprisingly, by latitude and longitude, the practice usually followed by larger advanced atlases. The index is pure and does not include such information as population statistics, although these and other vital data will be found in the brief summaries for each country.

SCOPE, CONTENTS, AND ARRANGEMENT

A detailed list of contents is provided in the prefatory pages. Every map is listed, and the scale at which each is drawn is clearly stated. The atlas is arranged in four distinct sections: (a) prefatory material, introduction, list of contents, etc.; (b) general maps of the world; (c) maps of the various continents and countries; and (d) the index. Added features worthy of note are the three pages of early world maps; the special astronomy section (six pages); and the brief summaries of vital statistical data for every country, state, and territory, including the national emblem and flag, in color. The continents follow the order of: Europe, Russia, Asia, Africa, North America, South America, Australasia.

SUMMARY

Despite the several political and cultural changes which have taken place since 1967, the *Pergamon World Atlas* remains a monumental and outstanding collection of highly detailed maps of the world which will be of special value to larger public, college, university, and special libraries, and in some instances, to specialist cartographers, geographers, and business executives. However, because of the advanced nature of the contents, the specialized approach, and its high cost, it is unlikely to appeal to the average home user or to smaller public libraries. The cartography is excellent, sometimes superb, although the ten delicate shades of layer tints on an off-white creamy paper will not appeal to everyone. The printing is exceptionally good, very clear, and easy to read. The double and treble page spreads of the fold-out maps provide a broad and well-detailed coverage and overall view of the most important areas of the world, at a large scale. Although originally prepared by Polish topographic authorities and printed in Poland, careful editing of this Anglicized version uses English spellings throughout, as well as the official local spellings. Because of its Eastern European origin, it tends to emphasize coverage of European countries, with particularly detailed coverage of Russia and neighboring Iron Curtain countries. This emphasis is demonstrated by the provision of 150 pages for Europe as against 70 for the whole of the Americas: North, Central, and South. For reference purposes, however, this may well be an advantage in that it does provide a considerable amount of useful statistical data and geographic information for East European countries which will not usually be found in atlases produced in the western hemisphere. Noteworthy features of this good atlas are the provision of excellent large-scale plans for each of the world's major cities; the provision, in full color, of the national emblem and flag of each of the world's countries; and the brief summaries of useful statistical data on all countries, such as area, latest population census figures (but none, of course, later than 1967), capital cities and seats of government, languages, currency, and administrative divisions. Critics of the *Pergamon World Atlas* will point out that areas are given in square kilometers rather than miles, and that on the maps, elevations are given in meters, not feet, although this latter criticism is countered by the provision of a simple conversion scale on each map. Overall, it is an impressive work, providing an astonishing total of some 1,500 well-executed maps of all types. Some criticism has been leveled also at its awkward method of loose-leaf binding (borne out to some extent by the failure of the publishers to provide updating sheets), and the considerable weight (12 lbs.), flaws that do not detract from its inherent quality. It is an important reference tool which, because of its comprehensive coverage, excellent cartography, and valuable sources of geographic information, warrants consideration for inclusion in all important map collections in public, government, college, university, special, and research libraries, with the one reservation that it is now becoming dated in some areas.

CRITICAL REVIEWS AND INFORMATIVE ARTICLES
American Reference Books Annual, 1970, p. 98.
College and Research Libraries, March 1970, p. 116.
Library Quarterly, July 1969, p. 282.
Choice, May 1969, p. 344.
Reference Quarterly, Spring 1969, p. 211.
Catholic Library World, April 1969, p. 502.
Library Journal, March 15, 1969, p. 1129.
Best Sellers, January 1, 1969, p. 415.
Saturday Review, November 16, 1968, p. 61.
Sunday Times, August 18, 1968, p. 13.

OTHER SOURCES OF INFORMATION
Cheney. *Fundamental Reference Sources.* 1971.
Lock. *Modern Maps and Atlases.* 1969.
Walford. *Guide to Reference Material.* 2nd ed. 1966–1970.
Winchell. *Guide to Reference Books.* 8th ed. 1967; 2nd supplement 1967–1968.

McGRAW-HILL INTERNATIONAL ATLAS

Merit Rating: 17
Group Two—Above Average Quality: *HIGHLY RECOMMENDED*

PUBLISHER
McGraw-Hill Book Co., 1221 Ave. of the Americas, New York, N.Y. 10020.

PUBLISHING HISTORY AND REVISION PROGRAM
First published under its present (Anglicized) title in the United States in 1964, but originally published in Europe in 1961, as the *Der Grosser Bertelsmann Weltatlas.* This was revised, updated, and adapted for the United States and other English-speaking countries. The only edition to date, unfortunately, is that of 1964, and there is no announced policy of a revised and updated new edition.

EDITORS, CARTOGRAPHERS, AND CONTRIBUTORS

Edited originally by Dr. Werner Bormann, assisted by a worldwide staff of cartographers and geographers, all of whom are listed on page xii of the atlas.

HOME SALE AND RETAIL PRICES

Available in one edition only, at $59.50 in the United States, and at £17.85 in the United Kingdom (through McGraw-Hill Limited, Maidenhead).

PURPOSE AND AGE SUITABILITY

This is an advanced major reference atlas for specialist use, advanced research, and for use by students from the age of 15 through high school, college, and university levels. The use of non-English terms tends to render the atlas more difficult for younger students, although the text is printed in English, French, and German.

SIZE AND NUMBER OF PAGES

The single-page bound size is 16 by 12 in., but most of the maps are spread over two facing pages for an actual display of 16 by 24 in. minus the margins. The atlas is comprised of a total of 544 pages and plates, not consecutively paginated, but broken down into groups of xii, 20, 20, 252, 188, and 52 pages, a rather inconvenient arrangement.

TOTAL MAP PAGES AND TYPES OF MAPS

The atlas proper, i.e. the maps, are contained in 126 plates (252 pages) and are comprised of multicolored (eight shades) physical–political maps of the countries and regions of the world, with relief shown by a well-executed series of layer tints and hill shading, although some indistinct boundaries were noted and the shading on some maps did not fully emphasize mountainous areas. A wealth of detail is presented on each map, and as most of these are spread over two facing pages, the full range of roads, railroads, and many other cultural and natural features are clearly seen, including rivers, airports, and canals. The projections employed are clearly specified on each map and there is a good explanation of these in the introductory section. Scale is shown both as a numerical fraction and on a scale bar which gives both miles and kilometers. A complete list of map symbols and the abbreviations employed is also provided at the beginning of the main atlas section. Only one thematic map is provided, a world economic map on pages 8 and 9. A particularly commendable feature is the practice of indicating in the margins the page numbers of the adjoining maps. Another commendable feature is the detailed introduction to the plan of the atlas, the explanations of the scales and projections employed, the principles of nomenclature adopted, and a key to languages and names. Note that for the continents, political maps are provided.

SCALE

Although the entire world is covered in great detail, there is at the same time a mixture of scales at which the maps are drawn, and there is a decided emphasis on Europe. The United States, for example, is quite well mapped at a scale of 1:4,000,000, but Canada, on the other hand, is dealt with in only one map at a scale of 1:12,000,000. Europe is exceptionally well mapped, with most of it covered at a scale of 1:2,000,000, including the British Isles. Russia is also well done at a scale of 1:2,000,000. The emphasis on Europe is demonstrated by the special section for Central Europe, where the maps are at a scale of 1:800,000, plus one very large scale map of the industrial region of North Rhine, Westphalia, at 1:400,000. For Asia, the important areas are mapped at 1:4,000,000 but the remoter areas are rather poorly scaled at 1:12,000,000. Australia, New Zealand, and Oceania are also small at scales of 1:12,000,000 and 1:24,000,000 (just two maps). Africa is mapped in three regions at 1:4,000,000 and in two regions at 1:12,000,000. Central America is almost dismissed, with just one map at a scale of 1:12,000,000. South America does better, however, with two maps at 1:12,000,000, but most of the maps are at the larger scale of 1:4,000,000.

BALANCE

Here there is also a decided emphasis on Europe, which is allocated 30 plates (60 pages) in the main atlas section, plus an additional 20 plates (40 pages) in the special section for Central Europe. North America, conversely, and this includes Central America, is allocated 14 plates (28 pages) only. Russia and Eastern Europe are allocated six plates (12 pages); Asia 22 plates (44 pages); Australia and Oceania two plates (four pages); Africa ten plates (20 pages); and South America seven plates (14 pages). Of the 100 plates in the main atlas, Europe is allocated almost one third, a decided imbalance in favor of Europe.

INDEXING

The indexes are in two distinct sections. The first and most important index is that of the entire world, which is 188 pages long and contains about 150,000 entries. The second relates to the special Central European section of maps and contains approximately 25,000 entries in its 52 pages. The indexing is comprehensive and detailed, including geographic features, and variants and older forms of place names. Place names are given in each country's own language with cross-references provided. The main index is printed on white paper, the second index on a tinted paper. Both are provided with short updating supplements.

SCOPE, CONTENTS, AND ARRANGEMENT

A detailed list of contents is provided in the front of the atlas, and this clearly specifies the scale for each listed map. Preceding the atlas section proper is an excellent introductory section, including a preface which gives a brief history of atlases, the problems faced by cartographers, and a sound explanation of map projections and scale. The map section is divided into six broad sections: the world, Europe, Asia, Australia, Africa, and America (North and South). The main map section is followed by a special map section for Central Europe. Completing the atlas are the two index sections.

SUMMARY

The *McGraw-Hill International Atlas* is, without question, one of the finest reference world atlases ever produced, with superb physical-political maps of outstanding quality, legibility, and beauty. It has a fine series of layer colors and shaded areas which are highly effective. No less than eight shades were used to depict relief. It contains a wealth of topographic and cultural detail, with surface forms and relationships especially prominent, although political, industrial, and cultural data are presented in more than adequate detail also. Printed in Germany, and originally compiled there, it understandably leans towards a coverage of Europe, especially Central Europe. This tends to imbalance the coverage of the rest of the world, although it is all represented in good detail. Nevertheless, an atlas which devotes half its maps to one continent is far less effective as a world atlas, splendid though it may be for one area. The text sections are in three languages: English, French, and German. This makes it a truly international atlas, but at the same time, tends to enlarge the contents to a sometimes unnecessary extent, which has to be paid for. Three features worthy of note are the giving of place names in the country's own language (e.g., Norge—Norway); the comprehensive glossary of geographic terms; and the outstandingly comprehensive index of some 175,000 entries (although split into two sections) which refers the user from his own language to the valid term, particularly important in view of the fact that the names on the maps are quite often only in German. An atlas in the purest sense of the term, with little in the way of nonmap material and a minimum of nongeographic maps, beautifully produced, extremely well detailed and comprehensive, the *McGraw-Hill International Atlas* is still essential for reference purposes in libraries of all types. The one reservation about it now is its age. Since it is almost ten years old, users will not find in it political or cultural changes which have taken place since 1964.

CRITICAL REVIEWS AND INFORMATIVE ARTICLES

Choice, July-August 1969, pp. 625–630.
Booklist, December 15, 1965, pp. 378–382.
Library Journal, November 15, 1964, p. 4509.

OTHER SOURCES OF INFORMATION

Barton. *Reference Books.* 7th ed. 1970.
Cheney. *Fundamental Reference Sources.* 1971.
Katz. *Introduction to Reference Work.* 1969.
Lock. *Modern Maps and Atlases.* 1969.
Walford. *Guide to Reference Material.* 2nd ed. 1966–1970.

UNIVERSAL REFERENCE ATLAS

Merit Rating: 16 (Provisional)
Group Two—Above Average Quality: *HIGHLY RECOMMENDED*

PUBLISHER

Pergamon Press Limited, Headington Hill Hall, Oxford OX3 OBW, England. Will be distributed in the United States, but no final arrangements had been made at time of going to press.

PUBLISHING HISTORY AND REVISION PROGRAM

The Universal Reference Atlas is to be published in mid- or late 1973. Although entirely new in several ways, it is based on the excellent maps contained in the larger, more comprehensive *Pergamon World Atlas*. There has been no stated policy of revision as yet but it is probable that, at this low cost, revised editions will be forthcoming at regular intervals.

EDITORS, CARTOGRAPHERS, AND CONTRIBUTORS

Principal editor is Stanley Knight, F.R.G.S., Head of the Cartographic Department of the Pergamon Press. See also the entry under the *Pergamon World Atlas* on which this new work is based.

HOME SALE AND RETAIL PRICES

Not finalized at time of compilation of survey, but expected to retail in the United Kingdom at between £6.00 and £7.00, and in the United States at from $15.00 to $17.50.

PURPOSE AND AGE SUITABILITY

Designed as an intermediate-sized yet comprehensive atlas for all-round general use by laymen as well as specialists. The suggested age range is from 12 years of age through college. Smaller public and branch libraries should find it a useful acquisition where larger works cannot be afforded.

SIZE AND NUMBER OF PAGES

Single-page bound size will be 13½ by 9½ in., with a considerable number of maps spread over two facing pages for an overall view of 13½ by 19 in. before margin loss. It is expected to be comprised of a total of 300 pages.

TOTAL MAP PAGES AND TYPES OF MAPS

According to the publishers, at least 176 pages of the atlas will be devoted to maps of all types. The main series will be physical-political maps. These will be in full color but, in an interesting innovation, the editors are designing an entirely new series of layer tints to break away from the traditional green base of physical maps. On the first proof offered for evaluation the base color is yellow, with higher land shown in increasing shades of brown.

Green is being used for land below sea level. This format, however, has not yet been finalized. A color key to the shades used is provided on each map, with the heights and depths shown in both feet and meters. The maps will be exceptionally well detailed, showing both expressways (motorways) and other classes of highways, railroads, airports, canals, and a variety of topographic features. The methods of projection employed are clearly stated on the map pages, as is the scale at which the map is drawn. This is shown as a numerical fraction and also on a bar scale in both miles and kilometers.

SCALE

Not enough data have been provided to assess whether the atlas will be adequately scaled. If, however, it is based on the *Pergamon World Atlas* series of scales, it will be uniformly scaled throughout the world, based on the population density formula used in the larger atlas.

BALANCE

Similarly, there are insufficient data yet available to assess the balance of coverage. It is unlikely, however, to be as pro-European as the *Pergamon World Atlas*, and there should be a more even representation of the entire globe. On the other hand, because of its restricted size, it must inevitably be more selective in its large-scale maps.

INDEXING

There will, according to the publishers, be a comprehensive index of about 90,000 entries, more than adequate for an atlas of this size and purpose.

SCOPE, CONTENTS, AND ARRANGEMENT

Insufficient data available to describe in detail. There will be 176 pages of maps, however, and the index will occupy about 100 pages, leaving about 24 pages for the introductory or additional material.

SUMMARY

Due to the fact that this new atlas is not yet available for a detailed analysis and evaluation, a provisional assessment and rating has been made based on some of the advance, but not finalized material. In terms of quality it is anticipated that this will be a very good medium-sized atlas, with excellent detail and more than adequate indexing. Because it is based on the excellent *Pergamon World Atlas*, it will include well-executed maps which will cover the entire earth at a uniform and well-selected scale. Certainly, judging from the first advance proofs, it will contain a wealth of detail and in that respect alone will be a work of great reference usefulness, especially when combined with an index of some 90,000 entries.

What may well come as a surprise is the radical departure from the traditional methods of layer coloring to show relief. This may be disconcerting at first glance. The proof sheet, for example, showed the British Isles on a yellow base surrounded by a deep blue sea; on first glance, this suggested a desert island in the Pacific. It was only on a further examination and adjustment of standard values that the merit of the new coloring became apparent, with the excellent black type standing out exceptionally clearly, having none of the cluttered appearance sometimes associated with maps of many colors. Superhighways, other roads, railroads, canals, and similar features were equally clearly seen. Overall, the new *Universal Reference Atlas* has all the appearances of being an excellent reference atlas in the intermediate range, and cartographers at least will appreciate the new color arrangement. Departing from the traditional colors, however, may not be appreciated by others less versed in cartographic techniques. This is a risk which the publishers are apparently prepared to accept, and credit is due to them for this bold break with tradition.

CRITICAL REVIEWS AND INFORMATIVE ARTICLES

None yet available, but they should be most interesting when they appear.

OTHER SOURCES OF INFORMATION

None yet available.

THE OXFORD ATLAS
and
THE CANADIAN OXFORD ATLAS OF THE WORLD

Merit Rating: 15
Group Two—Above Average Quality: *HIGHLY RECOMMENDED*

PUBLISHER

In the United States: Oxford University Press, Inc., 417 Fifth Ave., New York, N.Y. 10016. In Canada: Oxford University Press, 70 Wynford Drive, Don Mills, Toronto, Ontario. In the United Kingdom: The Oxford University Press, Ely House, 37 Dover Street, London WIX 4AH, England.

PUBLISHING HISTORY AND REVISION PROGRAM

Both atlases were first published in 1951, as was also the now defunct *American Oxford Atlas* (q.v.). The *Oxford Atlas* is issued periodically in revised and updated new printings, the latest of which, at the time of compiling this survey, was 1970. There is no announced policy of revision, however, and the atlases, basically, are those specially created in 1951.

EDITORS, CARTOGRAPHERS, AND CONTRIBUTORS

The *Oxford Atlas* is edited by Brigadier General Sir Clinton Lewis and Colonel J. D. Campbell, with the assistance of D. P. Bickmore and K. F. Cook.

The *Canadian Oxford Atlas* has the same editors and cartographers as for the parent edition, but includes an additional section on Canada edited by E. G. Pleva, Professor of Geography at the University of Western Ontario. Maps were made by the staff of the Cartographic Department of the Clarendon Press, although none of these are named in either atlas.

HOME SALE AND RETAIL PRICES

The *Oxford Atlas* retails at £4.50 in the United Kingdom. The *Canadian Oxford Atlas*, with its additional pages, retails at £6.30. In the United States the *Oxford Atlas* retails at $16.50 but, surprisingly, the *Canadian Oxford*, despite the additional material, is cheaper at $14.95.

PURPOSE AND AGE SUITABILITY

Designed mainly for high school, college, and university students, and the more serious home user. Relatively advanced in presentation, its suggested beginning age is 15 years, continuing through college and university to fairly advanced use by specialist adults.

SIZE AND NUMBER OF PAGES

The single-page bound size is 15½ by 10½ in., but the margins in this atlas are rather wide and the actual map pages measure 13 by 8½ in. On the other hand, as with most of the better atlases, nearly all the maps are spread over two facing pages, which gives an overall map coverage of 13 by 18 in. The original British edition is comprised of 214 pages. The Canadian edition is identical except for the addition of 28 pages of maps and a gazetteer of Canada.

TOTAL MAP PAGES AND TYPES OF MAPS

The *Oxford Atlas* contains 110 pages of physical-political maps in six colors (95 are double spread), plus a further 24 pages of thematic and special-purpose maps on precipitation, population, vegetation, rainfall, geological structure, predominant land use, air routes, and similar items for the world, Europe, Great Britain, the United States, Canada, and Asia. The Canadian edition has the same contents, plus an additional seven pages of thematic maps, 13 physical-political maps of Canada, and an eight-page gazetteer of Canada. The main series of maps in both atlases consists of the excellent Oxford physical maps, with relief shown by six layer tints and hill shading, but no contour lines. A key to the layer tints is provided for each map. Detail is good, with a full array of lines of communication, political divisions, boundaries, etc. The scale at which each map is drawn is clearly shown, as are the projections used. A particularly commendable feature is the provision of footnotes giving full particulars of the projections used on each map, and the incidence of scale errors and corrections. An excellent explanation of map projections is provided on pages 6–7 of the atlas. Most map pages are accompanied by detailed inset maps of the most important areas of the world.

SCALE

This is relatively large throughout, but there is a decided emphasis on Europe generally and Britain in particular. Europe is mapped mostly at 1:2,000,000 (France, northern Germany, and the Low Countries), but with some areas (Spain, Italy, Central Europe, and Scandinavia) at 1:4,000,000. Britain is especially well mapped in four regions, at a scale of 1:1,000,000. The United States, conversely, is mapped at 1:5,000,000 for the eastern and central states, but at only 1:8,000,000 for the western states. European Russia is mapped at a scale of 1:10,000,000 but the rest, including Eastern Russia, is at the relatively small scale of 1:18,000,000. Asia varies from 1:4,000,000 for the Middle East to 1:10,000,000 for the Far East. Southeastern Australia is quite well detailed at a scale of 1:5,000,000, but central and western Australia are at only half this scale, at 1:10,000,000. The scale for Africa also varies, from 1:4,000,000 for southern Africa to 1:8,000,000 for the other regions. Areas of South America are mapped at either 1:8,000,000 or 1:16,000,000. In the Canadian edition, the 13 physical maps of Canada vary from 1:1,500,000 for the Upper St. Lawrence area through 1:4,000,000 for the most important regions, and 1:5,000,000 for British Columbia, Ontario, eastern Canada, and the Prairie Provinces.

BALANCE

There is again a distinct emphasis on European coverage, especially Great Britain, Europe, and, in the Canadian edition, Canada also. Of the 88 physical maps pages in the original edition (excluding the thematic world maps), 13 are general maps allocated to the Arctic and Antarctic regions, the Atlantic, Pacific, and Indian Oceans, Eurasia, Europe, and Western Asia. These are followed, in order, by ten pages for the British Isles, with a further 16 pages for other European countries. Four pages are provided for a coverage of the U.S.S.R.; 14 for Asia and the Middle East; 6 for Australia, New Zealand, and the Pacific Islands; ten for Africa, and three for Central and South America. The United States, in comparison, is allocated only eight pages, with an additional four for Canada. In the Canadian edition, however, there are an additional 13 pages of maps for Canada. Both editions provide a 24-page section of thematic maps, augmented in the Canadian edition by a further seven pages of thematic maps for Canada.

INDEXING

Both atlases provide a fairly comprehensive index-gazetteer of the world, comprised of approximatley 50,000 entries, which list every town, village, settlement, and geographic feature named on the map pages. Alternative spellings and historical names are included where applicable. An unusual and useful feature of the index is the provision of reference panels for sovereign states and larger colonial possessions and territories, giving such pertinent information as population, area, and other vital administrative data. The Canadian edition provides a supplementary eight-page gazetteer index of approximately 5 000 entries for Canadian cities, towns, etc.

SCOPE, CONTENTS, AND ARRANGEMENT

A detailed list of contents is provided in the front of the atlas, which lists each map and the scale at which it is drawn. Both editions are arranged in the same way, the first eight pages being devoted to the list of contents, an explanation of map projections, a list of states and territories, and introductory notes. These are followed by the main series of physical maps arranged by the continents, beginning with Europe and ending with South America. These are followed by the 25-page section of distribution and special-purpose maps, and the index. In the Canadian edition, the front matter is comprised of seven pages of special thematic maps of Canada, 13 pages of physical maps of Canada, and an eight-page gazetteer of Canada.

SUMMARY

The largest of the Oxford series of general-reference world atlases, and one of the best medium-sized atlases produced in Britain. Well edited under a carefully formulated plan, the atlas was compiled with the cooperation of several well-known geographers, geologists, economists, historians, and statisticians. Handsomely produced, with excellent topographic maps in a range of six pleasing shades, it maps the entire world at a relatively large scale, although, as with most atlases, the country and continent of origin are given preferential treatment. The maps are well detailed, with the political and administrative divisions clearly marked with bold red boundary lines, and clearly defined lines of communication included. Features worthy of special note are (a) the excellent series of 24 pages of natural and human distribution maps (several of them at quite a large scale), which will be especially useful to college and university students; (b) the footnotes with each map giving detailed particulars of the projections employed; and (c) the well-detailed, informative reference panels in the gazetteer index. Prospective purchasers should take careful note that although the two titles are identical in their basic contents, the Canadian regional edition contains an additional 28 pages of maps and information on Canada. There appears to be an anomaly in the cost of the Canadian edition, however. If purchased in Britain it will cost more than the basic *Oxford* edition, but if purchased in the United States it is actually cheaper by $1.55 than the British edition. Overall, however, the *Oxford Atlas*, with or without the additional material on Canada, is a good medium-sized atlas, with excellent maps and no extraneous material. It is reasonably well balanced, despite the preferential treatment allocated to the British Isles. Also it is particularly useful when physical maps with an emphasis on regions of the world rather than individual countries are required. Libraries may wish to add either edition (but not both) to their map reference collections but should bear in mind that because the most recent publication date is more likely to be a revised reprint than an entirely new edition, the up-to-dateness of political changes may be suspect in some areas. Inexpensive abridged editions of the *Oxford Atlas* are the *Concise Oxford Atlas* (q.v.), the *Oxford Home Atlas*, the *Little Oxford Atlas*, and the school, desk, and Canadian regional editions of some of these.

CRITICAL REVIEWS AND INFORMATIVE ARTICLES
None have been traced in recent years.

OTHER SOURCES OF INFORMATION
Lock. *Modern Maps and Atlases.* 1969.
Walford. *Guide to Reference Material.* 2nd ed. 1966–1970.

THE ATLAS OF THE EARTH
and
THE CAXTON ATLAS OF THE EARTH

Merit Rating 15
Group Two—Above Average Quality: *HIGHLY RECOMMENDED*

PUBLISHERS
For *The Atlas of the Earth* (the trade edition), publishers are George Philip and Son Limited, 12–14 Long Acre, London WC2E 9LP, England. The United States·distributors are the Denoyer-Geppert Co., 5235 Ravenswood Ave., Chicago, Ill. The *Caxton Atlas of the Earth* (a subscription edition) is published under the imprint of International Learning Systems Corporation Limited, 72–90 Worship Street, London EC2, England, and will probably be available in the United States through the Purnell Library Service, 850 Seventh Ave. New York, N.Y. 10019.

PUBLISHING HISTORY AND REVISION PROGRAM
The *Atlas of the Earth* was first published in 1972. It is a new work, with new maps and new text, and bears no relation, other than a common ownership, to the much older *Caxton World Atlas.* It is comprised of two distinct works, an atlas proper, which was produced and copyrighted by George Philip and Son, and an encyclopedia of the earth, which bears the copyright of Mitchell Beazley Limited, who, it is worth noting, also produced the well-received *Atlas of the Universe.* There is no stated policy of revision, although doubtless new printings will be implemented as and when needed.

EDITORS, CARTOGRAPHERS, AND CONTRIBUTORS
A number of people are listed as editors, some for the atlas, and others for the text section. Harold Fullard is listed as the cartographic director (Dr. Fullard is the Cartographic Director of all atlases made by George Philip and Son); with Christopher Dorling as editorial director. For the text section Tony Loftas is listed as editor, with Martyn Bramwell as deputy editor, Bill Gunston as text editor, and Max Monsarrat as assistant text editor. Also listed are 32 Chief Editorial Consultants and Advisors, which includes three Americans and one Swede. Many of these are well known and well qualified

authorities in their respective subject fields. Two, for example, are executives of Rand McNally and Co., Chicago. Most of the authorities, however, have contributed to the text section rather than to the actual maps, which have been produced by George Philip and Son Limited, under the direction of Dr. Harold Fullard.

HOME SALE AND RETAIL PRICES

Both editions are understood to be available at one price only, although the outward appearance of each is different. The *Caxton* edition is in red imitation leatherette with gold stamping. Both are priced at £13.95 in the United Kingdom, and estimated at $35.00 for the United States.

PURPOSE AND AGE SUITABILITY

A combination of two separate yet related works, the *Atlas of the Earth* is clearly intended more for home and general use than for the library or the specialist user. The suggested age range is from 12 through college, but younger children will probably find the encyclopedic section attractive and interesting. The maps, on the other hand, are more sophisticated. More than just an atlas, being an encylcopedia of the environment also, it will appeal to the entire family, meeting their map-reference and geographic interests in an interesting and motivating format.

SIZE AND NUMBER OF PAGES

Single-page size is 14½ by 10½ in., but margins reduce this to 12¼ by 10 in., except for the double-page spreads, which measure 12¼ by 20 in. It contains a total of 446 pages, made up of 144 pages of encyclopedic text and illustrations, 176 pages of maps, 16 pages of climatic graphs, maps of national parks throughout the world, and an index to the text section, culminating in an index section of 110 pages.

TOTAL MAP PAGES AND TYPES OF MAPS

The *Caxton Atlas of the Earth* contains 176 pages of multicolored maps, plus four black and white maps of the national parks of the world, and a number of special thematic maps in the Good Earth encyclopedic section. The main series of maps is physical, but they are overlaid with adequate political detail. Relief is shown on these by an excellent series of layer tints and hill shading, with a color key in both feet and meters provided in the page margins. Detail is excellent, with a full range of lines of communication, airports, and similar features. The main series of maps is supplemented by a good variety of thematic maps on density of population, rainfall, natural vegetation, geology, and other similar material, on both a world level and a continental level, with preferential treatment given to the British Isles. There are also occasional inset maps for important or overlapping areas. The projections employed are clearly stated on each map, along with the fractional scale. The work would have been improved, especially for home use, if the fractional scale were also provided in its equivalent of miles per inch, together with explanations of scale and map projections. Scale bars, however, are given in both miles and kilometers. Useful also are the small locator and comparative maps provided in the pleasantly colored gray margins.

SCALE

Scales throughout are quite large and adequate although there is an emphasis on Europe. The British Isles are exceptionally well scaled at 1:800,00, as also is the important Sambre-Meuse-Ruhr region of Central Europe. Europe, as a whole, is mapped at the good scale of 1:2,000,000. Central and south European Russia is also well scaled at 1:4,000,000, but Asia is less favorably treated, with scales ranging from 1:4,000,000 for southern Japan, through 1:4,750,000 for India, to 1:8,000,000 for most of the rest of Asia. A notable exception is the Holy Land, mapped at a scale of 1:800,000. Africa is reasonably well scaled at 1:6,500,000, and special attention is given to southern Africa at 1:3,250,000. Australia is at almost the same scale, 1:6,000,000, with the important southeastern corner done at 1:3,500,000. New Zealand is much better off, the two islands being scaled at 1:2,750,000. The rest of the world, however, seems to have been packed into the remaining pages. Central America, Mexico, and the West Indies are poorly detailed at 1:9,500,000. South America is even more poorly detailed at 1:12,750,000 with the exception of central South America at 1:6,500,000. Canada is dealt with in four pages at a scale of 1:5,500,000, and the United States is only slightly better detailed at 1:4,750,000, with the important northeast region at 1:2,000,000.

BALANCE

The emphasis on Europe is even clearer in this context. Europe is allocated 66 pages in all, of which the British Isles alone receive 21. The United States, much larger, is allocated only ten pages. The U.S.S.R. receives eight pages, and Canada six. Asia is covered in only 23 pages, and Africa is allocated only 21. Australasia, on the other hand, is well treated in 12 pages. The two areas most poorly covered are Central America, in only two pages, and South America in only seven pages.

INDEXING

Although there is a reasonably comprehensive index of some 65,000 entries, this is perhaps smaller than would be expected of an atlas of this size, which has more than 170 fairly large-scale maps. Places and features are located by their exact degrees of latitude and longitude. There are no population figures or other types of gazetteer information in the index, but the approximate sizes of cities are indicated on the maps. Note that a smaller separate index of some 2,000 entries is provided for the Good Earth encyclopedic section.

SCOPE, CONTENTS, AND ARRANGEMENT

The work, as a whole, is divided into two main sections: the encyclopedic text section entitled The Good Earth, and the atlas proper. The former is

comprised of 144 pages and is to all intents and purposes an entirely separate work. There are two lists of contents: the first, at the front of the atlas,
refers for the most part to the encyclopedic section, and the second, which is
on the page immediately preceding the maps (p. 144), is a detailed list of
the maps in the atlas, showing the scale for each. The encyclopedic section
is broken down into (1) The Earth in Space, (2) The Structure of the Earth,
(3) Life on Earth, (4) The Resources of the Earth, and (5) Man on Earth.
This section includes several thematic maps. The atlas proper is arranged in
the following order: (1) General World Maps, (2) Europe, (3) Asia, (4) Africa, (5) Australasia, and (6) the Americas.

SUMMARY

The *Atlas of the Earth* and the *Caxton Atlas of the Earth* are identical in
every respect but title. It is more than just a collection of maps, being, in
fact, a general world atlas "married" to an encyclopedia of the earth, or two
quite separate works in one. The first section, the encyclopedic Good Earth,
is a beautifully illustrated, superbly produced history of the development of
the earth and its inhabitants, beginning with the formation of the earth and
its place in the universe, proceeding in stages through its structure and geology, the origin of life and its evolution to the present time, the resources of
the earth, and finally man and his environment, concluding with a timely
treatment of the problems of pollution and how they can be resolved. Strictly speaking, this is not atlas material, but it is done exceptionally well by the
makers of the *Atlas of the Universe* (Mitchell Beazley) and is well worth the
additional cost for those who would make use of it. The atlas proper takes
up the second part of the volume, and is comprised of 176 pages of well-
drawn, accurate, and up-to-date maps which are on a reasonably large scale
and are well detailed but, as has already been noted, contain an imbalance
of coverage in favor of Europe. These are supplemented by a wide variety
of useful thematic and political maps, some of which are on quite a large
scale. This is a good quality atlas, combined with a good encyclopedia of the
earth, and it should interest children and others in the average family, for
whom it is recommended. It would have been better still if the publishers
had thought to add to its usefulness to younger readers by providing explanations of projections, scale, and the use of an atlas. Libraries are unlikely to want to acquire it for their map reference collections at this price, especially as they can duplicate the encyclopedic section with alternative titles.

CRITICAL REVIEWS AND INFORMATIVE ARTICLES

None yet available.

OTHER SOURCES OF INFORMATION

None yet available.

ALDINE UNIVERSITY ATLAS

Merit Rating: 14
Group Two—Above Average Quality: *HIGHLY RECOMMENDED*

PUBLISHER

Aldine Atherton Inc., 529 South Wabash Ave., Chicago, Ill. 60605; and George Philip and Son Limited, 12–14 Long Acre, London WC2E 9LP, England.

PUBLISHING HISTORY AND REVISION PROGRAM

First published under this title in 1969, but actually an American adaptation of the highly successful *University Atlas* published in Britain by George Philip and Son Limited, which was first published in 1936 and was in its 14th edition in 1972. There is no announced policy of revision, but all of the Philip atlases are revised at frequent intervals and this will doubtless follow suit.

EDITORS, CARTOGRAPHERS, AND CONTRIBUTORS

Listed as the principal editors are Harold Fullard, H. C. Darby, and Norton Ginsburg. Mr. Fullard is the Cartographic Director of George Philip and Son Limited, Dr. Darby is Professor of Geography at the University of Cambridge, and Mr. Ginsburg, who is the consulting editor for this work, is Professor of Geography at the University of Chicago.

HOME SALE AND RETAIL PRICES

Available in one binding only, the *Aldine University Atlas* is sold at $8.50 in the United States, and at £3.75 in the United Kingdom.

PURPOSE AND AGE SUITABILITY

This is essentially a school and college atlas. It can be used from the age of ten through the last year of high school and even into college, although at that point the need for a larger work will become more apparent. It is equally suitable for all-round family use and as a desk atlas.

SIZE AND NUMBER OF PAGES

A relatively small atlas in format, the single-page size is 11½ by 9½ in., but the majority of the excellent physical maps are spread over two facing pages for a map coverage of 10 by 16 in. after allowing for margins. It is comprised of 318 pages in all, broken down into three units of eight pages of prefatory material, 208 pages of maps and graphs, and a 102-page index.

TOTAL MAP PAGES AND TYPES OF MAPS

There are 192 pages of maps of all types. The main series consists of excellent physical-political maps of the world, and these are supplemented by a wide variety of well-selected thematic maps. The cartography is superb and at quite a large scale throughout. Relief is shown by an excellent series of layer colors and shading which is tasteful, eye-catching, and meaningful. A key to the layer colors is provided on each page, with heights and depths shown in both feet and meters. The maps are unusually well detailed, showing boundaries, principal highways and railroads, tunnels, canals, pipelines, air routes, airports, shipping routes, rivers, locks, swamps, wells, ice, mountain passes, and other features. The heights and depths shown on the maps are in feet, but a conversion scale is supplied with the excellent list of map symbols on a plate preceding the maps. The projections employed are given on each map, as also are the scales, both as a representative numerical fraction and on a bar distance scale in both miles and kilometers. It would have been of use to students to have had the equivalent miles-per-inch scale provided. A very useful supplementary pamphlet is provided with the atlas. Entitled *The Use of an Atlas*, it provides excellent explanations of projections and scale, and other useful aids to map-reading skills.

SCALE

For what is a relatively small-format atlas, the scale is exceptionally large and uniform. The United States is scaled mainly at 1:6,000,000, with the exceptions of the northeastern United States at 1:2,500,000 and Hawaii at 1:5,000,000. The eastern side of Canada is mapped at 1:7,000,000, but the only map which includes western Canada is at 1:15,000,000. The British Isles are well mapped at 1:2,000,000, with the southeastern corner at 1:1,000,000. Most of Europe is at 1:2,500,000, but with some important regions at 1:1,000,000 and areas of lesser importance at 1:5,000,000. European Russia is covered in two maps at 1:5,000,000 and one at 1:10,000,000. The scales for Asia vary widely, from 1:1,000,000 for the Holy Land and 1:6,000,000 for the Near and Middle East. China is scaled at 1:6,000,000 and 1:10,000,000; Japan at 1:5,000,000 and 1:10,000,000. Other areas vary from 1:7,500,000 for Java to 1:10,000,000 for southern Asia. Africa is mapped at 1:4,000,000 in the Nile Delta, but at 1:8,000,000 for other regions, and at 1:15,000,000 for the uninhabited areas. Southeastern Australia is mapped at 1:4,500,000, but the other areas are at 1:7,500,000. New Zealand is more detailed at 1:3,500,000. Some small islands are mapped at the surprisingly large scale of 1:250,000.

BALANCE

On the whole, the atlas is well balanced, although Europe and North America between them take up almost half the map pages. Thirty-two pages are allocated to North America, of which 11 are allocated to the United States only, and six to Canada. Europe is allocated 52 pages, of which nine pages are devoted to a coverage of the British Isles. Asia gets 25 pages, Africa 19, and Australasia 11. Russia and South America are each allocated eight pages, with a further two for Central America. Twenty pages are given over to general world and continental maps, and six pages to the Polar regions and the oceans.

INDEXING

Another good feature considering the size of this atlas. There are 102 pages containing approximately 50,000 entries, which include features as well as places, and these are exactly located by the correct degrees of latitude and longitude. Reference is made to the largest-scale map when a place or feature is on one or more maps. Preceding the index is a list of alternative spellings of place names and a list of the abbreviations used. The index is pure and contains no gazetteer information or population statistics.

SCOPE, CONTENTS, AND ARRANGEMENT

A well-arranged atlas, with a minimum of nonatlas material. A detailed list of the contents is provided in the usual forefront, and this shows the scale for each map listed. The first eight pages are comprised of the list of contents and an excellent Introduction to Atlases. The first 29 pages of the map section contain a wide and extrememly well-selected range of thematic maps of the world, many of which will not be found in much larger atlases. Beginning then with North America, the physical-political maps (accompanied by a further series of regional thematic maps) proceed through Central and South America, Europe, the U.S.S.R., Asia, Africa, and Australasia. The atlas proper is followed by a 16-page text section which provides a useful list of international organizations, and world statistical information, arranged alphabetically by country, giving area, population, production, manufactures, and trade. Finally there is the index, which is separately paginated 1–102.

SUMMARY

The *Aldine University Atlas* is an excellent smaller school, college, and university atlas and is probably the best of its kind presently available. The maps are of an exceptionally high quality, with firm but pleasing colors and excellent detail, and which, because of their development over a period of years, are more accurate, more reliable, and better designed than those usually found in new atlases. For these and other reasons it is an atlas of real value (especially at the low cost) for college-level courses. It will, inevitably, be compared to the fine *Goode's World Atlas* which has been, for more than forty years, by far the best medium-sized atlas in the United States. The *Aldine* is better in a number of respects. It has a few less pages than *Goode's* but is more than $2.00 cheaper. The maps are more detailed, and there are eight more pages of them, but perhaps the most obvious superiority lies in the indexes, with the *Aldine* providing some 15,000 additional entries. Designed though it is for school and college use, *Aldine University Atlas* will be just as useful in homes, libraries, and offices. As such, it is highly recommended as the most inexpensive alternative to one of the more comprehensive large-scale atlases.

CRITICAL REVIEWS AND INFORMATIVE ARTICLES

Choice, March 1970, p. 40.
Reference Quarterly (RQ), Summer 1969, pp. 284–285.

OTHER SOURCES OF INFORMATION

American Reference Books Annual, 1970, p. 96.

GOODE'S WORLD ATLAS

Merit Rating: 13
Group Two—Above Average Quality: *HIGHLY RECOMMENDED*

PUBLISHER

Rand McNally and Co., P.O. Box 7600, Chicago, Ill., 60680

PUBLISHING HISTORY AND REVISION PROGRAM

First published in 1922, when it was known as *Goode's School Atlas.* It continued under this title until 1949 when it was amended slightly to become *Goode's World Atlas.* The latest edition is the 13th (1970), and the edition analyzed here is the second revised printing of the 13th edition. It is maintained under a program of continuous revision and is reprinted annually, at least, to incorporate all significant political and other changes.

EDITORS, CARTOGRAPHERS, AND CONTRIBUTORS

Goode's World Atlas was originally compiled by and named after John Paul Goode (died 1932). It is now edited by Dr. Edward B. Espenshade, Jr., with the map research and compilation by the staff of the Cartographic Division of Rand McNally, with R. Forstall as Senior Research Editor, J. Leverenz as Cartographic Editor, and J. Smutnik as Chief of Geographic Research. A complete list of ten cooperating specialists, and a list of acknowledgments which includes reference to sources of information, is on p. vi of the atlas.

HOME SALE AND RETAIL PRICE

Available in two editions, the trade or general edition which retails at $10.95, and the text or educational edition which is available to educational institutions only at $7.95. Note that the paper dustcover or jacket is entitled *Rand McNally World Atlas: Goode's Edition.* The title page and spine both describe it correctly as *Goode's World Atlas.*

PURPOSE AND AGE SUITABILITY

Although specially designed for school and college use, from the age of ten through the final senior school year, *Goode's World Atlas* has found equal favor for reference work in libraries and as an atlas for general family use.

SIZE AND NUMBER OF PAGES

Relatively small in format, it measures 11½ by 9½ in. in its single-page size but, as with most of the better quality atlases, the majority of the maps are spread over two facing pages for maximum span. The total number of pages in the current edition is 327 (27 more than in the 12th edition).

TOTAL MAP PAGES AND TYPES OF MAPS

Goode's World Atlas is now comprised of 184 pages of excellent multicolored physical maps with improved new colors, which provide a striking new dimension. The basic series of maps is the fine Goode-originated topographic maps with political features. Relief is shown by a well-blended combination of contours, layer tints, and shaded hill drawing to produce a pleasing three-dimensional effect. A color key to the layer tints is provided on each map page, with heights and depths shown in both feet and meters, although actual spot heights on the maps are in feet only. Detail is excellent and sharply defined, with roads, railroads, airports, dams, pipelines, pyramids, ruins, lakes, swamps, rivers, aqueducts, canals, etc., all clearly shown. A legend of the map symbols employed is provided on a prefatory page. The map projections employed are clearly stated on each page and there is, additionally, an excellent explanation of map projections in the introductory material. The scale at which each map is drawn is given both as a representative numerical fraction and (a most useful feature) in its equivalent in miles per inch. A scale bar is also provided which shows distances in both miles and kilometers. In addition to the main series of maps there are excellent inset maps of metropolitan areas and a fine collection of more than 100 special-purpose thematic maps for (a) the world, (b) each of the continents, and (c) the more important countries. New to this edition are several special-subject world maps, new general-reference maps of Canada, new landform maps of the world, and a world portrait map. The typography has also been improved with a much cleaner look to the map pages.

SCALE

Very good throughout, although there is a tendency to favor the United States. The United States is mapped mostly at a scale of 1:4,000,000 with metropolitan areas at 1:1,000,000. Europe is mapped at exactly the same scale, as also are the major European cities. Similarly, the most important areas of Russia are at a scale of 1:4,000,000, with Moscow and Leningrad at 1:1,000,000. Asia is scaled at different sizes. Part of eastern China and southern Japan are both at 1:4,000,000 but the remainder, including India, eastern China, Korea, and Japan are at 1:10,000,000, with some remoter areas at 1:16,000,000. Australia and New Zealand are much less detailed, however, at 1:16,000,000, except for southeastern Australia at 1:8,000,000. Africa is reasonably well covered in three regions at 1:4,000,000, and in three others at 1:16,000,000, but note that the Suez Canal is at 1:1,000,000. Both Central and South America are mapped mostly at 1:4,000,000, but some of these are insets in the smaller-scale regional maps at 1:16,000,000. All cities appear to be mapped at 1:1,000,000.

BALANCE

Good overall, but there is a decided emphasis on North America, which is allocated 48 pages, including 21 for the United States and seven for Canada. Europe, which should be approximately the same, is allocated only 26 pages, of which the British Isles is allocated only one. Twenty pages are allocated to Asia, ten to the U.S.S.R., seven to Africa, and four to Australasia. The emphasis on the western hemisphere is again demonstrated by the provision of eight pages for Central America (including Mexico) and six for South America. Included in the allocations are the series of thematic maps for each continent.

INDEXING

Good for an atlas of this size, with a total of 35,000 entries for places, features, and points of interest. Local official names are used for nearly all cities and towns. Location of all entries is made exactly by the provision of the correct degrees of latitude and longitude. A useful feature is the provision of a pronouncing gazetteer. The index in this edition is some 20 percent larger than that in the previous 12th edition.

SCOPE, CONTENTS, AND ARRANGEMENT

The first 12 pages contain an exceptionally well detailed list of contents (with the scale shown for every listed map), a list of acknowledgments and the names and qualifications of the ten cooperating or contributing specialists, an excellent introduction, and a list of map symbols. These are followed by three pages on the universe and a fine explanation of map projections. The maps are presented first in a world section of 53 pages, which includes the fine collection of thematic maps; then physical and thematic maps of Canada, the United States, Central America, South America, Europe, the U.S.S.R., Asia, Australasia, and Africa are presented. Following the maps are three pages of text on world comparisons, a list of countries of the world, with useful data, a glossary of foreign geographic terms, a list of abbreviations, and the pronunciation of geographic names and, finally, the index.

SUMMARY

Goode's World Atlas is an outstanding school atlas, long a favorite with both pupils and teachers, and a basic work of geographic reference in schools and educational materials centers. It is currently on more approved lists than any other atlas now available, although it may well be challenged for this place by the new *Aldine University Atlas*. Professionally, it is considered to be one of the finest atlases available in this category and price range, and at its present regular trade cost of $10.95, is one of the best inexpensive atlases for students and nonspecialist general and home use. A good atlas from its first publication in 1922, it has undergone extensive revisions with almost every subsequent edition. The present edition, the 13th, is the biggest and best ever and shows a substantial improvement over even its immediate predecessor. Maintained as it is under a program of continuous revision, it is at all times thoroughly up-to-date, reflecting with a high degree of accuracy all major political and administrative changes. The physical maps, overlaid with political and cultural features, are exceptionally good, clear, easily read, and unusually attractive in the new stronger layer tints, pronounced hill shading, and sharply defined contour lines which produce a striking three-dimensional effect. Boundaries are clearly marked in red as also are major conurbations. The printing on the maps has been improved and, despite the stronger layer tints, is as clear and legible as ever, with the names of places frequently given in both their native and English forms. Noteworthy features of this fine school atlas are the many maps of metropolitan areas and important regions at a uniform scale of 1:1,000,000; the excellent explanation of map making and the none too easy subject of map projections; the series of special-subject maps of the world; and the much improved index. A pure atlas in the sense that it contains little or nothing of an encyclopedic or nonatlas nature, *Goode's World Atlas* (which is one of only four atlases listed in the *Choice Opening Day Collection*) is highly recommended for personal use as well as for schools, colleges, and libraries requiring a medium-sized, relatively well balanced world atlas.

CRITICAL REVIEWS AND INFORMATIVE ARTICLES
American Reference Books Annual, 1971, p. 173.
Science Book News, December 1971.

OTHER SOURCES OF INFORMATION
Cheney. *Fundamental Reference Sources.* 1971.
Deason. *AAAS Science Book List.* 3rd ed. 1970.
Katz. *Introduction to Reference Work.* 1969.
Lock. *Modern Maps and Atlases.* 1969.
Walford. *Guide to Reference Material.* 2nd ed. 1966–1970.
H. W. Wilson Co. *Children's Catalog.* 12th ed. 1971
H. W. Wilson Co. *Junior High School Libraries Catalog.* 2nd ed. 1970.
H. W. Wilson Co. *Senior High School Libraries Catalog.* 9th ed. 1967.
H. W. Wilson Co. *Public Library Catalog.* 5th ed. 1968.
Winchell. *Guide to Reference Books.* 8th ed. 1967.
Ziskind. *Reference Readiness.* 1971.

THE UNIVERSITY ATLAS
and
THE LIBRARY ATLAS

Merit Rating:12
Group Two–Above Average Quality: *HIGHLY RECOMMENDED*

PUBLISHER
George Philip and Son Limited, 12-14 Long Acre, London WC2E 9LP, England. Distributed in the United States by the Denoyer-Geppert Co., 5235 Ravenswood Ave., Chicago, Ill.

PUBLISHING HISTORY AND REVISION PROGRAM

One of the most popular atlases in Britain, it was first published in 1938 and is now into its 10th edition as the *Library Atlas* and into its 13th edition as the *University Atlas*. It was completely redesigned in 1959 and again in 1967. It is kept up-to-date by a program of frequent reprintings with revisions, and new editions appear at frequent intervals, about every three or four years. Derived directly from the *Library Atlas/University Atlas* is the *Aldine University Atlas*, but this contains material of special value to students in North America. Identical to the atlas section proper, but 20 percent larger, is the *Atlas of the Earth* (q.v.).

EDITORS, CARTOGRAPHERS, AND CONTRIBUTORS

Edited by Harold Fullard (editor of all George Philip atlases), H. C. Darby, and the cartographic staff of George Philip and Son Limited. Dr. Fullard and Dr. Darby are also the editors of the *Aldine University Atlas*, which is basically the same as these two titles but with some additional material adapted for use in the United States.

HOME SALE AND RETAIL PRICES

The *Library Atlas* retails in the United Kingdom at 3.75, and in the United States at $8.50 (the same price as the *Aldine University Atlas*). The *University Atlas*, which differs from the *Library Atlas* only in that it omits 32 pages of economic maps dealing with land use, industry, and the distribution of commodities, retails in the United Kingdom at £3.00 and in the United States at $7.50.

PURPOSE AND AGE SUITABILITY

Designed for the serious student from the ages of 10 through 18 and also in college and the university. Can be used equally well in the home, office, and school libraries.

SIZE AND NUMBER OF PAGES

The single-page size of both atlases is 11½ by 9½in., but the actual map area for each page is 9¾ by 8 in. Most maps are, however, spread over two facing pages for a real coverage of 9¾ by 16 in. The *Library Atlas* contains 344 pages: 24 pages of prefatory material, 208 pages of maps, and a 112-page index. The *University Atlas* is identical except for the omission of 32 pages of thematic maps, pages 177 to 208 of the *Library Atlas*. Pagination of the *University Atlas* is 24 prefatory pages, 176 map pages, and 112 index pages, for a total of 312 pages.

TOTAL MAP PAGES AND TYPES OF MAPS

The *Library Atlas* has 208 pages of maps, but these include 32 pages of special world thematic maps. Both atlases have basically 176 pages of physical-political maps of the world on a quite large scale, supplemented by a judicious variety of thematic maps. The cartography is superb, with relief shown by an excellent series of layer tints and shading which is meaningful, eye-catching, and tasteful. A key to the layer tints is provided on each map page, with heights and depths shown in both feet and meters. The maps are exceptionally well detailed and show boundaries, principal highways, railroads, tunnels, canals, pipelines, air routes, airports, shipping routes, and the usual natural features: rivers, lakes, swamps, wells, ice areas, mountain passes, etc. The projections employed are identified on each map, as also are the scales, both as a representative numerical fraction and a bar distance scale in both miles and kilometers. There is a good introductory section which explains projections and scale, but the provision of a scale equivalent in miles per inch on the map pages would have been more meaningful, to younger students at least.

SCALE

Very good for what is a relatively small- to medium-sized atlas. Europe is given preference for obvious reasons, but most areas of the world are dealt with in good detail. The British Isles are mapped mainly at 1:4,000,000, but with the most important regions at the large scale of 1:1,000,000. Most of Europe is at 1:2,500,000, except for the important Sambre-Meuse-Ruhr region at 1:1,000,000. The United States is uniformly mapped in three areas at 1:6,000,000, except for the northeastern region at 1:2,500,000. Canada is mapped at 1:7,000,000, Central America mostly at 1:8,000,000, while the mapping of Mexico is at 1:12,000,000 and the Panama Canal region and Bermuda at 1:1,000,000. South America, however, is less well detailed, with only one map for the central area at 1:8,000,000 and two for the northern and southern regions at 1:16,000,000. Russia is quite well mapped, with two maps at 1:5,000,000 and one at 1:10,000,000. The scales for Asia vary somewhat. Palestine is well detailed at a scale of 1:1,000,000, and southern Japan is reasonably well detailed at 1:5,000,000. The Indo-Gangetic Plain, southern India, and Ceylon are mapped at 1:6,000,000, but there is a change to much smaller-scale maps at 1:10,000,000, for the Indian subcontinent, eastern China, and Korea. The important areas of Africa (The Nile Delta, southern Africa, and the Transvaal) are mapped at 1:4,000,000, and the remainder at 1:8,000,000. The Australasia area also varies from 1:3,500,000 for New Zealand, through 1:4,500,000 for southeastern Australia, to 1:7,500,000 for the rest of Australia and the surrounding islands.

BALANCE

Again very good but again, understandably, with some emphasis on Europe, which is allocated 66 pages (21 for the British Isles alone), as against only 20 for all of North America (ten for the United States, and six for Canada). Mexico and Central America are allocated two pages, and South America seven. Asia is reasonably well treated with 23 pages, as also is Africa with 21. Australasia, with 12 pages, is allocated as much page space as the United States and Central America together. Included in these totals are pages of thematic maps.

INDEXING

A very adequate index, identical in both titles, contains 50,000 entries for features and places, which are exactly located by the correct degrees of latitude and longitude. There is no extraneous material such as population statistics or gazetteer information.

SCOPE, CONTENTS, AND ARRANGEMENT

A detailed list of contents is provided in the forefront of the atlases, with the scales shown for every map listed. The first 24 pages in both works contain a preface, a list of contents, a list of alternative spellings, an explanation of the climate graphs, and a list of the 14 projections used. Following a short number of pages on map symbols, thematic maps of the world, maps of the oceans and the world generally, the main series of physical maps, accompanied by regional thematic maps, begins with Europe, then the U.S.S.R., Asia, Africa, Australasia, North America, Central America, and South America. At this point the atlases differ. The *Library Atlas* continues with a fine selection of world thematic maps for a further 32 pages. These are of special interest to students. Both titles conclude with the 112-page index, which includes a list of abbreviations.

SUMMARY

The *Library Atlas* and its shorter version, the *University Atlas*, are excellent medium-sized reference atlases for detailed study in schools, colleges, and universities, with the former title more useful at the advanced level. It has been in existence for many years and has earned an enviable reputation for accuracy, comprehensiveness, and the beauty of its maps. Particularly noteworthy is the map of the Himalayas, which gives a striking three-dimensional effect of the whole mountain range. Detail is excellent, and superior in many instances to atlases which are larger and more comprehensive. British and European users certainly will prefer the *Library Atlas* or the *University Atlas,* for either home or school use, but North American users will want to acquire the similar *Aldine University Atlas* which, as well as being specially designed for the North American market, has one or two superior features. Of interest is the fact that the atlas section per se—the physical-political maps (but excluding the thematic maps)—is also contained in the same publisher's *Atlas of the Earth,* but the maps have been enlarged in size by some 20 percent. The two atlases have been widely and justifiably acclaimed as among the best available for educational purposes. They are both highly recommended as excellent, inexpensive world atlases for student and home use, especially where none of the larger, more detailed, and more comprehensive works can be afforded.

CRITICAL REVIEWS AND INFORMATIVE ARTICLES

None are recorded for these titles, but see also *Aldine University Atlas.*

OTHER SOURCES OF INFORMATION
Lock. *Modern Maps and Atlases.* 1969.
Walford. *Guide to Reference Material.* 2nd ed. 1966–1970.

PANORAMIC WORLD ATLAS

Merit Rating: 12
Group Two—Above Average Quality: *HIGHLY RECOMMENDED*

PUBLISHER
Hammond Inc., Maplewood, N.J. 07040.

PUBLISHING HISTORY AND REVISION PROGRAM
First published in the United States in 1967, but first copyrighted in 1966 by
the London cartographic firm of Geographical Projects (a division of the
London-based publishers, Aldus Books Limited). Hammond publishes and
distributes this atlas in the United States but is not the copyright owner, and
this particular title is not a Hammond atlas per se, although included as a
title in their "New Perspective" series. There is no announced program of
revision, reprinting, or updating, and the 1966 edition is the only edition so
far recorded.

EDITORS, CARTOGRAPHERS, AND CONTRIBUTORS
Designed and created by Geographical Projects, London, from original map
techniques by Frank Debenham. Named as editor is Shirley Carpenter, with
Romek Marber as designer, and H. A. C. Lewis, I. Dawson, Colin Ronan,
and Gordon Manley as consultants.

HOME SALE AND RETAIL PRICE
According to the publishers, available in one edition only, at $8.95. It is
probably available in the United Kingdom also, but no details are available.

PURPOSE AND AGE SUITABILITY
Designed as a general-purpose physical atlas for home, school, and library
use. Suggested beginning age is 12, to extend through high school and college.

SIZE AND NUMBER OF PAGES
Single-page bound size is 12½ by 9½ in., and there are 205 pages.

TOTAL MAP PAGES AND TYPES OF MAPS

There are 147 pages of maps in full color, including a number of unique three-dimensional models of every area of the earth, specially created and photographed in the United Kingdom. Two maps are given for each continent, one showing the relief features, the other showing political boundaries. Each continental section is followed by excellent physical maps of the countries and regions of the area. Relief features are shown by hill shading and tinting. These are accompanied by special thematic maps on climate, soils, land uses, fuel resources, and histories of the continents. The projections employed are shown on each map as are the scales, both as a representative fraction and on the usual bar distance scale in both miles and kilometers.

SCALE

These are shown clearly on each map and, for the most part, are large enough to show good detail. They do, however, vary considerably from area to area, and there is a decided emphasis on European countries.

BALANCE

Understandably, there is an emphasis on Europe and European countries, as evinced by the allocation of no less than 39 pages of maps to Europe, as opposed to only 17 pages for the entire North American continent: the United States, Canada, and Mexico. Aside from this, however, the entire earth is well represented, with a reasonable balance of maps for the remaining continents.

INDEXING

Rather limited for an atlas of this size and purpose, with only 25,000 entries in the 44-page section. It is, however, pure, and lists only the places and the physical features on the maps. Location is by means of a grid reference system of numbers and letters. Population statistics are not given here or elsewhere in the atlas, a practice which differs radically from the traditional Hammond practice of providing very detailed population statistics in the indexes to their own series of atlases.

SCOPE, CONTENTS, AND ARRANGEMENT

The atlas covers the entire world, continent by continent, with a fine series of physical maps for the continents, the regions, and the countries. These are accompanied by a well-chosen series of thematic maps, but political maps are provided for the continents only. Pages 1–25 contain a list of the editors and consultants; a detailed list of contents (with the scale shown for each listed map); a section About this Atlas; an explanation of map projections; a section on space exploration and the world from space; and a world section of special maps. Pages 26–65 are allocated to Europe; pages 66–89 to Asia; pages 90–105 to Africa; pages 106–123 to North America and Central America; pages 124–137 to South America; and pages 138–153 to Australasia. Pages 154–160 contain a further selection of special maps of the world, and pages 161–205 comprise the general index.

SUMMARY

The *Panoramic World Atlas* is well thought of professionally, as evinced by its inclusion as an outstanding academic publication in the *Enrichment Collection* of the Xerox College Library Book Program, and the good reviews which have heralded its appearance. It is a unique atlas in several respects. It is the first ever to use shadow relief maps, which were specially created for this atlas from models made in England, and then photographed to provide a striking three-dimensional effect by the employment of special lighting devices. It is also a rare departure from the traditional Hammond series of basically political atlases. It was brought into the "New Perspective" series because of its unusual method of manufacture and the high praise accorded its initial publication in Europe. This particular edition has been printed in the United States with only a few scattered changes of a minor nature, and the original British spellings have been retained in the text material, which, although it may at times be disconcerting to readers in the western hemisphere, does not detract from the considerable merit of the atlas. The coverage of the world is reasonably well balanced although there is, as in most atlases, a tendency to favor the country of origin, in this case the British Isles. The arrangement is by six large groupings of the continents, with each group containing a series of special-purpose thematic maps embracing such material as geographic, economic, climatic, and historical information, soils, land use, power resources, population density, and religions, followed by fine physical maps of the more important individual countries or regions. Those with a special interest in the physical features of this planet will find the *Panoramic World Atlas* instructive and of more than passing interest.

CRITICAL REVIEWS AND INFORMATIVE ARTICLES

Choice, February 1968, p. 1363.
Saturday Review, November 18, 1967, p. 39.

OTHER SOURCES OF INFORMATION

Winchell. *Guide to Reference Books.* 8th ed. 1967, 2nd supplement 1967–1968.

WORLD BOOK ATLAS

Merit Rating:11
Group Two—Above Average Quality: *HIGHLY RECOMMENDED*

PUBLISHER

Field Enterprises Educational Corporation, 510 Merchandise Mart Plaza, Chicago, Ill. 60654.

PUBLISHING HISTORY AND REVISION PROGRAM

One of the most recently published world atlases now available, the *World Book Atlas* was first published and copyrighted in 1964, although the basic series of Cosmo maps have been available for some years previously. Further copyrights were issued in 1965, 1968, 1970, and 1972. A number of changes and improvements have been implemented in each new edition, particularly noteworthy being the entirely new series of world thematic maps in 1968, and the introduction of an excellent pronouncing gazetteer, specially edited by Dr. Clarence L. Barnhart, the well-known compiler of the Thorndike-Barnhart series of dictionaries. New in 1972 is a useful section on automobile travel in the United States, Canada, and Mexico, and a very much up-to-date section on the moon. Carefully and responsibly edited, always accurate and up-to-date, the atlas is maintained under the same meticulous program of continuous revision as is implemented for the *World Book Encyclopedia* and the *World Book Dictionary*.

EDITORS, CARTOGRAPHERS, AND CONTRIBUTORS

Specially compiled by the editorial staff (24 listed) of the *World Book Encyclopedia*, which the atlas is designed to complement and supplement, in association with the Cartographic Staff and Research Staff of Rand McNally and Co. (four listed). Dr. William H. Nault is listed as editorial director, with Robert Zeleney as executive editor, the same positions they have for other products of Field Enterprises. Also listed is a Cartographic Advisory Board, comprised of six well-known professors from American universities, and a Library Committee of seven well-qualified librarians and educators.

HOME SALE AND RETAIL PRICES

The *World Book Atlas* is usually sold (at a discount) in combination with the *World Book Encyclopedia* and/or other educational titles, but it can also be purchased separately. It is available in two editions: a cream, brown, and gold Aristocrat binding at $31.20 when purchased separately, but reduced to $26.20 when purchased in combination with the encyclopedia; and now also in a recently introduced Renaissance binding at $36.20 as a separate item, or at $29.20 in the combination deal.

PURPOSE AND AGE SUITABILITY

Although intended to complement and supplement the *World Book Encyclopedia*, this atlas is a reference work in its own right and can be used independently. It is designed mainly for home and library use by elementary, junior, and senior high school students from the age of 10 through 18. It is equally suitable for general adult use, but will probably not be entirely suitable at college and university level.

SIZE AND NUMBER OF PAGES

Including the margins, the single-page bound size is 14 by 11¼ in. Some of the maps are spread over two facing pages, but most are contained on a single page. The 1972 edition is comprised of 424 pages.

TOTAL MAP PAGES AND TYPES OF MAPS

The atlas proper is comprised of 167 full-page maps, but to these must be added a further 46 pages which are part maps, part text and diagrams. The basic series of political-physical maps is copyrighted by Rand McNally and Co., and is derived from their well-known Cosmo series, which converts basically political maps to show terrain and physical features by means of layer tints, hachures, and, in the historical maps, hill shading. Keyed color scales are provided on each map page for a ready interpretation. Each main section is preceded by a shaded relief map of the region. These were specially prepared for the atlas by the well-known cartographer, Richard Edes Harrison. Each is followed by a physical features map showing the natural features of the region, and a political map showing the boundaries of countries, states, and provinces. These are then followed by a series of historical maps showing the region from ancient times to the present. The main part of each section is comprised of a series of physical-political general-reference maps which focus on the most important areas, the relief on these being shown by color layer tints. In addition to these there are 30 thematic maps dealing with such subjects as health, literacy, education, and population. An outstanding feature of the atlas, these thematic maps have been most carefully and thoughtfully prepared.

The range of maps is wider than is usual in an atlas of this size, and a notable feature is the provision of 75 historical maps for the main regions. Locator maps are provided as small inset maps, relating the mapped area to larger regions. Most of the maps, however, are on a relatively small scale, which restricts the amount of detail which can be shown. Railroads, for example, are shown clearly, but the important communications network of highways and roads is not. The projections employed are identified on each map page, as also are the scales, both as a representative numerical fraction and as a bar distance scale in both miles and kilometers. Heights, however, are given in feet only.

SCALE

This varies quite considerably and is a weak point of an otherwise excellent school atlas. Both the United States and Canada are mapped in some detail but the scales vary widely from, for example, 1:731,000 for the state of Connecticut to 1:4,096,000 for Texas. This is due to each being allocated the same single-page size, although Texas is more than five times the size of Connecticut. Similarly, the provinces of Canada range from 1:4,255,000 for British Columbia to a much larger scale for Quebec at 1:929,000. The rest of the world is more uniformly mapped, but not at impressively large scales. Europe is allocated two scales, so that the British Isles, the Low Countries, Denmark, Central Germany, and Switzerland are mapped at 1:2,000,000, but France, Spain and Portugal, and Italy are less well detailed at 1:4,000,000. Most of Asia is at 1:8,000,000, as is also the western U.S.S.R., southeastern Australia, and New Zealand. Africa, however, is poorly detailed at a scale of only 1:11,000,000. Latin America is mostly at a scale of 1:8,000,000, except for Central America, which is much better detailed at 1:6,000,000.

BALANCE

Excluding the special thematic and historical maps, there is a heavy weighting in favor of North America, and a subsequent imbalance for the rest of the world. The United States alone is allocated 54 pages out of a total of 148, and this is augmented by a further 14 pages for Canada. Europe, conversely, is allocated only 23 pages. Asia is rather roughly dealt with in only 14 pages, but the rest of the world is reasonably well covered, with 11 pages for Africa, eight for Australasia, 11 for South America, and four for Central America. This decided imbalance is due to the practice of allocating one full page to each of the 50 states of the United States. The atlas would have been much improved if the United States were mapped by regions, allowing greater coverage of the other areas of the world.

INDEXING

Perhaps the best feature of this atlas. The comprehensive 110-page index (conveniently printed on green tinted paper) contains at least 82,000 entries, in one straight alphabetical listing of places and physical features. Not given, however, are the degrees of latitude and longitude, and places are located by the grid number–letter system which, although easier to use, is less exact. The index in itself does not provide population statistics, but these are given in detail in three preceding sections : (1) 3,000 world cities outside the United States and Canada, (2) the 1966 census figures for all Canadian counties, cities, towns, and incorporated villages, and (3) the 1970 census figures for all United States counties, cities, towns, and villages. In the two latter sections, the places are listed not alphabetically, but under the state or province in which they are located.

SCOPE, CONTENTS, AND ARRANGEMENT

The *World Book Atlas* is comprised of 14 distinct sections. A detailed list of the contents is provided at the front of the atlas, but a weakness of this is that the scales at which the individual maps are drawn are not given. The first 20 pages are particularly useful and include the valuable advice on How to Get the Most out of the *World Book Atlas* (how to find places, how to find directions, how to understand symbols, etc.). This is followed by a superb series of thematic maps of the world, of special value to students, and containing a wealth of detail. The basic series of reference maps which comprise the main part of the atlas are arranged in the order of Europe, Asia, Africa, Australasia, the Polar Regions, Latin America, Canada, and finally the United States. A useful feature which should be noted is the practice of color coding the different sections for quick reference to the required part of the atlas. New in the 1972 edition is a travel guide to the United States, Canada, and Mexico which provides a highways and distance table and map; and maps for the tourist regions of the Northwest, Northeast, Southwest, Southeast, New England, Alaska, and Hawaii. Preceding the travel guide is another new section on the moon, with maps and photos of the moon's surface, facts about the moon, and landings on the moon.

Concluding the atlas is a 52-page population statistics section, and the 110-page index.

SUMMARY

The *World Book Atlas* is beautifully made, carefully compiled, and thoughtfully edited. It is accurate, reasonably comprehensive although weighted in favor of North America, simply presented, reasonably well detailed although lacking highways and roads, and packed with a wealth of useful geographic information. As such it will be a useful and an interesting atlas in the home, school, and library. It has been specially designed and edited to complement and supplement the same publisher's well-known *World Book Encyclopedia*, but this in no way detracts from its usefulness as a world atlas in its own right. It is geared to meet all but the most advanced reference needs of students, teachers, parents, and librarians, especially those in the United States and Canada. The maps have been drawn from the *Cosmo* series made by Rand McNally and there is a similarity between this atlas and the *Cosmopolitan World Atlas* which also uses the *Cosmo* series of maps. These have been commended for their clarity (but not abundance) of detail and the layer colors which generally are pleasing, although sometimes overbright. A particularly commendable feature of the *World Book Atlas* is the unique and exceptionally well written, well illustrated section on How to Get the Most out of the World Book Atlas, which is again of special interest to students and parents and to teachers for group instruction use. This good section is augmented by the equally useful tests of map reading skills and the questions at the front of each major map grouping entitled "What is your IQ of. . .", the answers to which are provided on an end page of the atlas. Other features worthy of note are the exemplary series of world thematic maps, the interesting series of historical maps, and the useful travel guide to the United States, Canada, and Mexico. Despite its shortcomings, the most serious of which are the wide variations in scales, the limited detail on the maps and the heavy imbalance in favor of North America, the *World Book Atlas* is a good school atlas which will appeal especially to children and young people. Widely accepted professionally, it is included on almost every standard list of approved reference books.

CRITICAL REVIEWS AND INFORMATIVE ARTICLES

American Reference Books Annual, 1972, pp. 197–198.
American Reference Books Annual, 1970, p.99.
Choice, July-August 1969, pp. 625–630.
Booklist, January 15, 1965, p.412.

OTHER SOURCES OF INFORMATION

Cheney. *Fundamental Reference Sources.* 1971.
Deason. *AAAS Science Book List.* 3rd ed. 1970.
Walford. *Guide to Reference Material.* 2nd ed. 1966–1970.
H. W. Wilson Co. *Children's Catalog.* 12th ed. 1971.

H. W. Wilson Co. *Junior High School Library Catalog.* 2nd ed. 1970.
H. W. Wilson Co. *Senior High School Library Catalog.* 9th ed. 1967.
H. W. Wilson Co. *Public Library Catalog.* 5th ed. 1968.
Katz. *Introduction to Reference Work.* 1969.
Reference Services Division. *Reference Books for Small and Medium Sized Libraries.* 1969.
Winchell. *Guide to Reference Books.* 8th ed. 1967.
Ziskind. *Reference Readiness.* 1971.

COSMOPOLITAN WORLD ATLAS

Merit Rating:10
Group Two—Above Average Quality: *HIGHLY RECOMMENDED*

PUBLISHER

Rand McNally and Co., P.O. Box 7600, Chicago, Ill. 60680. It is distributed in the United Kingdom by Geographia Limited, London.

PUBLISHING HISTORY AND REVISION PROGRAM

First published in 1949 when the new series of *Cosmo* maps were introduced. The title was changed slightly to the *New Cosmopolitan World Atlas* in 1965 but has now reverted to its original title. As with all Rand McNally atlases, it is maintained under a program of continuous revision and is reprinted annually to incorporate all major political and statistical changes. The 1971 edition, called the "Enlarged Planet Earth Edition," in particular, shows quite extensive revision. Eliminated are: (1) the eight-page section of thematic maps on climate, natural vegetation, population, races of mankind, languages, and religion; (2) an outdated 16-page section on space and the moon; (3) the 26-page section on World History in Maps; and (4) America's Heritage in Maps. Taking the place of these is an excellent 48-page section on the earth, the moon, and outer space, most of which has been taken from the fine *Atlas of the Universe;* a fine new series of oceanographic maps; and a well-done series of maps of major metropolitan areas, both foreign and U.S., on a uniform scale of 1:300,000.

EDITORS, CARTOGRAPHERS, AND CONTRIBUTORS

None are named in the atlas, but they have been specified by the publishers as the Cartographic Division Staff of Rand McNally and Co., with R. Forstall as the senior research editor; J. Leverenz as the cartographic editor; and J. Smutnik as chief of geographic research.

HOME SALE AND RETAIL PRICES

The *Cosmopolitan World Atlas* is available in two distinct editions, a standard trade edition at $19.95 and a deluxe edition in a slip case (which does nothing to improve the contents) at $25.00.

PURPOSE AND AGE SUITABILITY

Like the *World Book Atlas* which it closely resembles, the *Cosmopolitan World Atlas* is designed mainly for home and library use by elementary, junior, and senior high school students from the age of 10 through 18. It is suitable for general adult use also, but at college and university level it will be less useful, especially when considerable detail is required.

SIZE AND NUMBER OF PAGES

Single-page bound size is 14 by 11¼ in. It is comprised of 428 pages, made up of variously paginated sections. Most of the maps are contained on a single page, but a small number of world and continental maps are spread over two facing pages for a map area of 14 by 22 in.

TOTAL MAP PAGES AND TYPES OF MAPS

The *Cosmopolitan World Atlas* is comprised of 130 pages of the political-physical *Cosmo* series of multicolor maps of the world, Canada, and the United States. These are supplemented by 13 pages of well-executed relief maps of the continents, 19 pages of maps of the major metropolitan areas of the world, and ten pages of U.S. metropolitan areas. On the main series of maps, which are basically political, major elevations are shown by hachures and mountain symbols, but these are augmented by purely physical maps of (a) the world, (b) the continents, and (c) the United States, with the relief features in these shown by a pleasing series of layer tints and hill shading. Locator maps are provided on all the regional maps, which are also useful for comparative purposes. Clearly identified are the methods of projection employed; the bar distance scales in both miles and kilometers; heights in both meters and feet (on the physical maps); and the scale at which the maps are drawn, the equivalents given in miles per inch. Detail is relatively good, showing railroads, tunnels, parks, points of interest, dams, and bridges, but not highways and roads. A legend to the map symbols employed is printed on a prefatory page, as also is a good explanation of map projections and scale. A noteworthy feature in this edition is the series of maps of the ocean floors. There are no longer, however, any thematic maps, except for such odd items as comparative time zones.

SCALE

Curiously mixed. Some of the scales, although perhaps small, are rational enough in even progression, but in other areas, and this applies particularly to Canada and the United States, the page size has determined the scale, with all sorts of odd fractions as a result. The regional maps of Europe vary from 1:1,000,000 for Switzerland through 1:2,000,000 for England, Wales, and Scotland, the Low Countries, western and central Germany, and the Alpine Regions; 1:4,000,000 for Ireland, France, and most other countries in Europe, except Scandinavia, which is at 1:8,000,000. For Russia there are only two maps, one at 1:8,000,000 and one at 1:11,000,000. The Mediterranean area is at 1:8,000,000 also, but the important regions of Israel and the northern United Arab Republic are at 1:2,000,000. Asia is rather poorly treated, no areas being mapped at a scale larger than 1:8,000,000, while some are at 1:16,000,000. Africa is allocated seven maps, all at the same but somewhat odd scale of 1:11,400,000. Southeastern Australia, rightly, is at 1:8,000,000, but the continent as a whole is at 1:16,000,000. South America is also evenly mapped at the quite good scale of 1:8,000,000. The greatest imbalance is in the maps of Canada and the United States. Each province and state, with just one or two exceptions, is allocated a full page, and the area is reduced or enlarged to fit the page. The scales then vary widely from an excellent scale of 1:731,000 for Connecticut to 1:4,118,000 for Texas, with all odd scales in between, rendering comparison extremely difficult. The physical maps are also somewhat varied from an odd 1:9,631,000 for the United States and Canada to 1:32,567,000 for Africa and South America. The best maps are those of the metropolitan areas, the 47 world cities and 12 American cities, all at the same good scale of 1:300,000.

BALANCE

Heavily in favor of the United States and Canada. The United States alone is allocated 50 pages, with an additional ten for Canada (and this excludes the metropolitan area maps) for a total of more than 50% for the North American continent. Europe gets only 19 pages, of which four are allocated to the British Isles. Russia is contained in three pages, as also are the Mediterranean lands and Australasia. Asia is very harshly treated in only nine pages, and Africa is not treated much better in eight pages, the same as for South America. Much the same balance applies to the maps of the metropolitan areas, with ten pages for the United States and 19 for the rest of the world.

INDEXING

One of the best features of the atlas is the well-compiled 100-page index containing more than 82,000 entries, which includes physical features (differentiated by italic type). Also included are U. S. and Canadian national parks. Places and features are located by the simpler letter-number grid system, not by the more exact degrees of latitude and longitude. Population statistics are not given in the index now (they were in previous editions), but these will still be found in the sections for geographic facts about (a) the world, and (b) the United States and Canada.

SCOPE, CONTENTS, AND ARRANGEMENT

The *Cosmopolitan World Atlas* can be divided into three broad sections: (1) the introductory material and the Planet Earth section; (2) the series of world, regional, state, and provincial maps; the statistical data and metropolitan area maps; and (3) the index. The first section is comprised of 55 pages and contains the list of contents (in which the scales of the maps are not given); the Planet Earth section, a well-illustrated and interesting survey extracted from the publisher's *Atlas of the Universe*; maps of the Moon; maps of the oceans and ocean floors and the Polar Regions; an explanation of map projections and scales, and a list of map symbols. Pages 1–140 are comprised of the main series of physical and political-physical maps of the world, beginning with Europe and progressing through Russia, the Mediterranean, Asia, Africa, Australasia, South America, Canada, and the United States. Pages 141–153 offer a mass of statistical data such as world political information, world comparisons, and population statistics. These are followed by large-scale maps of 47 major metropolitan areas of the world (excluding the United States) and world population statistics. Pages 201–204 are allocated to geographic, historical, and general statistical information about the United States. Following immediately are large-scale maps of the 12 major U.S. metropolitan areas, and an index to these. Completing this second section are 32 pages of population statistics for U.S. cities, towns, and villages, arranged under each state. The third section is the index, and a list of abbreviations.

SUMMARY

The *Cosmopolitan World Atlas* is only one of many published by Rand McNally and Co. In size it ranks below only the far superior *The International Atlas*. Abridged directly from it is the *Premier World Atlas* (q.v.). The *Cosmopolitan World Atlas* is professionally regarded as one of the best in the medium-sized, medium price range, and this is borne out by its inclusion and citation in nearly all of the "most approved" lists of reference books. It is well produced and well printed, with clear, easy-to-read maps of better than average quality, conveniently and logically arranged for maximum usefulness. It opens with a very good, specially produced section on the Planet Earth (this edition is called the *Enlarged Planet Earth Edition*), which is literally a work of art in its own right that will attract, entertain, and educate users. The several photos in it are excellent, many of them taken from outer space. Most of this section, however, is drawn from the highly recommended *Atlas of the Universe*, also published by Rand McNally, but actually produced in Britain by Mitchell Beazley, and edited by Patrick Moore, the well-known British astronomer. This is followed by an equally interesting section on the moon, again illustrated with excellent photos. A new feature is the excellent section on the Ocean World, with diagrams, text, photos, and specially drawn maps of the floors of the Atlantic, Pacific, and Indian Oceans, and the Arctic and South Polar Regions. Preceding the atlas proper there is an excellent, well-illustrated explanation of map projections, scale, and the symbols used on maps.

The atlas proper is comprised mainly of political-physical maps of the world, and all of the individual states and provinces of the United States and Canada. These are supplemented by fine relief maps of the continents and another new feature, the series of large-scale maps of the major metropolitan areas of the world and the United States. A comprehensive index of more than 82,000 entries locates every place and feature appearing on the maps. Worthy of note also are the highly informative geographic facts, figures, and information about the world, and the similar section of geographic and historical facts about the United States. The *Cosmopolitan World Atlas* is a very good atlas. It falls short of being a great atlas because of its bewildering mixture of scales, especially those used for the United States and Canada, and its overemphasis on these two countries. For those seeking a relatively complete coverage of the United States and Canada, it is one of the best atlases available, but as a general world atlas it can be a poor choice. Nevertheless, it is popular and reputed to be one of America's best-selling atlases, and it may be useful to students from the upper elementary grades through high school, and for all-round family use. College and university students and libraries will certainly, however, prefer the much superior *The International Atlas,* albeit at almost double the cost.

CRITICAL REVIEWS AND INFORMATIVE ARTICLES

American Reference Books Annual, 1972, p. 196.
Reference Quarterly (RQ), Spring 1972, p. 267.
Library Journal, February 1, 1972, p. 468.
Choice, July-August 1969, p. 625-630.
Saturday Review, May 18, 1968.
Booklist, October 15, 1966, p. 199.

OTHER SOURCES OF INFORMATION

Barton. *Reference Books.* 7th ed. 1970.
Deason. *AAAS Science Book List.* 3rd ed. 1970.
Katz. *Introduction to Reference Work.* 1969.
Lock. *Modern Maps and Atlas.* 1969.
Walford. *Guide to Reference Material.* 2nd ed. 1966-1970.
H. W. Wilson Co. *Children's Catalog.* 12th ed. 1971.
H. W. Wilson Co. *Junior High School Library Catalog.* 2nd ed. 1970.
H. W. Wilson Co. *Senior High School Library Catalog.* 9th ed. 1967.
H. W. Wilson Co. *Public Library Catalog.* 5th ed. 1968.
Winchell. *Guide to Reference Books.* 8th ed. 1967.

AMBASSADOR WORLD ATLAS
MEDALLION WORLD ATLAS
and
HALLMARK WORLD ATLAS

Note: These three atlases are to all intents and purposes the same work, and two are in fact identical in every respect except price. The third differs only in that it omits a 30-page section on the environment and a 144-page "Atlas of the Bible Lands."

Ambassador World Atlas Merit Rating: 9
Group Two—Above Average: *HIGHLY RECOMMENDED*
Medallion World Atlas Merit Rating: 6
Group Three—Average Quality: *RECOMMENDED*

Hallmark World Atlas   Merit Rating: 3
Group Three—Average Quality: *RECOMMENDED*

PUBLISHER

Publisher of all three atlases is Hammond Inc., Maplewood, N. J. 07040. Usually distributed in Britain through Macdonald, London.

PUBLISHING HISTORY AND REVISION PROGRAM

Both the *Ambassador* and the *Medallion* atlases were first published in 1966, in what was entitled the New Perspective Series, although the title of *Ambassador* had been used for previous Hammond atlases of a different character. The *Hallmark* title was introduced for the first time in 1971 under the series title of New Census edition. The basic series of maps, identical in all three works, was, according to the publishers, in preparation for four years. As with the majority of Hammond atlases, they are maintained under a program of continuous revision and are frequently reprinted with updating material.

EDITORS, CARTOGRAPHERS, AND CONTRIBUTORS

The only persons named are the 13 members of the Hammond Publications Advisory Board, to each of whom is assigned an area of the world or a special subject. Most are professors of geography at various American universities. Also contained in the prefatory pages is a list of sources and acknowledgments. Actual cartography is by the staff of the Cartographic and Research Division of Hammond Inc.

HOME SALE AND RETAIL PRICES

There is a considerable variation in the costs of the three titles. The *Ambassador World Atlas* is the cheapest, at $14.95, and is considered a better value than the other two, although there are 174 fewer pages. The *Medallion World Atlas* and the *Hallmark Atlas* are priced at $24.95 and $39.95 respectively, although the contents, apart from a slight rearrangement, are identical. The *Medallion* however, is in one volume, with a padded cushion-type cover. The *Hallmark*, for an additional $15.00, comes in two volumes, again with padded cushion covers, and a slipcase. For these reasons the *Ambassador* is considered the best buy. The additional $10.00 for the *Medallion* buys only a 30-page section on the environment and 144 pages containing an atlas of Bible lands, a world history atlas, and a U. S. history atlas, none of which is essential atlas material. An even greater difference of $15.00 lies between the *Medallion* and *Hallmark* editions, for exactly the same work in two volumes and a slipcase. The *Ambassador* is therefore rated at 9, the *Medallion* at 6, and the *Hallmark* at 3.

PURPOSE AND AGE SUITABILITY

All three atlases are general-purpose reference and political atlases, designed for use by students from the age of 12 through college, as well as for general family use. The two more expensive editions contain a wider range of ency-clopedic material, which will make them of more interest for home use, but libraries, schools, and serious users will find that the *Ambassador* provides all that is necessary for geographic studies.

SIZE AND NUMBER OF PAGES

There was a radical change in the size of Hammond atlases in 1971. The single-page bound size of these three titles is now 12½ by 9½ in. as opposed to the 15¼ by 11¾ in. format of the editions from 1966 to 1970. On the other hand, the number of pages in the *Ambassador* has been increased from 364 to 496, and in the *Medallion* and *Hallmark* editions from 459 to 672. The pages in the two larger editions are not sequentially numbered, having the following additional sections, E32, B32, H48, and U64, inserted for the environmental section, the atlas of the Bible lands, the world histori-cal atlas, and the United States History atlas.

TOTAL MAP PAGES AND TYPES OF MAPS

An exact count of the total map pages is difficult, due to the fact that in all three titles, maps, text, statistical data, and additional material such as na-tional flags (in color) are also provided on the map pages, with some occa-sional pages with no maps at all. In the atlas section proper, however, iden-tical in all three editions, there are 320 pages, excluding the special historical sections in the two larger editions. The main or basic series of maps is strictly political. These maps show international and internal boundaries and capital cities, but detail is otherwise limited, with neither roads nor railroads (except for some special maps) shown. Accompanying each main political map is a much smaller topographic map which, in well-executed layer color-ing, depicts the relief and physical features of the country or region mapped. The continental maps are accompanied also by a series of thematic maps on population distribution, vegetation, rainfall, and temperature. Some of the country or regional maps are also accompanied by thematic and special-purpose maps such as agriculture, industry and resources, historical maps, language maps, and road and rail transportation maps. Inset maps show large metropolitan areas or significant regions. Locator maps are pro-vided in the margins of each map page, which is a useful feature, and a short legend of map symbols is also provided. For the relief maps, heights and depths are given in both feet and meters, with a key to the layer tints. Every map is accompanied by a great deal of additional information such as the individual indexes to each map; and information tables showing the area, population, largest city, capital city, highest point, monetary unit, ma-jor language, and major religion. Also provided is a full-color illustration of the national flag of each country. The projections employed are shown on each map and there is an exceptionally good explanation of map projections by Erwin Raisz on an end page following the index. Some maps are bled to the edges of the pages but very few overlap into a second facing page. The maps generally are small.

SCALE

Probably the worst feature. The publisher states that each country has been portrayed at a scale commensurate with its political, social, economic, or tourist importance, but the exact scale at which each map has been drawn is not stated as a representative numerical fraction. A bar distance scale is given for each map in both miles and kilometers and it would be possible, but highly inconvenient, to work out the exact scale from this. There is no valid reason for the scale not being properly shown, which makes comparison of areas difficult and mitigates against the other merits of the atlas. On the relief maps and the inset maps, the bar distance scale is given in miles only. It is clear, however, that most maps are on a relatively small scale, except those for the United States. Areas of dense settlement or importance are enlarged and shown on a larger scale as inset maps, but are still not satisfactory.

BALANCE

Overwhelmingly weighted in favor of the United States and Canada, with 50 percent of the available pages allocated to North America. The United States alone is allocated 133 pages. Canada is allocated 26. Europe, conversely, is allocated only 42 pages, of which eight are for the British Isles. Central America is quite well treated with 16 pages, and South America is well mapped in 26 pages. Russia, however, is contained in six pages, and Asia in 32. Australasia is allocated 16 (same as Central America) and Africa is allocated 18. In all instances, these pages contain statistical and other data as well as maps.

INDEXING

Certainly the best feature in all three editions is the really well-compiled, comprehensive index of some 110,000 entries contained in 142 pages. This is particularly useful in that it provides zip code numbers for all American cities, towns, and villages, which will be as useful outside the United States as it will be internally. Places and features are located by the simple system of a letter-number grid. Degrees of latitude and longitude are not given. Mention should be made also of the individual indexes with each map which also provide the latest population statistics for the area mapped. In the *Medallion* and *Hallmark* editions, small 2-page indexes are provided for the world and United States historical maps sections.

SCOPE, CONTENTS, AND ARRANGEMENT

In all three editions, the first 16 pages are identical and contain: a list of the Hammond Publications Advisory Board; a list of contents (quite detailed but not stating the scales for each map); a gazetteer-index of the world; an introduction to the maps and indexes; a list of sources and acknowledgments; and a glossary of abbreviations. The next section, numbered E1–E32. is provided at this point in the *Medallion World Atlas* only. It is also provided in the *Hallmark World Atlas*, but at the end of Volume 2. It is omitted entirely from the *Ambassador World Atlas*. Pages 1–320 are identical in all three editions and are comprised of the atlas proper, political and topographic maps, and accompanying text. The section begins with a series of world maps, then progresses continent by continent from Europe, through Russia, Asia, Australasia and Oceania, Africa, South America, Central America, Canada, and the United States. Pages 321–480 are also identical. These contain the index (142 pages); black and white zip code zone maps for 22 American cities or metropolitan areas (12 pages); an excellent explanation of map projections by Erwin Raisz (three pages); and world statistical tables, world geographic comparisons, and a table of geographic terms (three pages). The *Ambassador World Atlas* is completed at this point, but the *Medallion* and *Hallmark* editions go on to include an illustrated Atlas of the Bible Lands (32 pages); a World Historical Atlas, from 3,000 B.C. to the present time (48 pages); and a United States History Atlas, from 1600 to the present time. This last section includes several maps of economic usefulness. A two-page index concludes the works.

SUMMARY

The Ambassador, Medallion, and Hallmark world atlases are major reference sources of geographic and geopolitical information which will, in one edition or another, be found in all larger map reference collections. Hammond atlases have been in existence now for some 70 years, but this new series, entitled the New Perspective or, more recently, New Census series, is vastly superior to all their previous publications, not only cartographically, but in method of presentation also, employing an entirely new concept which may well become a standard practice in the future. The *Medallion/Hallmark* edition is by far the most comprehensive atlas in the Hammond range, followed closely by the *Ambassador World Atlas,* basically the same work. For each country, a political and physical map are shown side by side. Both are clear, well executed, accurate, up-to-date, and in a pleasing blend of colors, especially the topographic maps. An essential difference between the Hammond and other atlases is that each and every main map is accompanied by text in the form of an individual index and statistical information. The outstanding feature of the atlases is the logical and convenient arrangement of the maps and all the pertinent information relating to them on immediately adjacent pages, thus grouping together the basic political and physical reference maps, the index to the maps, statistical information, and other pertinent data, such as thematic and special-purpose maps.

Other features worthy of commendation are: (a) the comprehensive index of 110,000 entries for the ready location of all places and physical features on the maps, (b) the inclusion of zip codes for all U. S. cities, towns, and villages, and (c) the excellent, up-to-date population statistics. There are few atlases without one drawback or another, however, and the *Ambassador/ Medallion/Hallmark* atlases are no exception. Otherwise excellent for general reference use, one must nevertheless have reservations about (a) the failure of the makers to identify the scale at which each map is drawn, rendering comparison unduly difficult; (b) the considerable imbalance of the maps in favor of the United States and Canada; (c) the difference in size between the main political map and its equivalent-area physical map; and (d) the duplication of the indexes. This latter feature—useful though the separate indexes are for each map—has the disadvantage of taking up a considerable portion of the map pages, which could have been better utilized for larger-scale maps. These criticisms apart, the works are good reference atlases and the *Ambassador,* in particular, has a place in every library map reference collection. Both the *Medallion* and *Hallmark* versions contain everything that the *Ambassador* does, and more, but at greatly inflated prices for what is really nonessential material. In order of preference and value for money, the *Ambassador World Atlas* is first choice, especially for libraries. Home users may prefer the more ency-clopedic *Medallion/Hallmark* editions, but even then, the *Medallion* is a far better value than the deluxe *Hallmark.*

CRITICAL REVIEWS AND INFORMATIVE ARTICLES

American Reference Books Annual, 1972, pp. 193–197.
Wilson Library Bulletin, April 1972, pp. 741–742.
Library Journal, March 1, 1972, pp. 862–863.
Library Journal, January 1, 1972, p. 59.
College and Research Libraries, January 1972, p. 46.
Choice, July-August 1969, pp. 625–630.
Booklist, April 1, 1968, pp. 877–884.
Reference Quarterly (RQ), Spring 1967.

OTHER SOURCES OF INFORMATION

Barton. *Reference Books.* 7th ed. 1970.
Cheney. *Fundamental Reference Sources.* 1971.
Deason. *AAAS Science Book List.* 3rd ed. 1970.
Katz. *Introduction to Reference Work.* 1969.
Reference Services Division. *Reference Books for Small and Medium Sized Libraries.* 1969.
Walford. *Guide to Reference Material.* 2nd ed. 1966–1970.
H. W. Wilson Co. *Junior High School Library Catalog.* 2nd ed. 1970.
H. W. Wilson Co. *Public Library Catalog.* 5th ed. 1968.
Winchell. *Guide to Reference Books.* 8th ed. 1967. 1st supplement 1965–1966.
Ziskind. *Reference Readiness.* 1971.

Group Three:
AVERAGE QUALITY ATLASES

ODYSSEY WORLD ATLAS
and
ODYSSEY WORLD ATLAS—UNIVERSAL EDITION

Merit Rating: 8
Group Three—Average Quality: *RECOMMENDED*

PUBLISHER

Western Publishing Co. Inc., 850 Third Ave., New York, N.Y. 10022. The atlases are actually published under the imprints of Odyssey Books and Golden Press, division of the Western Publishing Co. They are also available from the Denoyer-Geppert Company.

PUBLISHING HISTORY AND REVISION PROGRAM

When this atlas was first published (in the larger edition) in 1966, it was a completely new reference world atlas, completed after six years of careful preparation. It was reprinted in 1967 with corrections and additions and, at the same time, the smaller *Universal* edition was launched. It was then intended that the atlases would be maintained under a program of frequent revision and updated with each new printing. This has regrettably not been the case, and within the next year or so, as the remaining stocks are exhausted, it will go completely out of print.

EDITORS, CARTOGRAPHERS, AND CONTRIBUTORS

The cartography is by the General Drafting Company, Inc. (the creators of the well-known "Esso" maps). Relief renderings are by the well-known cartographer, Richard Edes Harrison. A panel of 14 well-known specialist consultants and professors of geography from 11 universities is printed in the prefatory material.

HOME SALE AND RETAIL PRICES

When first published in 1966–1967, the *Odyssey World Atlas* was available in two editions: The standard or large size edition, which retailed at $24.95, and the *Universal* smaller edition at $9.95. There is no difference whatsoever in content between the two, but the *Universal* is reduced by 20 percent in physical size, measuring 13¼ by 10 in. as compared with the 16¼ by 12¼ in. of the standard edition. The publishers have stated, however, that the larger edition is now out of stock completely and will not be reprinted, and that although the smaller edition is still available this will also cease to exist when the present stock is exhausted. Note, however, that both editions are still listed in the current Denoyer-Geppert catalog at $14.98 and $7.48 respectively.

PURPOSE AND AGE SUITABILITY

The *Odyssey World Atlas* was designed to meet the relatively advanced needs of libraries and also to serve the requirements of the entire family, beginning at age 12 and continuing through college and advanced adult use. Younger children could use it in parts, but would otherwise find it difficult.

SIZE AND NUMBER OF PAGES

As already stated, the atlas comes in two formats, the standard large size at 16¼ by 12¼ in., and the smaller *Universal* at 13¼ by 10 in. Both atlases contain 318 pages, including the prefatory material and index. Most maps are contained on a single page, but the continental maps are spread over two facing pages for greater clarity of detail.

TOTAL MAP PAGES AND TYPES OF MAPS

There are 169 pages of well-executed maps, broken down into 107 full-page political maps, 22 full-page shaded relief maps, 40 pages of special-subject thematic maps, and 57 relief-map insets. The basic series consists of political maps (for countries), but with physical maps as insets. For the continents and large geographic areas, there are excellent double-page physical maps. These are followed by the political regional maps, and a series of thematic maps showing the natural resources, air, water, rail, and road features. The maps are well done, with pleasing colors and excellent legibility, and an uncluttered appearance. They do not, however, show either highways or railroads and, as a result, towns stand isolated, seemingly bereft of lines of communication. The margins are adequate, and a good feature is that the place names are given both in the language of the country (Romanized alphabet) and in the Anglicized version. The strong feature of the map arrangement is the separation of the political and physical relief maps, although their relationship is clearly shown. Relief is by hill shading, and heights are given in both feet and meters. The projections employed are clearly identified on each map page, as also are the scales on which the maps are drawn. There is a particularly good three-page explanation of map projections, illustrating 40 different methods. A striking feature is the profusion of carefully chosen thematic maps, particularly beneficial to students. Although most maps are drawn on relatively small scales, there are larger-scale insets of metropolitan and important areas.

SCALE

The merits of this good atlas are somewhat diminished by the confusing mixture of scales. No attempt appears to have been made to standardize these and they are far from being uniform in application. Asia, for example, is mapped at the odd scale of 1:15,400,000; Africa at 1:14,100,000, and South America at 1:11,700,000.

BALANCE

Although the world is quite well represented, the maps of the United States in particular, and North America, generally, predominate. The United States alone is allocated 42 pages, almost one third of the entire page allocation. Canada is allocated a further 12. In comparison with other areas this is a heavy weighting in favor of North America. Europe, in contrast, has to make do with only 22 pages. Russia is contained in eight pages (quite good), but Asia is allocated only 18 pages, Africa ten pages, Australasia 12 pages, Central America 12 pages, and South America ten pages.

INDEXING

Easily the best feature of the atlas is the excellent, comprehensive index of 105,000 entries in one straight alphabetical listing. This is contained in 128 pages, and places are located by page number and the grid system of letters and numbers. Official spellings are used throughout, and the entries include political entities, populated places, physical, and cultural features. Dating the index, however, are the population statistics of the time.

SCOPE, CONTENTS, AND ARRANGEMENT

The atlas is divided into 12 major sections, preceded by 11 pages of introductory material. It covers the globe by continents and subcontinents, allocated on the basis of political and economic importance. Particularly commendable is the coverage of remote areas and smaller islands. Included in the introductory material is an explanation of map projections and map symbols. The maps are arranged in the following order: the world, North and Central America; South America and Atlantic Ocean; Europe; the U.S.S.R.; Asia; Africa; Australasia and the Indian and Pacific Oceans. Following the maps but preceding the index, are eight pages of miscellaneous appendixes of such material as world facts and figures, a glossary of geographic terms, a table of foreign geographic terms, and a list of abbreviations. On the end papers of the atlas are mapped the standard time zones of the world.

SUMMARY

Because this atlas will shortly be completely out of print, it needs to be summarized as a work which no longer exists. It still retains a great deal of useful information, however, and remains a good buy, especially in the smaller edition. It has provided an adequate coverage of all areas of the world, a logical and convenient international arrangement, and a thorough, easy-to-use index. It was almost unanimously acclaimed, at the time of its first publication, as an excellent atlas, considered to be one of the best ever produced in the United States. This is reflected in its selection as one of only four atlases to be listed in the *Choice Opening Day Collection*. It was beautifully made, with superb maps of an outstanding degree of legibility, uncluttered, in pastel shades of a pleasing blend, and exceptionally well printed. It was a really serious attempt to be a distinguished, authoritative, and comprehensive atlas and, despite its shortcomings in not showing lines of communication and employing such a mixture of scales, it reflected credit on its originators, editors, and cartographers. It is a matter of regret that the publishers have decided not to bring out a new and improved edition. Although it remains a useful atlas and will do for some time yet, it can no longer be considered as an atlas of top quality. It is recommended, but with reservations.

CRITICAL REVIEWS AND INFORMATIVE ARTICLES

Choice, July-August 1969, pp. 625-630.
Booklist, November 1, 1967, pp. 281-288.
College and Research Libraries, July 1967, pp. 296-297.
Library Journal, April 15, 1967, p. 1575.
Reference Quarterly (RQ), Spring 1967.
Professional Geographer, July 1966.

OTHER SOURCES OF INFORMATION

Barton. *Reference Books*. 7th ed. 1970.
Cheney. *Fundamental Reference Sources*. 1971.
Katz. *Introduction to Reference Work*. 1969.
Reference Services Division. *Reference Books for Small and Medium Sized Public Libraries*. 1969.
Walford. *Guide to Reference Material*. 2nd ed. 1966-1970.
H. W. Wilson Co. *Public Library Catalog*. 5th ed. 1968.
Winchell. *Guide to Reference Books*. 8th ed. 1967; 1st Supplement 1965-1966.
Ziskind. *Reference Readiness*. 1971.

PHYSICAL WORLD ATLAS
or
EDINBURGH WORLD ATLAS
or
ADVANCED ATLAS OF MODERN GEOGRAPHY

Merit Rating: 8
Group Three—Average Quality: *RECOMMENDED*

PUBLISHER

There are three separate publishers, each using a different title for the same work. As the *Physical World Atlas* it is published in the United States by the American Map Company, Inc., New York, under their "Colorprint" trademark. As the *Edinburgh World Atlas* it is published in Great Britain by the original makers, John Bartholomew and Son Limited. Again in the United States, it is published by the McGraw-Hill Book Co. as the *Advanced Atlas of Modern Geography*.

PUBLISHING HISTORY AND REVISION PROGRAM

This can be somewhat confusing. The *Edinburgh World Atlas* was first published in 1954, and is now in its seventh edition, which was published, with several changes, in 1970. The *Physical World Atlas* is believed to be the same. The *Advanced Atlas of Modern Geography* however, although the same work, was first published in 1949, but this is described as being in its ninth (Metric) edition, published in 1971. All three titles, however, are maintained under a program of frequent reprinting and updating. The most recent editions of all three titles include a number of new thematic world maps as well as new thematic maps for the British Isles. Another change is that contour lines have been deleted for greater clarity. Most measurements, such as heights and depths, have been converted to meters, and temperatures to centigrade from Fahrenheit. New editions have been appearing at intervals of approximately three years.

EDITORS, CARTOGRAPHERS, AND CONTRIBUTORS

Only one person is named, John C. Bartholomew, Director of the Geographical Institute, Edinburgh, but the atlas is, of course, the product of the cartographic staff of John Bartholomew and Son Limited, who are also the makers of the internationally acclaimed *Times Atlas of the World*.

HOME SALE AND RETAIL PRICES

These vary from title to title. The *Physical World Atlas* is retailed at $14.95 (soon to be $16.95). The *Advanced Atlas of Modern Geography* is much lower priced at $9.95 in a text edition, but this may be an older edition. In the United Kingdom the *Advanced Atlas* retails at £2.60 and the *Edinburgh World Atlas* at £2.50.

PURPOSE AND AGE SUITABILITY

This is basically a school atlas, designed for students from the age of 12 through college, but it will be useful also to scientifically minded users requiring a well-detailed general reference atlas for home, office, and library use.

SIZE AND NUMBER OF PAGES

Physically a large-format atlas with a single-page size measuring 15 by 10 in., and most of the maps are spread over two facing pages for an excellent

area of 15 by 20 in., subtracting the quite narrow margins. All three titles
have a total of 165 pages.

TOTAL MAP PAGES AND TYPES OF MAPS

Excluding a few smaller maps in the text section, there are six pages of 47
two-color thematic maps and star charts, and 100 pages of full-color maps
of the world. The basic series of maps is the well-known series of Bartholomew physical-political maps, well drawn and adequately detailed, with good
rendering of political and cultural features. These are supplemented by a
fine selection of thematic maps of the world, for each of the continents, and
for several of the major countries, usually as insets with the principal series
of maps. Detail is very good and includes international and state boundaries, main roads and railways, with elevations shown by pleasing shades of
layer coloring. A color key to the shading is provided in the margin for each
map, with heights and depths shown in both meters and feet. The projections employed are identified on each map, and a good explanation of these
is given in the prefatory material. The scale of each map is given in the
usual style of a representative fraction, and as a bar distance scale in both
miles and kilometers.

SCALE

Quite even and well selected for areas of importance. There is a distinct
weighting in favor of the British Isles, which is mapped uniformly at
1:1,250,000, as also is most of Europe, except for central and southern Europe, which is at a scale of 1:3,000,000. European Russia is quite well detailed at a scale of 1:6,000,000, but Asia varies from 1:2,500,000 for the
Middle East through 1:4,000,000 for the densely populated areas of India;
1:6,000,000 for Japan and east China; and 1:10,000,000 for other areas of
Asia. Africa is the least well detailed, being mapped in only three regions at
1:12,500,000. Both the United States and Canada are quite well represented
at a uniform scale of 1:5,000,000 with the exception of the Middle Atlantic
States, at twice that scale at 1:2,500,000. Southeastern Australia is quite well
detailed at 1:5,000,000, but Central America at 1:10,000,000, and South
America at 1:12,500,000, are not so well detailed.

BALANCE

There is here again a heavy bias favoring Europe generally and the British
Isles in particular. The United States, for example, is allocated nine pages,
exactly the same as for the British Isles. Europe as a whole is spread over 28
pages, but the continent of North America, including Mexico and Central
America, gets only 14 pages. The remainder of the world is reasonably well
balanced, Asia being allocated 14 pages, Russia four, Africa seven, South
America four, and Australasia six.

INDEXING

There is a fairly comprehensive index of about 26,000 entries in 51 pages.
This is in two sections: (a) the general index to the world, about 24,000 en-

tries, and (b) a supplementary index to the maps of the United States, with an additional 2,000 entries. Places and features are located by special "hour" coordinates, which are fully explained in the introductory material. The degrees of latitude and longitude are not given, nor are population statistics.

SCOPE, CONTENTS, AND ARRANGEMENT

Well organized, the atlas begins with a four-page foreword and a detailed list of the contents, showing the scale for each listed map. These are followed by 12 pages of text material on the "hour" coordinates; a list of geographic terms; climate tables; a list of states and countries; exploration maps of the "Old" and "New" worlds; an explanation of 22 methods of map projection; a world airways map; and star charts to the northern and southern skies. The atlas proper begins with 19 pages of thematic maps of the world in full color, spanning a wide range of subjects. These are followed by the basic series of physical-political maps of Europe, Russia, Asia, Africa, North and Central America, South America, and Australasia. The end papers are utilized to provide (a) a map index to the world maps and (b) a facsimile of a map of the world made by Edmund Wright for the 1599 edition of Hakluyt's *Voyages and Discoveries.*

SUMMARY

The *Edinburgh World Atlas* (and its variant titles) has long been held in high regard by schools, colleges, and universities as an accurate and well-executed world atlas combining physical and political geography with a judicious use of economic information. This is not surprising when it is appreciated that it comes from the same famous cartographic firm which produces the superb *Times Atlas of the World.* The *Edinburgh World Atlas* is a good clear atlas with an emphasis on physical features, and is a fine example of expertly done color printing, with relief being shown by as many as 17 different layer tints. The maps are well detailed, with political and cultural features, and are frequently revised to keep them up-to-date. The balance of coverage is generally good, although there is an overemphasis on the British Isles specifically and Europe generally. The scale of the maps is relatively uniform, especially within each continent, and is adequate for the most important areas at least. Features worthy of special note are the excellent thematic maps of the world; the well-written and well-illustrated section explaining 22 different methods of map projection or ways to draw a map of the world; and the broad area of continental maps illustrating the density of population, and the vegetational, climatic, and physical backgrounds. This is certainly one of the best of the medium-sized atlases and is recommended for public, college, and university libraries, schools, and homes as an atlas of merit, with unique material not readily found in similar atlases, and a distinguished example of fine color printing. It should be noted, however, that both American editions are considerably more expensive than the British editions.

CRITICAL REVIEWS AND INFORMATIVE ARTICLES
Booklist, December 1, 1962.

OTHER SOURCES OF INFORMATION
Katz. *Introduction to Reference Work.* 1969.
Lock. *Modern Maps and Atlases.* 1969.
Walford. *Guide to Reference Material.* 2nd ed. 1966–1970.

CONCISE OXFORD ATLAS

Merit Rating: 7
Group Three—Average Quality: *RECOMMENDED*

PUBLISHER
United States: Oxford University Press, Inc., 417 Fifth Ave., New York, N.Y. 10016.
Canada: Oxford University Press, 70 Wynford Drive, Don Mills, Toronto, Ontario.
Great Britain: Oxford University Press, Ely House, 37 Dover Street, London WIX 4AH, England.

PUBLISHING HISTORY AND REVISION PROGRAM
Based on the larger *Oxford Atlas,* this *Concise* edition was published one year later for the first time in 1952. A second, substantially revised edition was published in 1958. Since then there have been frequent revisions with each reprinting, the latest of which is dated 1970, but it is still basically the second edition.

EDITORS, CARTOGRAPHERS, AND CONTRIBUTORS
Listed as editor is D. P. Bickmore. The historical notes and contemporary data are by T. K. Derry. Cartography is by the Cartographic Department of the Clarendon Press, although none are named.

HOME SALE AND RETAIL PRICES
In one edition only, it retails at $8.00 in the United States, and at £2.50 in the United Kingdom.

PURPOSE AND AGE SUITABILITY
Designed particularly for use in homes, offices, and libraries when only a medium-sized atlas is required. It makes a good desk atlas and one for all-round family use, from about the age of 12 through college.

SIZE AND NUMBER OF PAGES

The *Concise Oxford Atlas* is considerably smaller than the *Oxford Atlas* measuring only 10 by 7½ in. Nearly all the maps are spread over two facing pages, but due to the rather wide margins, the map coverage is only 9¼ by 14 in. It contains 288 pages, several more than the *Oxford Atlas*, but only 120 of these are given over to maps.

TOTAL MAP PAGES AND TYPES OF MAPS

There are 120 pages of maps of all types. The main series is comprised of the fine physical-political maps in six colors, nearly all of them spread over two pages for maximum effect. Relief is shown by an excellent series of layer tints and hill shading, but no contour lines are used. A key to the colors is contained on each page. Detail is excellent for an atlas of this relatively small format, with a full array of lines of communication, international boundaries, political divisions, etc. The scale at which each map is drawn is clearly stated, as also are the projections used. Of special interest are the historical maps of Roman Britain, Medieval Britain, and Britain from the fifteenth to the nineteenth century.

SCALE

There is a decided emphasis on Britain and Europe. Britain is mapped at a scale of 1:1,000,000, and most of Europe is mapped at 1:2,000,000. The United States, on the other hand, is mapped in regions at a much smaller scale of 1:5,000,000 for the most part, and at 1:8,000,000 for the less important, less densely populated areas. Eastern Russia is rather inadequately mapped at 1:10,000,000. Asia varies, with some areas at 1:4,000,000 but others ranging up to 1:10,000,000. Southeastern Australia is at 1:5,000,000 but the rest of Australia is at only 1:10,000,000. Africa, like Asia, varies from 1:4,000,000 to 1:8,000,000. South America is also rather poorly scaled at either 1:8,000,000 or 1:16,000,000.

BALANCE

Very British and very European in content. Excluding the historical and other special maps of Britain, 15 pages of the main series of physical maps are allocated to seven regions of the British Isles. The rest of Europe, including a historical map, is allocated 19 pages. Eurasia and Russia are allocated a further eight pages. North America, conversely, is allocated only 14 pages, with only two pages for all of Canada, and ten pages for all of the United States and Mexico. Asia, including the Near, Middle, and Far East, is contained in 13 pages; Australasia in five pages; Africa in ten pages; and Central and South America in only six pages.

INDEXING

There are two indexes. The first, which is for the British Isles only, is at the front of the atlas, and contains some 11,500 entries. The second or main index of the world, is contained in 119 pages, and provides about 40,000 entries, good for an atlas of this size. For towns and countries and larger areas, both indexes provide information on population, area, currency, etc. Places are located by means of the National Grid, a full explanation of which is provided in the prefatory material.

SCOPE, CONTENTS, AND ARRANGEMENT

The atlas is divided into three main sections: the 40 pages of introductory material, the 120 pages of maps, and the final section of 128 pages, which includes statistical data and the index-gazetteer of the world. The first six pages of introductory material provide a list of the contents, but this does not specify the scale for each map listed; a list of principal states and territories; an explanation of the National Grid; and a list of the abbreviations used. The remaining 34 pages of the first section contain an index-gazetteer of the British Isles, with about 11,500 entries. The first 32 pages of maps are devoted entirely to the British Isles, and include seven pages of historical maps; special material on population, climate statistics, climate, scenery, recreations, and roads (ten pages); and then 15 pages of physical-political maps of seven regions of Great Britain and a map of Greater London. The remaining maps of the world are arranged in the order of Europe, Russia, Asia, Australasia, Africa, North America, Central America, and South America. These are followed by general world maps and a number of thematic maps, including two pages on the moon. Preceding the world index are six pages of general information on climatic statistics, countries of the world, and abbreviations.

SUMMARY

The *Concise Oxford Atlas* is a well-produced reference atlas in a handy format, with excellent physical-political maps, and useful special maps showing population, climate, sea and air communications, etc., plus a considerable amount of useful miscellaneous information. It is based on the larger and more authoritative *Oxford Atlas*, but is reduced in size by about 20 percent. It lays special emphasis on the British Isles and, to a lesser extent, Europe. This limits its usefulness to users outside the British Isles except where there may be a special interest. For this reason, it is recommended with reservations. Small libraries may find it useful for reference work, but its usefulness in schools and homes will be restricted to British users.

CRITICAL REVIEWS AND INFORMATIVE ARTICLES

None were traced for the most recent printings.

OTHER SOURCES OF INFORMATION

Lock. *Modern Maps and Atlases.* 1969.
Walford. *Guide to Reference Material.* 2nd ed. 1966–1970.
Winchell. *Guide to Reference Books.* 8th ed. 1967.

READER'S DIGEST GREAT WORLD ATLAS

Merit Rating: 7
Group Three—Average Quality: *RECOMMENDED*

PUBLISHER

Reader's Digest Association, 380 Madison Ave., New York 10017, and Reader's Digest Association Limited, 7-10 Old Bailey, London.

PUBLISHING HISTORY AND REVISION PROGRAM

There is no announced policy of revision, but new editions are appearing at reasonably regular intervals. It was first published in Great Britain in 1961, and a second printing followed in 1962. By 1964 its popularity had taken it into a fifth printing. A new third edition appeared in 1969. With some additional material, and redesigned and re-edited to conform with the needs and interests of American users, it was first published in the United States in 1963. The publishers have stated that a revised United States edition is tentatively scheduled for 1973.

EDITORS, CARTOGRAPHERS, AND CONTRIBUTORS

Originally published in Britain under the editorship of Frank Debenham. The maps were prepared by John Bartholomew and Son Limited, Edinburgh (makers of *The Times Atlas of the World*); the Aero Service Corporation; and the Babson Institute. The American edition, edited for the Special Book Division of Reader's Digest, names Alfred S. Dashiell as editor, with Charles B. Hitchcock, Director of the American Geographical Society, as joint consulting editor with Frank Debenham.

HOME SALE AND RETAIL PRICES

The trade edition, when published in 1968, retailed at $17.00 and was sold through Random House, Inc. According to information received from the publishers in March 1972, the third edition (1969) retails at $11.97, but this is most probably the special price available only to subscribers to the *Reader's Digest*. In Great Britain the prices are £4.50 and £3.15 respectively.

PURPOSE AND AGE SUITABILITY

The aim of the editors has been to stimulate interest in the universe and to demonstrate man's place in it. As such, this is a multipurpose, general world atlas, designed not for the specialist but rather for all-round family use, by children from the age of 12 through general adult and family use.

SIZE AND NUMBER OF PAGES

A large volume, the single-page size is 15½ by 10¼ in., but many of the maps are spread over two facing pages for a map area of 13 by 18½ in., after allowing for margins. The atlas is comprised of 232 pages in toto, all numbered sequentially.

TOTAL MAP PAGES AND TYPES OF MAPS

There are 115 pages of major maps, supplemented by a small number of special-purpose maps. The basic series of reference maps, between pages 46 and 136, are excellent physical-political maps, made by John Bartholomew and Son Limited, Edinburgh, and are based on those contained in the *Times Atlas of the World*. Elevations are shown by an excellent series of layer tints, a key to which is provided on each map page, together with the scales and projections employed. Detail on the main maps is very good, showing both natural and cultural features such as roads and railroads, although none show main seaways or air routes. In addition to the Bartholomew maps there are 22 pages of relief maps by the Aero Service Corporation, but these are rather crude in comparison.

SCALE

On the whole, even and quite large, showing good detail. In the American edition the maps of the United States are very well scaled at 1:2,500,000. Europe is also very good, with most of it at 1:3,000,000, excepting Scandinavia at 1:4,500,000. Most of the rest of the world, however, is at a smaller scale than is desirable, with Africa, Australasia, and South America all at 1:12,500,000. Other areas, including parts of Asia, are at still smaller scales, the poorest being 1:17,500,000.

BALANCE

In the American edition there is a decided emphasis on North America, which, including Mexico, is allocated 46 pages. Europe, in comparison, is allocated only 18 pages, although this excludes Russia, which is allocated a further four pages. Asia is harshly dealt with in only 11 pages, as also is Africa, with only five pages. Australasia and South America are covered in three pages apiece.

INDEXING

There are three separate indexes; a main index of some 22,000 entries for the world, excluding the United States, a larger index for the United States with some 50,000 entries, which also gives population figures; and a small index to the general text, persons, and geographic features.

SCOPE, CONTENTS, AND ARRANGEMENT

Including the three index sections, the *Reader's Digest Great World Atlas* can be broken down into the following sections: (a) The Universe and the Earth, (b) The Countries of the World, and (c) The World about Us. Pages 1–8 provide a list of the contents and an introduction. Pages 9–21 contain a Space section, including the geography of space, the solar system, the moon, and star charts. Pages 22–24 are relief maps of the United States,

Canada, South America, Europe, Africa, Asia, and the Great Oceans. Pages 45–136 comprise the atlas proper, with physical-political maps of the United States, Canada, Mexico, and Central America, followed by South America, Europe, Russia, Africa, Asia, and Australasia. Pages 137–152 is the special world section The World About Us, which describes its structure, ages and treasures of the earth, climates, vegetations, exploration, populations, and comparative geographic data. Pages 153–232 are the three index sections.

SUMMARY

Much more encyclopedic in character than most atlases, unconventional but imaginative, and with a considerable visual impact, the *Reader's Digest Great World Atlas* contains a great deal of impressive, useful, and interesting material, pleasantly and attractively arranged in a manner which would motivate an interest in the earth sciences. It contains particularly good material on space and space activities, and interesting, though not too well executed relief maps of the world and the continents. The Bartholomew maps are accurately drawn and well colored to show physical features and elevations as well as political boundaries. As with most atlases of European origin, the United States is mapped by regions rather than by individual states, but this has tended to give some of the maps of the more densely populated areas a cluttered appearance. The indexes, although good overall, are inconveniently arranged in two separate sections for (a) the United States and (b) the rest of the world, mitigating against the reference merits of the atlas. The most outstanding features are the relief maps which have been created from three-dimensional models, the views of the earth from 25,000 miles out in space, the photo-relief maps of the ocean floors, and the color photo-relief model of the United States. In conclusion, although the *Reader's Digest Great World Atlas* is recommended, it is done with reservations. It contains much nonatlas material. This is interesting, attractively arranged, and useful, but it can be found elsewhere, and the inclusion of this sort of material in an atlas lessens its reference usefulness. It is good but not good enough.

CRITICAL REVIEWS AND INFORMATIVE ARTICLES

Choice, July-August 1969, pp. 625–630.
Booklist, July 1, 1964.
Geographical Journal, September 1961, pp. 378–379.

OTHER SOURCES OF INFORMATION

Deason. *AAAS Science Book List*. 3rd ed. 1970.
Lock. *Modern Maps and Atlases*. 1969.
Walford. *Guide to Reference Material*. 2nd ed. 1966–1970.

THE WORLD ATLAS

Merit Rating: 6
Group Three—Average Quality: *RECOMMENDED*
Note: As the distributor did not supply a copy of this atlas for a detailed examination, and did not reply to a request for specific information, a full analysis cannot be provided, and the information presented below has been abstracted from published sources.

PUBLISHER

Actually made and published in Russia, but distributed in the United States by the Telborg Book Corporation, P.O. Box 545, Sag Harbor, N.Y. 11963.

PUBLISHING HISTORY AND REVISION PROGRAM

It is believed that this English-language edition of the famed *Atlas Mira* was first published in 1967, although it is described as the second edition. As the *Atlas Mira*, it was first published in Moscow in 1954, with a second edition in 1967. There is no announced policy of revision. The present edition does not incorporate the several changes which have occurred since 1967.

EDITORS, CARTOGRAPHERS, AND CONTRIBUTORS

A. N. Baranov is listed as editor in chief, along with 18 other Russian cartographic specialists. No information is available on who was primarily responsible for this English-language edition.

HOME SALE AND RETAIL PRICE

Understood to be available in one edition only, at $76.50 ($85.00 with separately published index) in the United States, and £30.00 in the United Kingdom.

PURPOSE AND AGE SUITABILITY

One of the world's most advanced atlases, it is designed for use by learned adults and specialist geographers. The minimum suggested beginning age is 15, and even then only by the most able students.

SIZE AND NUMBER OF PAGES

One of the largest atlases available, it measures 20 by 13 in., and is comprised of 262 pages. A commendable feature is that there is no extraneous or nonatlas material.

TOTAL MAP PAGES AND TYPES OF MAPS

In this second edition of the *World Atlas* there are 250 pages of maps, slightly less than in the original edition of 1954, due to the reduction of the number of maps for the Soviet Union and the number of historical maps. The basic series of maps consists of physical-political maps of exceptional beauty, showing relief by a wide range of hypsometrical tints. Contours are in brown, and on some maps there is oblique shading into violet. Accompanying these are some general, political, and communications maps. A noteworthy feature is the provision of numerous city plans at a large scale as well as larger-scale maps of important areas as insets. An extensive range of map symbols is employed and the detail shown on the maps is quite exceptional, considered by some to be superior to any other atlas currently available. Railways in red, for example, are a prominent feature. The second edition differs from the first in that it incorporates the results of Russian surveys of ocean floors, and the maps are unhinged and no longer open flat, as they did in the 1954 edition.

SCALE

Quite exceptionally large and beautifully balanced, perhaps the best balanced of all world atlases. The entire world is shown at never less than 1:7,500,000. Europe is especially well detailed at 1:2,500,000. Asia is at either 1:3,000,000 or 1:5,000,000; and the United States is mapped in regions at a scale of 1:5,000,000. This is very good indeed for a single-volume atlas although there is, naturally, a tendency to favor the Soviet Union and, to a lesser extent, countries of East Europe and Asia.

BALANCE

Insufficient data does not enable a thorough comparison to be made between countries and continents. In this second edition, the number of pages allocated to the Soviet Union has been reduced, but even so it is still heavily favored, by the allocation of 54 map pages to Russia, more than 20 percent of the total pages containing maps.

INDEXING

Magnificently comprehensive but at the same time very limited. More than 215,000 place names appear on the 250 pages of maps but, as yet, the index to these is available only as a separate volume. The Russian-language index volume is 534 pages long; the English-language version was unavailable for examination. Another drawback is that there is a confusing treatment of nonwestern place names. The cost of the atlas ($76.50 or £30.00) does not include the index-gazetteer to the maps.

SCOPE, CONTENTS, AND ARRANGEMENT

The World Atlas maps the entire world in very considerable depth and in great detail. It is a pure atlas in the real sense of the word, containing only 12 pages of essential prefatory matter and 250 pages of physical-political maps, but no index.

SUMMARY

The World Atlas or, as it is probably better known, the *Atlas Mira* is one of the great atlases of the world and indeed, considered by some specialists to be the best world atlas ever produced. It is beautifully made with superbly drafted maps showing great detail. It is considered by many to be the best-balanced atlas in print, although this is debatable, with no area of the world shown at less than 1:7,500,000. Russia, however, is exceptionally well detailed (better than any other country) with regional maps at the large scale of 1:1,500,000. Other noteworthy features are the extensive range of map symbols to show a wealth of detail; the numerous city plans; and the separate index gazetteer of 215,000 entries. These are its praiseworthy points.

Offsetting these, however, are (a) the confusing treatment of nonwestern place names, seriously limiting its usefulness to non-Russian users and (b) the misrepresentation of locations of certain portions of the Soviet Union. Although this latter is believed to be deliberate policy, it nevertheless makes the atlas suspect in other vital areas. *The World Atlas* will be of value to the specialist cartographer and geographer, and to large reference libraries, for whom it is recommended. For the less advanced user, however, it will be a relatively difficult atlas to use and understand.

CRITICAL REVIEWS AND INFORMATIVE ARTICLES

Choice, July-August 1969, pp. 625–630.

OTHER SOURCES OF INFORMATION

Barton. *Reference Books.* 7th ed. 1970.
Cheney. *Fundamental Reference Sources.* 1971.
Walford. *Guide to Reference Material.* 2nd ed. 1966–1970.
Winchell. *Guide to Reference Books.* 8th ed. 2nd supplement 1967–1968.

PREMIER WORLD ATLAS

Merit Rating: 5
Group Three—Average Quality: *RECOMMENDED*

PUBLISHER

Rand McNally and Co., P.O. Box 7600, Chicago, Ill. 60680. Distributed in the United Kingdom by Geographia Limited, London.

PUBLISHING HISTORY AND REVISION PROGRAM

First published under this title and in this format in 1967, replacing the now defunct *International Atlas* by Rand McNally as the second largest atlas in the Rand McNally catalog. The specific title of "Premier" has, however, been used previously in 1952, for another quite different Rand McNally publication. This new 1972 edition is subtitled the *New Census Edition.* (It was formerly the *New Portrait Edition*). The larger *Cosmopolitan World Atlas* is subtitled the *Enlarged Planet Earth Edition.*

EDITORS, CARTOGRAPHERS, AND CONTRIBUTORS

None are named in the atlas but they have been specified by the publishers as the Cartographic Division staff of Rand McNally and Co., with R. Forstall as the senior research editor; J. Leverenz as the cartographic editor; and J. Smutnik as chief of geographic research. These are the same as those listed in the *Cosmopolitan World Atlas* and other Rand McNally atlases.

HOME SALE AND RETAIL PRICES

Understood to be available in one edition only, at $14.95. Note that it is identical in most respects to the *Cosmopolitan World Atlas*, which is priced at $19.95 in a regular edition and $25.00 in a deluxe edition. The *Cosmopolitan* contains 428 pages, and the *Premier* 336, but the map pages are identical, as also is the index.

PURPOSE AND AGE SUITABILITY

Like the larger *Cosmopolitan World Atlas* from which it is directly derived, the *Premier World Atlas* is designed mainly for home and library use by elementary, junior, and senior high school students from the age of 12 through 18. It is suitable for general adult use also, but will be less useful at college and university level where more detailed maps are a prime requirement.

SIZE AND NUMBER OF PAGES

The single-page bound size is the same as the *Cosmopolitan*, 14 by 11¼ in. It is comprised of 336 pages, made up of three variously paginated sections of xvi, 220, 100x pages and there are also some additional pages numbered a, b, c, etc. Most of the political maps are contained on a single page, except for the few world and continental maps which are spread over two facing pages for a map area of approximately 14 by 22 in.

TOTAL MAP PAGES AND TYPES OF MAPS

The *Premier World Atlas* is comprised of 130 pages of the *Cosmo* series of political-physical maps of the world, Canada, and the United States, all of which are in full color. These are supplemented by 13 pages of well-executed relief maps of the continents, and ten pages of maps of U.S. metropolitan areas. On the main series of political-physical maps, major elevations are shown by hachures and mountain symbols. These are supplemented by purely physical maps of (a) the world, (b) the continents, and (c) the United States, with the relief on these shown by a pleasing series of layer tints and hill shading. Locator maps are provided on all the regional and state maps, which are also useful for comparative purposes. Clearly identified are the methods of projection employed, and the scale at which each map is drawn, shown as (a) a representative fraction, its equivalent in miles per inch, and (c) a bar distance scale in both miles and kilometers. On the physical maps, heights are given in both feet and meters, and a key to the layer colors used is provided. Detail is relatively good. Railroads, tunnels, parks, points of interest, dams, and bridges are shown, but not, unfortunately, main and secondary roads. A legend to the map symbols employed is printed on a prefatory page, as also is a good explanation of map projections and scales.

SCALE

A confusing mixture. Some of the scales, although relatively small, are logical enough in an even progression, but in other areas, especially the United States and Canada, the page size determines the scale, and all sorts of odd fractions have resulted. The regional maps of Europe vary from 1:1,000,000 for Switzerland (very good); through 1:2,000,000 for the British Isles, the Low Countries, western and central Germany, and the Alpine Regions; 1:4,000,000 for Ireland, France, and most other countries in Europe, excepting Scandinavia at 1:8,000,000. For Russia there are only two maps, one at 1:8,000,000 and one at 1:11,000,000. The Mediterranean is also at 1:800,-000, except for the important regions of Israel and the northern United Arab Republic at 1:2,000,000. Asia is rather poorly treated, with no area being mapped at a scale larger than 1:8,000,000, while several areas are smaller still at 1:16,000,000. Africa is mapped uniformly but at the rather odd scale of 1:11,400,000. Southeastern Australia, correctly, is mapped at 1:8,000,000, but the remainder of the continent is at only 1:16,000,000. South America is evenly mapped at the quite good scale of 1:8,000,000. The greatest variation in scales occurs in the maps of Canada and the United States. Each province and state (with just one or two exceptions), is allocated a full page regardless of the size of the area, which is enlarged or reduced to fit the page. Because of this the scales vary widely and wildly from an excellent 1:731,000 for Connecticut to a relatively small scale of 1:4,118,000 for Texas. In between, for the other states and provinces, are all sorts of odd scales, making comparison difficult and inconvenient. The physical maps are also somewhat varied, from an odd 1:9,631,000 for the United States and Canada to a minute 1:32,567,000 for Africa and South America. The best maps are those of the U.S. metropolitan areas, all at the same good scale of 1:300,000.

BALANCE

Heavily weighted in favor of the United States and Canada. The United States alone is allocated 50 pages (excluding the metropolitan area maps), and a further ten pages for Canada means that more than 50 percent of the total map pages are given over to a coverage of the North American continent. Europe gets only 19 pages, four of which are allocated to the British Isles. Russia is contained in three pages, and also the Mediterranean lands and Australasia. Asia is harshly dealt with in only nine pages, and Africa is not much better treated with eight, the same as for South America. The favoring of North America is even more in evidence with the provision of ten pages of maps of metropolitan areas of the United States, but none for other major world cities.

INDEXING

This is easily the best feature of this otherwise mediocre atlas. More than 82,000 entries are contained in the 100-page index section, and these include physical features, differentiated by italic type. Also included are U.S. and Canadian national parks. Places and features are located by the simple letter-number grid system. The exact degrees of latitude and longitude are not given. Population statistics are no longer given in the index as in previous years, but most of these will still be found in the sections of geographic facts about the world, the United States, and Canada.

SCOPE, CONTENTS, AND ARRANGEMENT

The *Premier World Atlas* is made up of three broad sections: (1) the 16 pages of introductory material, (2) the 220 pages of maps and tables of statistical data, and (3) the 100-page index. The first 16 pages contain a detailed list of contents, but it does not specify the map scales; a section on The Planet Earth, the solar system, star charts for the northern skies, the moon, and good explanations of map projections and scales. Pages 1-149 are comprised of the main series of political-physical maps of the world, beginning with Europe and progressing through Russia, the Mediterranean, Asia, Africa, Australasia, South America, Canada, and the United States. These pages include a mass of statistical data such as world political information, world comparisons, and population statistics, for example. Pages 150-170 contain the populations of foreign countries, cities, and towns, listed under each country; geographic and historical facts about the United States; and general statistical information about the United States. Pages 171-186 are large-scale maps (1:300,000) of 12 metropolitan areas of the United States, with a six-page index to these. These are followed by the population of the United States, by cities, towns, counties, etc., arranged under each state. The 100-page index section completing the atlas is identical to that in the *Cosmopolitan World Atlas*.

SUMMARY

The *Premier World Atlas* is one of several published by the Rand McNally Co. In size it ranks third in their catalog, below the highly rated and far superior *The International Atlas*, and the work from which it is directly derived, the *Cosmopolitan World Atlas*. It is, in fact, purely and simply a scaled-down version of the *Cosmopolitan*, being identical to the larger work for nearly all of its 336 pages. The *Premier* differs from the *Cosmopolitan* only in that it: (1) contains a star chart of the Northern Skies, not included in the larger work; (2) alters the sequence slightly for the U.S. population section; (3) omits 40 pages of the *Cosmo's* introductory material, most of which was extracted from the same publisher's *Atlas of the Universe*; omits two pages of air and steamship distance tables; omits 19 pages of world metropolitan area maps and an eleven-page index to these. The rest of the atlas is identical to the *Cosmopolitan World Atlas*. Because of its omission of the metropolitan area maps of the world it is even more heavily weighted in favor of North America and is thus less useful than the larger work for reference purposes. It has the same less commendable features of limited detail and a confusing mixture of scales, especially for the United States and Canada. For those seeking a relatively complete coverage of Canada and the United States it has merit, but as a general-reference world atlas it is a mediocre work, despite its good index. Where cost is a limiting factor, and where coverage of North America is a prime requirement, the *Premier World Atlas* is recommended as an inexpensive alternative to the larger *Cosmopolitan World Atlas.*

CRITICAL REVIEWS AND INFORMATIVE ARTICLES

None for this title per se, but it is so similar to the *Cosmopolitan World Atlas* that the works are frequently treated together, and the reviews listed under the *Cosmopolitan World Atlas* apply equally to the *Premier World Atlas* insofar as the maps are concerned.

OTHER SOURCES OF INFORMATION

Because the *Premier World Atlas* is simply a scaled-down version of the *Cosmopolitan World Atlas*, the larger work is that usually cited in standard bibliographies of reference books. For those interested, it is worth checking the list provided for the *Cosmopolitan.*

FAMILY EDITION WORLD ATLAS
and
WORLDMASTER ATLAS

Note: These two atlases are identical for the first 247 pages, which is the full size of the *Worldmaster Atlas.* The *Family Edition World Atlas* goes on to provide an additional 81 pages.

Family Edition World Atlas Merit Rating: 4
Group Three—Average Quality: *RECOMMENDED*

Worldmaster Atlas Merit Rating: 4
Group Three—Average Quality: *RECOMMENDED*

PUBLISHER

Both atlases are published by Rand McNally and Co., P.O. Box 7600, Chicago, Ill. 60680.

PUBLISHING HISTORY AND REVISION PROGRAM

The *Family Edition World Atlas* was first published in 1964. It is based upon and derived from the *Cosmo* series of political-physical maps contained in the same publisher's larger *Cosmopolitan* and *Premier* world atlases. The

Worldmaster Atlas was also first published in 1964, but the present work appears to differ quite considerably from the earlier edition which was, in fact, reported out of print in 1968. As with all Rand McNally atlases, they are maintained under a program of continuous (usually annual) revision and updating.

EDITORS, CARTOGRAPHERS, AND CONTRIBUTORS

None listed in the atlases, but specified by the publishers as the Cartographic Division staff of Rand McNally and Co., who also compile other atlases by Rand McNally, the most notable of which are the *Cosmopolitan World Atlas* and the *Premier World Atlas*. The Universe sections, however, (pages viii–xxiv) were written by Stuart M. Kaminsky and Charles E. Yoder, in cooperation with the Office of Public Information of the University of Chicago.

HOME SALE AND RETAIL PRICES

The *Family Edition World Atlas* is available in two distinct bindings, a regular binding in cloth at $9.95, and in an "Imperial" edition with Lexatone deluxe binding at $12.95. The contents, of course, are identical, the editions differing only in their external appearance. The *Worldmaster Atlas*, which differs from the *Family Edition* only in that it excludes the historical and thematic maps, is considerably cheaper at $6.95.

PURPOSE AND AGE SUITABILITY

Both atlases are designed more for browsing and casual use than for serious reference work, although they contain a wide variety of maps and encyclopedic material. They can be used by children from the age of 12, as well as for general family use, but are limited in value for college work or advanced reference work.

SIZE AND NUMBER OF PAGES

Both atlases are the same single-page size of 12½ by 10 in. After allowing for the margins, the map area of each single page is 10¾ by 7¾ in. A few maps are spread over two facing pages for a better map area of 10¾ by 16 in. The *Family Edition World Atlas* contains 328 pages (xl, 288). The *Worldmaster Atlas* contains 247 pages, all of which are identical to the first 247 pages of the larger work.

TOTAL MAP PAGES AND TYPES OF MAPS

Including the global view relief maps, there are 103 pages of maps in both atlases (some with accompanying text), of which 89 comprise the basic series of political reference maps derived directly from the well-known *Cosmo* series utilized in nearly all Rand McNally atlases. Although essentially political in character, elevations are shown by hachures and mountain symbols. In the *Family Edition* there are, additionally, seven special thematic maps dealing with world population, transportation, climate, languages, religions, natural vegetation, and landforms, and also a series of historical maps. These are omitted from the *Worldmaster Atlas*. Except for the United States and Canada, all areas of the world are mapped by regions rather than by individual countries. Worthy of note are the many inset maps of metropolitan areas and important regions. A bad feature of the maps is that because they have been reduced in size by approximately one fifth from the *Cosmopolitan World Atlas*, the fractional scales are not given, a considerable disadvantage only partially offset by the provision of a bar distance scale in miles and kilometers. The reduction in size has also resulted in smaller type faces which are more difficult to read and tend to give the maps a cluttered appearance. As with the major *Cosmo* maps, detail is somewhat limited. Roads, for example, are not shown, although railroads are. Spot heights are given on the maps, but in feet only, with no metric equivalent. The projections used on each map are clearly stated, but there is no explanation of these elsewhere in the atlas. A list of map symbols is provided on page 90, immediately after the main series of maps, which is not a convenient location.

SCALE

This is very poor and very difficult to compare. The usual fractional scale is not shown on any map, nor in the list of contents, nor in the equivalent of miles per inch. The maps, however, are the same as those in the *Cosmopolitan* and *Premier* world atlases, but reduced by some 20 percent. The scales in those two atlases were a confusing mixture which varied widely and wildly, and the same remarks can be applied to the *Family Edition* and *Worldmaster* atlases.

BALANCE

Also very poor, and heavily weighted in favor of North America, which takes up more than 50 percent of the available space. The United States alone is allocated 45 of the 103 map pages, and almost every state is allocated one full page. Canada is allocated a further nine pages, with again one page for almost every province. Europe is allocated only nine pages, with the British Isles occupying one solitary page. The Soviet Union is covered in two pages, Asia in seven, Africa in four, Australasia in two, South America in six (which is better coverage), and Central America in two pages. A further 17 pages are allocated to the global view relief maps, and general maps of the world and the continents. The *Family Edition World Atlas* provides a further series of maps on history and special themes, again weighted in favor of the United States.

INDEXING

These atlases have identical indexes of 96 pages, containing some 30,000 entries for cities and towns, etc., with up-to-date population statistics. The index is located in both atlases between pages 94 and 189, immediately following the main series of maps. It is followed in both atlases by a further 18 pages of geographic statistics and other geographic information and, in the *Family Edition*, by a further 81 pages of historical and thematic maps.

SCOPE, CONTENTS, AND ARRANGEMENT

The first 40 pages in both atlases are virtually identical, differing only slightly in that the *Worldmaster Atlas* omits the list of credits and has a shorter contents list. Pages viii–xxv are identical, being the special Universe section, which includes: The Earth in Perspective; Historical Background; Planets and other Solar System Bodies; The Moon (map and index); The Sun; The Stars; The Galaxies; and a Space Glossary. Pages xxvi–xl are the special global view relief maps of Europe, Asia, Africa, Australasia and Oceania, South America, North America, the United States, and an introduction to the political maps. Pages 1–89 are comprised of the main series of political-physical maps beginning with Europe and progressing through the Soviet Union, Asia, Africa, Australasia, South America, Central America, Canada, and the United States. Pages 90–93 contain a list of map symbols and an explanation of the index system, geographic facts about the United States, historical facts about the United States, state areas and populations, a state general information table, and a list of abbreviations. Pages 94–189 contain the 30,000-entry index. Pages 190–207 provide further statistical data on a world scale: a glossary of foreign geographic terms, world political information table, world facts and comparisons, the largest metropolitan areas and cities, principal world cities and populations, principal discoveries and explorations, and world air and steamship distance tables. The *Worldmaster Atlas* is completed at this point, but the *Family Edition World Atlas* goes on to provide, on pages 208–219, a world history in maps; and American History in Maps, pages 220–233. These are followed by 55 pages of thematic world maps on various themes, accompanied by photographs and text.

SUMMARY

Although some of the text material is new, both atlases are basically scaled-down versions of the *Cosmopolitan* and *Premier* world atlases also published by Rand McNally. In effecting a 20 percent reduction in size, the publishers have sacrificed some of the better points of the two larger atlases. Particularly bad is the absence of a fractional representation of scale on each map, not in any way excusable by the provision of a bar distance scale. The maps are also more cluttered in appearance, and the smaller print makes them difficult to read in several instances. Both atlases do provide some useful and interesting supplementary material and good up-to-date statistical data, but this is insufficient to offset their cartographic deficiencies. Families will undoubtedly find them interesting and useful up to a point, but there are better atlases available in this price range. These atlases are good enough to earn a recommendation, but a very lukewarm and unenthusiastic one.

CRITICAL REVIEWS AND INFORMATIVE ARTICLES

Booklist, September 15, 1966.
Christian Century, October 6, 1965, p. 1237.

OTHER SOURCES OF INFORMATION

H. W. Wilson Co. *Junior High School Library Catalog.* Supplement 1966.
Winchell. *Guide to Reference Books.* 8th ed. 1967. 1st supplement 1965–66.

CITATION WORLD ATLAS
and
INTERNATIONAL WORLD ATLAS

Note: These two atlases are identical for the first 200 pages, which is the full
size of the *International World Atlas.* The *Citation World Atlas* goes on to
provide an additional 160 pages.

Citation World Atlas Merit Rating: 4
Group Three—Average Quality: *RECOMMENDED*

International World Atlas Merit Rating: 0
Group Four—Below Acceptable Standards: *NOT RECOMMENDED*

PUBLISHER

Both atlases are published by Hammond Inc., Maplewood, N.J. 07040, but
note that the *Citation World Atlas* is also published, with some additional
material, as the *Cram Modern World Atlas,* and the *International World Atlas* may be found under the imprints of other publishers, especially overseas.

PUBLISHING·HISTORY AND REVISION PROGRAM

The *Citation World Atlas* was first published in 1966, when Hammond introduced their new series of New Perspective atlases. At that time it was
smaller in format than the larger Hammond atlases, but now all are in the
same format of 12½ by 9½ in. The *International World Atlas* was also first
published in 1966, and is derived directly from the larger Hammond atlases,
but is designed for overseas use. It was at one time sold in Britain as *Newnes
International World Atlas: New Perspective Edition.*

EDITORS, CARTOGRAPHERS, AND CONTRIBUTORS

Actual cartography is by the cartographic staff of Hammond Inc., but also
named are 13 members of the Hammond Publications Advisory Board, to
each of whom is assigned an area of the world or a special subject. A full
list of these is also printed in the *Hallmark, Medallion,* and *Ambassador*
world atlases, from which these smaller works are derived. Most of the

named authorities are professors of geography in various American universities. A list of sources and acknowledgments is also given.

HOME SALE AND RETAIL PRICES

The *Citation World Atlas* retails in one edition only, at $10.95. It contains 160 pages more than the *International World Atlas*, which retails at $6.95.

PURPOSE AND AGE SUITABILITY

The *Citation World Atlas* is designed as a reference atlas for libraries, schools, colleges, offices, and homes as an inexpensive alternative to the *Ambassador World Atlas*, from which it is directly abridged. It can be used by students from the age of 12 through college. The *International World Atlas*, which can also be used from the age of 12, is designed more for overseas use, especially in English-speaking countries. It is far less useful in the United States and Canada because of the omission of the individual state maps.

SIZE AND NUMBER OF PAGES

Both atlases measure 12½ by 9½ in., in the single-page size. Neither provides double spread maps. The *Citation World Atlas* contains 360 pages. The *International World Atlas* contains only 200 pages, but these are identical to the first 200 pages of the *Citation*.

TOTAL MAP PAGES AND TYPES OF MAPS

The *Citation World Atlas* contains 320 pages of maps, but an exact count of these is difficult, due to the fact that also provided on the map pages is additional material such as text, statistical data, political and geographic information, and the national flag in color, and on some pages there are no maps at all. For want of a better term, this will be called the atlas section proper, and it should be noted that these are identical in every respect to the same 320 pages in the *Ambassador*, *Medallion*, and *Hallmark* world atlases (q.v.). The *International World Atlas* duplicates the first 192 pages of the other four atlases, and differs only in that it omits the pages allocated to the individual maps of the United States and provinces of Canada. For comments on the quality of the atlas section, the reader is referred to the analyses of the *Ambassador*, *Medallion*, and *Hallmark* world atlases. The merits and demerits are identical.

SCALE

See the details provided in the entries for the *Ambassador*, *Medallion*, and *Hallmark* world atlases. These are exactly the same for the *Citation World Atlas*. They apply equally to the *International World Atlas*, except for the comments on the maps of the United States and Canada.

BALANCE

Again, see the entries for the three larger atlases specified above, especially for the *Citation World Atlas*. The adverse balance in these four atlases, however, does not apply to the *International World Atlas*, which is not heavily weighted in favor of the North American continent.

INDEXING

Both atlases differ considerably in this respect. The *Citation World Atlas* has a general index of only 25,000 entries, very much shorter than the 105,000 entries in the three larger works. This makes it less useful for reference and serious work. The *International World Atlas* has no general index at all, although, as with all the other Hammond atlases, indexes to each map are provided on each map page.

SCOPE, CONTENTS, AND ARRANGEMENT

The atlas section in the *Ambassador, Medallion, Hallmark,* and *Citation* world atlases is identical in every respect from pages 1 to 320. The *International World Atlas* is also identical to the other four atlases, but only up to page 192.

SUMMARY

The *Citation World Atlas* is, at best, a mediocre general-reference world atlas, and is recommended only as an inexpensive alternative to the larger Hammond atlases from which it is abridged. The same criticisms apply: (a) the failure to indicate the scale at which each map is drawn; (b) the considerable imbalance of the maps in favor of the United States and Canada, although this is not applicable to the *International World Atlas*; (c) the differences in size between the main political series of maps and their accompanying physical maps; and (d) the duplication of the indexes on each map page, using up an inordinate amount of space which could have been better utilized for larger-scale maps. In the case of the *Citation World Atlas*, these deficiencies are further compounded by the much abbreviated index, which lists only the most important places and features. *The International World Atlas* has all of these disadvantages, even further compounded by the complete absence of a general index, and this cannot be recommended for any purpose.

CRITICAL REVIEWS AND INFORMATIVE ARTICLES

American Reference Books Annual, 1972, p.194.
Choice, February 1967, p.1111.
Library Journal, January 1, 1967, p. 101.
Wilson Library Bulletin, January 1967, p. 525.
Harper's, December 1966, p. 135.
Saturday Review, November 19, 1966, p. 51.
(See also the *Ambassador World Atlas*.)

OTHER SOURCES OF INFORMATION

Cheney. *Fundamental Reference Sources.* 1971
Walford. *Guide to Reference Material.* 2nd ed. 1966–1970.
(See also the *Ambassador World Atlas*.)

CRAM MODERN WORLD ATLAS

Merit Rating: 3
Group Three—Average Quality: *RECOMMENDED*

PUBLISHER

The George F. Cram Co., Inc., 301 La Salle St. South, Indianapolis, Ind. 46206. (Actually made by Hammond Inc.)

PUBLISHING HISTORY AND REVISION PROGRAM

An atlas entitled the *Cram New Modern World Atlas* was published in 1956, and the same work was retitled the *Cram Modern World Atlas* in 1962. The present work, however, although bearing the same title, is a quite different atlas. As already noted, it is in fact the Hammond *Citation World Atlas*, with 48 pages of additional material specially prepared by the George F. Cram Company.

EDITORS, CARTOGRAPHERS, AND CONTRIBUTORS

This atlas is identical for the most part to the *Citation World Atlas*. Like that, it is produced mainly by the cartographic staff of Hammond Inc., with some additional material by the editorial staff of the George F. Cram Company.

HOME SALE AND RETAIL PRICE

Understood to be available in one edition only, at $12.50. Note that the *Citation World Atlas*, which is identical except for the omission of the 48 pages added by Cram, is priced at $10.95.

PURPOSE AND AGE SUITABILITY

Like the *Citation World Atlas*, this slightly different Cram atlas is designed as a reference atlas for libraries, schools, colleges, offices, and homes as a medium-priced alternative to more comprehensive works. It can be used by students from the age of 12 through college.

SIZE AND NUMBER OF PAGES

The single-page bound size is 12½ by 9½ in. It is comprised of 408 pages, forming sections of 16, 358, and 34 pages. There are no double-page map spreads. Some of the maps take up a full page with no margins, but most are smaller than the actual page size.

TOTAL MAP PAGES AND TYPES OF MAPS

The map content in this atlas is identical to that contained in the *Citation*, *Ambassador, Medallion,* and *Hallmark* world atlases by Hammond, but it is supplemented by a small number of original maps by Cram. It has the same unique arrangement, which brings together as one unit the maps, text, statistical data, and national flags for each individual country or group of countries, and not all the pages have maps on them, making an exact count difficult. The main series of maps consists of the Hammond political maps, accompanied by smaller physical maps of the same region, and in some instances, by smaller thematic maps. The *Cram Modern World Atlas* provides an additional 32 pages of historical maps. As is the case with the other Hammond atlases mentioned above, roads and railroads are not shown on the maps, although special transportation maps are provided for some areas. Scale is shown only as a bar distance scale in both miles and kilometers, and never as a representative fraction nor in the equivalent mile-per-inch scale, making comparison difficult. Some locator maps are provided, but these are more often with the text than with the relevant map. The methods of projection employed are also not identified on the map pages, but a useful list of these is given in the prefatory pages, and the usual useful explanation of map projections by Erwin Raisz is provided on an end page. For a fuller analysis of the maps, see the entry for the *Ambassador World Atlas*.

SCALE

Very poor. The scales are not only not given on the map pages, but are obviously very mixed, especially for the United States and Canada. See the comments under "Scale" in the analysis of the *Ambassador World Atlas*.

BALANCE

Also very poor, and heavily weighted in favor of North America. As the main series of maps are the same, again see this analysis in the entry for the *Ambassador World Atlas*, and, of course, the *Citation World Atlas*, and several other Hammond atlases.

INDEXING

As with the *Citation World Atlas*, the Cram edition provides a somewhat limited index of some 25,000 entries, very much shorter than the 105,-000-entry indexes in the larger works, although the maps are identical. This makes it far less useful for reference work of a serious nature.

SCOPE, CONTENTS, AND ARRANGEMENT

Differs only slightly from the *Citation World Atlas*. The first 16 pages (different from the *Citation*) provide: an index to the contents, with map page number and latitude and longitude; a list of countries, states, and provinces; a condensed world gazetteer, with classification, capital city, area, population, and similar facts on the various countries of the world. Then follows a special Cram physical-political map of the world; a list of the largest cities of the world and a list of the largest cities of the United States; a physical-political map of the United States (by Cram cartographers); a list of U.S. national parks; a good section on how to use an atlas; and an article on the exploration and discovery of the Polar regions. This prefatory section is followed by the main series of Hammond political and topographic maps, each with its own index and statistics (pages 1–320). Pages 321–352 are also identical to the *Citation World Atlas*, containing the 24-page index, a list of geographic terms, airline distance tables, a table of geographic comparisons, and an explanation of map projections. The atlas is concluded with an additional section of original Cram material: a story of the Polar regions (continued from the prefatory section), the language of maps, definitions of geographic terms, and a world history section containing 32 pages of colored maps of the world from ancient times to the end of the Second World War.

SUMMARY

The *Cram Modern World Atlas* is, like the *Citation World Atlas*, at best a mediocre general-reference world atlas. To all intents and purposes it is just another Hammond atlas which the additional material from the George F. Cram Company does little or nothing to enhance. It has the same good points and the same bad points. The arrangement of the maps is good, and related material is well executed, bringing together, as it does, all the vital data for each specific country or area of the world. The maps themselves are clear and well printed, and the topographic maps, especially, are well designed. But the same criticisms apply here as for other Hammond atlases: (a) the failure of the cartographers to indicate the scale at which each map is drawn, (b) the considerable imbalance of coverage in favor of North America, (c) the difference in size between the main political map and its accompanying topographic map, and (d) the duplication of the indexes on each map page in the general index, further compounded by the fact that the general index is much too short for serious reference use. Because the *Cram Modern World Atlas* is virtually the same as the *Citation World Atlas*, it is included in those atlases rated about average in quality, but is rated slightly lower because of its higher cost and inclusion of less useful material.

CRITICAL REVIEWS AND INFORMATIVE ARTICLES

None for the *Cram Modern World Atlas* as such, but see the *Citation World Atlas* and the *Ambassador World Atlas*, the reviews of which can be applied almost equally.

OTHER SOURCES OF INFORMATION

Not listed in any bibliography under the title of *Cram Modern World Atlas*, but again, see the *Citation* and *Ambassador* world atlases.

Group Four:
ATLASES BELOW
ACCEPTABLE QUALITY

THE FABER ATLAS

Merit Rating: 1
Group Four—Below Acceptable Quality: *NOT RECOMMENDED*

PUBLISHER
Distributed by Faber and Faber Limited, 3 Queen Square, London WC1N 3AU, England, but actually made by Geo Publishing (Oxford) Limited.

PUBLISHING HISTORY AND REVISION PROGRAM
First published in 1956. A second edition appeared in 1959, a third in 1961, and a fourth in 1964, with revised reprints in 1966 and 1968. The current edition is the fifth, published in 1970.

EDITORS, CARTOGRAPHERS, AND CONTRIBUTORS
The only editor named is D. J. Sinclair, a Senior Lecturer in Geography at the London School of Economics, although there is also a foreword by Professor L. Dudley Stamp, a well-known authority on geography. The maps, according to a note on the verso of the title page, were produced by E. Holzel, of Vienna.

HOME SALE AND RETAIL PRICES
Available in one edition only, it retails in the United Kingdom at £3.00 and in the United States at $8.50. It is available in Canada through the exclusive agents, the Oxford University Press, Toronto.

PURPOSE AND AGE SUITABILITY
A quite attractive smaller atlas designed for general use in homes, high schools, colleges, libraries, and offices. Because of its strong emphasis on Britain and Europe, it will appeal only to those with a special interest in these areas.

SIZE AND NUMBER OF PAGES

Single-page size is 12¼ by 8¾ in., which is slightly larger than in the four previous editions. A small number of maps are spread over two facing pages for a map area, after allowing for margins, of 10½ by 16 in. The atlas is comprised of 204 pages, made up of eight prefatory pages, 152 pages of maps, and a 44-page index section.

TOTAL MAP PAGES AND TYPES OF MAPS

There are exactly 152 pages of multicolored maps. The majority of these are physical in nature, with political detail. Relief is shown by an excellent series of layer tints and also by hill shading. A legend to the colors is provided on each map, with heights and depths shown in both feet and meters. Thematic maps are plentiful, showing, among other things, geology, vegetation and land use, mining and industries, population density, economics, rainfall, climate, and religions. There are a few very good metropolitan area maps, with three foreign and seven British cities shown at the adequate scale of 1:200,000. Detail is good. On the larger-scale maps, roads, railroads, and canals are shown, as well as political boundaries. Scale is shown both as a numerical fraction and as a bar distance scale in both miles and kilometers. The projections employed are clearly and properly identified on each map.

SCALE

This varies considerably, and emphasizes Britain. Some regions of the United Kingdom are mapped at the excellent scale of 1:200,000, but other regions such as Scotland and Ireland are less well done at 1:1,250,000. Europe is quite well covered, most of the maps being at 1:2,500,000. There are some also at 1:5,000,000, but the more important regions are at the quite large scale of 1:200,000. Asia suffers in comparison, no region other than Japan and the Near East (at 1:5,000,000) being shown at a scale larger than 1:10,000,000. Australasia does a little better at either 1:3,000,000 or 1:5,000,000, but Africa is badly scaled and poorly detailed at either 1:10,000,000 or 1:20,000,000. The United States is inadequately mapped also, the best scale being at 1:5,000,000, but with other areas at the less uniform scale of 1:12,500,000. All of South America is at the inadequate scale of 1:10,000,000.

BALANCE

Heavily weighted in favor of Great Britain and Europe. No less than 31 pages are allocated to the British Isles (20 percent of the available space). A further 38 pages are allocated to other European countries. Asia is allocated only 22 pages, Australasia six, Africa ten, North America 13, and South America seven. As a general world atlas it is much too heavily weighted in favor of Europe.

INDEXING

This is somewhat limited, containing only some 20,000 entries, including physical features. Location is by page number and a letter-number grid system. Degrees of latitude and longitude are not given. The index is pure and does not provide extraneous information such as population statistics.

SCOPE, CONTENTS, AND ARRANGEMENT

A relatively small atlas, there are eight pages of prefatory material, including a list of contents which shows the scale for each map listed. This is followed by the 152 pages of world, regional, and resource maps, and a 44-page index.

SUMMARY

The *Faber Atlas* is a small, but quite useful and attractive desk atlas for general reference use. The maps in themselves are of good quality, with good detail and coloring which shows relief well, but its coverage is heavily imbalanced in favor of Europe in general (more than 50 percent of the total map pages) and the British Isles specifically (more than 20 percent). North America, in comparison, is offered only 10 percent of the available space. The scales of the maps vary widely also, and whereas Britain is well dealt with in a series of regional maps ranging from as large as 1:200,000 to 1:1,250,000, the United States and Canada are poorly detailed in only four regional maps, varying from 1:5,000,000 to 1:12,500,000 with the solitary exception of New York City at 1:200,000. Despite the good quality of the maps, the *Faber Atlas* is not a good atlas, and is not recommended.

CRITICAL REVIEWS AND INFORMATIVE ARTICLES

None recorded.

OTHER SOURCES OF INFORMATION

Walford. *Guide to Reference Material.* 2nd ed. 1966–1970.

HAMMOND CONTEMPORARY WORLD ATLAS

Merit Rating: 1
Group Four—Below Acceptable Quality: *NOT RECOMMENDED*

PUBLISHER

Doubleday and Co., Inc., 277 Park Ave., New York, N.Y. 10017, but actually made by Hammond Inc., Maplewood, N.J. 07040.

PUBLISHING HISTORY AND REVISION PROGRAM

First published in 1967 as an entirely new atlas, one of many in the much improved New Perspective series of Hammond atlases. All of the maps are abridged and derived from the several other larger Hammond atlases, from the *Ambassador* to the *Citation*. The maps, however, are smaller in format and are reduced about 20 percent in size. As with all Hammond atlases, it is maintained under a program of frequent revision and updating.

EDITORS, CARTOGRAPHERS, AND CONTRIBUTORS

No editors are named as such, but the atlas was compiled by the cartographic and research staff of Hammond Inc. Listed on the first page is the Hammond Publications Advisory Board, comprised of well-known educators and professors of geography from various American universities.

HOME SALE AND RETAIL PRICE

Apparently available in one edition only, at $12.50.

PURPOSE AND AGE SUITABILITY

A small atlas designed for general family and student use, from the age of 12. It is too limited for college use.

SIZE AND NUMBER OF PAGES

Single-page size is 11 by 8 in. (Most Hammond atlases are 12½ by 9½ in.) It is comprised of 288 consecutively numbered pages.

TOTAL MAP PAGES AND TYPES OF MAPS

Some pages are comprised of maps only, but most of the 252 pages which comprise the atlas section proper also contain statistical information, indexes, and national flags in full color, where applicable. The basic series of maps are political only, but each is accompanied by a smaller topographic map of the same area and some thematic maps on population, distribution, temperature, rainfall, vegetation, and similar features. For the United States, Canada, and some South American countries, special-feature highway maps are provided. The political maps are poorly detailed and vital communications networks such as roads and railroads are not given. The physical maps are better, but too small. Relief is shown on these by well-executed layer tinting and hill shading. A key to the color elevations is provided. As with other Hammond maps, the scale at which each map is drawn is not shown as a representative fraction, only in the unsatisfactory bar distance scale. The maps are exactly the same as those in the *Ambassador, Medallion, Hallmark, Citation,* and other Hammond atlases, but reduced in size by about 20 percent which gives them a cluttered appearance.

SCALE

Very unsatisfactory. The usual method of showing scale as a numerical fraction is not employed, and the only way of ascertaining this is by means of the bar distance scale. Although not given, the scales obviously vary considerably, especially for the United States, where each state is allocated a full page, irrespective of its size, so that a relatively small state such as Connecticut is mapped at a much larger scale than Texas.

BALANCE

Equally unsatisfactory. There is a considerable emphasis on North America, and the United States particularly, which is allocated no less than 131 pages, more than 50 percent of the entire atlas section. Europe is contained within 40 pages, the Soviet Union in six, Africa also in six, Asia in 27, Australasia and New Zealand in five, South America in 22, and North America and Central America (excluding the section on the United States) in 14.

INDEXING

By far the worst feature of this atlas. There is no general index as such and the location of places can only be made if the country is known, as each map is provided with its own classified indexes. These include political and administrative divisions such as counties, cities, towns, villages, and physical features, but in separate tables. If these were counted, there would be a total of some 80,000 entries. There is also a prefatory index-gazetteer of the world which lists some 300 countries and states.

SCOPE, CONTENTS, AND ARRANGEMENT

The atlas can be divided into three main sections, the four pages of prefatory matter, which lists the Hammond Publications Advisory Board, and an index-gazetteer of the world. This is followed by the 252 pages of maps, arranged on the unit system, whereby all pertinent and related maps, together with all relevant statistical information, are grouped together on facing or adjoining pages, continent by continent. The last section is a 32-page supplement entitled Environment and Life, and is identical to the same section in the *Medallion World Atlas,* but is in smaller print. There is no index.

SUMMARY

Like the several other Hammond atlases from which it is derived, the *Hammond Contemporary World Atlas* is logically arranged on the convenient unit principle, with each basic political map being accompanied by smaller maps showing the topography and resources of the area. The maps are then accompanied by relatively comprehensive classified indexes of inhabited places, physical features, and political subdivisions. Also with each map are tables of important data and glossaries of useful information such as area, population, currency, language, religion, and national flags in color. Special-feature maps include (for continents) climatic and population density maps. For all the individual states of the United States and for some of the larger countries, special major highway maps are provided. These are the better points of the atlas. It has many deficiencies, however, such as the lack of detail on the political maps, the failure to show the scale at which each map is drawn, the obvious variations in scale, and the too small physical maps. A major defect is the lack of a general cumulative index, which the individual classified indexes do not make up for. At $12.50 it is also quite expensive, as evinced by the fact that the much larger *Citation World Atlas,* containing much the same and more information, is priced at only $10.95. The *Hammond Contemporary World Atlas* is not recommended.

CRITICAL REVIEWS AND INFORMATIVE ARTICLES

None recorded for this title, but see the *Ambassador World Atlas* for reviews which are pertinent.

OTHER SOURCES OF INFORMATION

Deason. *AAAS Science Book List*. 3rd ed. 1970.
H. W. Wilson Co. *Senior High School Library Catalog*. 1971 supplement.

ADVANCED REFERENCE ATLAS

Merit Rating: 0
Group Four—Below Acceptable Quality: *NOT RECOMMENDED*

PUBLISHER

Hammond Inc., Maplewood, N.J. 07040.

PUBLISHING HISTORY AND REVISION PROGRAM

First published in 1949. Revised printings have appeared at regular intervals: 1956, 1957, 1959, 1961, 1962, 1964, 1966, and 1968. As with all Hammond atlases, it is maintained under a program of continuous revision and updating.

EDITORS, CARTOGRAPHERS, AND CONTRIBUTORS

There are no individuals named. Atlas is the product of the cartographic and research staff of Hammond Inc.

HOME SALE AND RETAIL PRICE

Available in one edition only, at $7.50 (has increased 50 percent in cost in past five years).

PURPOSE AND AGE SUITABILITY

Claimed by the publishers to be a complete social studies atlas, it is a binding of four separate works in one volume: *The Comparative World Atlas*, the *Historical Atlas*, the *American History Atlas*, and the *World Atlas for Students*. It can be used by children from the age of 12, and will be of some interest to other family users, but has little value as a general-reference world atlas.

SIZE AND NUMBER OF PAGES

Single-page size is 12½ by 9½ in. It contains 196 pages in all, variously paginated.

TOTAL MAP PAGES AND TYPES OF MAPS

There are 160 pages of maps of varying types. The basic series of maps consists of the usual Hammond political maps, with limited detail and no scales shown. There are also 90 pages of historical maps in two sections, one for the United States, and the other for the rest of the world. These are supplemented by relief maps, in layer shading, for the continents and large areas of the world, and a number of thematic maps on such facts as population distribution, temperature and rainfall, and vegetation. On the few maps with physical features, relief is shown by layer tinting or hill shading, or sometimes a combination of both. Detail is very limited and lines of communication, for example, are not shown.

SCALE

The fractional scales used on most atlases are not provided here, a usual Hammond policy. This makes comparison difficult, which the provision of a bar distance scale does nothing to alleviate.

BALANCE

Only two sections of the atlas are concerned with present-day general-reference world maps. The first section is a world geography section containing a number of thematic maps and miscellaneous atlas statistics and material. The second section is comprised of 32 pages of Hammond political maps of the world at the present time. Because of the small number of such maps there is no discernible imbalance.

INDEXING

There is no general index as such, and small, specific features and places are difficult to locate. A limited measure of guidance is provided by the three-page gazetteer-index of the world in the prefatory matter, which lists some 400 countries, states, provinces, and major geographic regions, giving for each its area in square miles, population, and capital or largest city. A small index of some 1,500 entries is provided for the *Historical Atlas.*

SCOPE, CONTENTS, AND ARRANGEMENT

This work is arranged in four clear and separate parts, all of which can be found, in one combination or another, in other Hammond Atlases. Part 1 (Pages 1–51) is the "Comparative World Atlas." This is a series of comparative maps for each continent, showing the political and physical features of each, together with thematic maps on vegetation, population, temperature and rainfall, world distribution, and resource maps. There is also a one-page explanation of map projections by Erwin Raisz. Part 2 (Pages H1–H49) is the "Historical Atlas" (of Western Civilization). This is comprised of a series of 49 maps depicting the history of the world from B.C. to the present time. Part 3 (Pages A1–A40) is an "Atlas of American History," portraying the growth and development of the United States in 40 pages of colored maps, accompanied by a gazetteer of states and territories. Part 4 (Pages 1–32) is the "World Atlas for Students." This is comprised of a series of postwar political maps of the various countries and regions of the world.

SUMMARY

The two sections of historical maps in this mixed-purpose atlas are of some interest and usefulness, but the atlas as a whole is awkwardly arranged, which decreases ease of use, and is seriously deficient in its provision of general-reference world maps. The lack of an index mitigates even further against any merits it may otherwise have. A compendium of four quite separate works, the *Advanced Reference Atlas* is a poor compromise which serves no one purpose well. There are many atlases available at this cost which are far more comprehensive and more conveniently arranged, including several within the Hammond range. Even where there is a special interest in historical maps, there are better alternatives available. The *Advanced Reference Atlas* is not recommended.

CRITICAL REVIEWS AND INFORMATIVE ARTICLES

American Reference Books Annual, 1972, p. 194.

OTHER SOURCES OF INFORMATION

Whyte. *Whyte's Atlas Guide*. 1962.
H. W. Wilson Co. *Senior High School Library Catalog*. 1957 edition.

ILLUSTRATED ENCYCLOPEDIA LIBRARY WORLD ATLAS
and
HAMMOND ILLUSTRATED FAMILY WORLD ATLAS

Merit Rating: 0
Group Four—Below Acceptable Quality: *NOT RECOMMENDED*

PUBLISHER

The Bobley Publishing Corporation, Glen Cove, Long Island, N.Y. 11542, in collaboration with Hammond Inc., Maplewood, N.J. 07040.

PUBLISHING HISTORY AND REVISION PROGRAM

This is not entirely clear. This work was first recorded under this title in 1969 and also as the *Hammond Illustrated Family World Atlas*. It is almost certainly a direct successor to the *Hammond Family World Atlas* (also in two volumes), which was first published in 1953 and retailed then by the Standard Reference Works Publishing Company until about 1967.

EDITORS, CARTOGRAPHERS, AND CONTRIBUTORS

No individuals named. Maps are by the cartographic and research staff of Hammond Inc. Some of the text material is probably by the editorial staff of the Bobley Publishing Corporation.

HOME SALE AND RETAIL PRICE

The only known edition (in two volumes) is stated to cost $11.72, but it is probably available at this price only as a subscription item with the *Illustrated World Encyclopedia*, or as a premium item.

PURPOSE AND AGE SUITABILITY

Designed for general home use and by children from the age of 12, it is not suitable for advanced work or serious reference use.

SIZE AND NUMBER OF PAGES

Single-page size is 12½ by 9½ in., the same as most of the Hammond atlases. Both volumes together total 376 pages. Volume 1 contains 192 pages, variously paginated, and volume 2 contains 184 pages, again variously paginated. The actual map sizes are usually smaller than the page sizes, and there are no maps spread over two facing pages.

TOTAL MAP PAGES AND TYPES OF MAPS

There is a total of 207 pages of maps, of which 86 are in volume 1, and 121 in volume 2. The majority of these are the basic Hammond multicolor political maps, but also included are a number of black and white resource-relief maps of the continents, a historical atlas of world civilization, and an atlas of the Bible lands, both in color. In addition, there are a small number of distribution and resource maps for the world and for the United States. Where relief is shown, the methods used are hill shading, layer tinting, or a combination of both. As is usual on Hammond maps, detail is limited, with neither roads nor railroads being shown. Omitted also is the numerical scale at which each map is drawn, although a bar distance scale is provided.

SCALE

Badly defined. The almost universal method of showing scale is by numerical fraction. This is not done in this atlas, and the only indication of distance is by the bar distance scale, an inadequate substitute. It is clear, however, that this atlas follows the usual Hammond practice of varying and unidentifiable scales, and comparison is very difficult. In the case of the United States, there is a full page allocated to almost every state, with the result that the state of Connecticut is mapped far more favorably than the much larger state of Texas.

BALANCE

Heavily weighted in favor of the United States, which takes up some 50 percent of the available space. Volume 1 contains 126 pages of maps and statistical tables for the world, excluding the United States, which is contained in volume 2 and occupies more than 150 pages. Europe, for example, and this includes the European Soviet Union, is allocated 16 pages. Asia, including Asiatic Russia, occupies only nine pages. Africa is very badly mapped in only two pages, Australasia also only in two pages, but Central and South

America are better dealt with in 19 pages. As a general world atlas, this work is badly imbalanced and inadequate for serious study.

INDEXING

There are two small and inconveniently arranged indexes. The first, which is for the world generally, is contained between pages 57 and 88 of volume 1. The second, which is for the United States only, is contained in volume 2 between pages 194 and 255. The world index contains some 12,000 entries, and the index to the United States about 30,000 entries. Both provide population statistics.

SCOPE, CONTENTS, AND ARRANGEMENT

Volume 1 deals mainly with the world. It begins with 16 pages of text and colored illustrations on space activities. This is followed by a three-page gazetteer-index to the world's major political units, and five pages of global views of the world, and general world political maps. Pages 9–56 are comprised of political maps of Europe and European countries; Asia and Asian countries; Africa; Australia and Pacific; Central and North America (excluding the United States); and South America and the West Indies. Immediately following the maps is a 32-page index to the world maps. Various supplementary material is included in volume 1, such as 32 pages of an illustrated geography of the world; six pages of black and white resource maps; and ten pages of social and economic tables. Separately paginated sections complete the first volume, comprised of Races of Mankind (pages D1–D12); world distribution maps (pages D13–D20); world statistical tables (Pages D21–D22); an explanation of map projections by Erwin Raisz (pages D23–D24); and finally, paginated C1–C16, a Historical Atlas of World Civilization. Volume 2 is given over almost entirely to the United States. The first 56 pages are political maps of each of the 50 states, and these are followed immediately by a 64-page index to the maps of the United States. Padding out this volume is a 32-page illustrated geography of the United States, and a 32-page Historical Atlas of the Bible Lands.

SUMMARY

The arrangement of this atlas in two relatively slim volumes is neither necessary nor convenient. All the maps and a great deal of the text material are drawn from the main Hammond series of world atlases, and the same criticisms apply: inadequate detail, imbalance of coverage, and failure to indicate the scales at which the maps are drawn. The retail or premium cost of $11.72 for the two volumes is unrealistic in comparison to other far more comprehensive, more accurate, better detailed, and more up-to-date atlases retailing in this price range. The atlas is very much smaller than the two volumes suggest and a great deal of nonatlas material or text and illustrations of minimal value pad the work. This is a poor atlas, badly indexed, and poorly arranged. It is not recommended in any edition.

CRITICAL REVIEWS AND INFORMATIVE ARTICLES
None recorded under either title.

OTHER SOURCES OF INFORMATION
None available for either title.

STANDARD WORLD ATLAS

Merit Rating: 0
Group Four—Below Acceptable Quality: *NOT RECOMMENDED*

PUBLISHER
Hammond Inc., Maplewood, N.J. 07040.

PUBLISHING HISTORY AND REVISION PROGRAM
This title was first used for a Hammond atlas in 1948, but the present work appears to be quite different and was first published in 1967, as one in the series of Hammond New Perspective atlases introduced in 1966.

EDITORS, CARTOGRAPHERS, AND CONTRIBUTORS
The cartographic and research staff of Hammond Incorporated. No individuals are named, but a list of acknowledgments is printed in the prefatory material.

HOME SALE AND RETAIL PRICE
In one edition only, at $12.50. Like the *Hammond World Atlas—Classics Edition*, it is designed for the premium and subscription markets, and will be more often sold as a subscription item in a package deal with other reference books than as a regular trade item. Other Hammond atlases, such as the *Citation World Atlas* (q.v.), contain all and more than is provided in this atlas, and at a lower cost.

PURPOSE AND AGE SUITABILITY
Designed for all-round family use, by students from the age of 12 through general adult use. It is certainly not suitable for advanced reference purposes.

SIZE AND NUMBER OF PAGES
The single-page bound size is 12½ by 9½ in., the standard size now for all Hammond atlases. There are 332 pages, made up of 12 prefatory pages and 320 pages of maps, indexes, and other information. Note that these are identical to the first 332 pages of the *Citation World Atlas*.

TOTAL MAP PAGES AND TYPES OF MAPS

The 320 map pages (which include indexes, tables of information, and national flags in color) are identical to the same 320 pages of maps in the *Ambassador, Medallion, Hallmark,* and *Citation* world atlases, the entries to which the reader is referred for further information.

SCALE

See the entries for the *Ambassador World Atlas* and *Citation World Atlas,* for a full description of scale.

BALANCE

See the entries for the *Ambassador World Atlas* and the *Citation World Atlas* for details.

INDEXING

The most serious deficiency of this atlas is that it does not provide a general index, and terminates abruptly at page 320. The *Citation World Atlas,* which is identical up to this point, goes on to provide a 28-page index section—at less cost! There are, of course, classified indexes provided with each map unit. In total, these are quite comprehensive, but it entails knowing which country the entry required is located in.

SCOPE, CONTENTS, AND ARRANGEMENT

Refer to the *Citation World Atlas* specifically, and also to the *Ambassador, Medallion,* and *Hallmark* world atlases. The *Standard World Atlas* is identical in every respect to the *Citation World Atlas* up to and including page 320. The map section proper, pages 1–320, are identical in all the atlases itemized.

SUMMARY

The *Standard World Atlas* is simply a shortened version of the *Citation World Atlas,* but offers much less for a little more money. The maps, as far as they go, are of good quality and are well arranged on the Hammond unit principle, but are still deficient in that they are inadequately detailed, poorly scaled and heavily imbalanced. Its most serious defect is the lack of a general index, which is the only difference in fact between this atlas and the *Citation.* The *Standard World Atlas,* for this reason alone, is a poor purchase, and is not recommended.

CRITICAL REVIEWS AND INFORMATIVE ARTICLES

None are recorded under this title, but see *Citation World Atlas.*

OTHER SOURCES OF INFORMATION

There are none for this title, but see *Citation World Atlas.*

HAMMOND WORLD ATLAS—CLASSICS EDITION

Merit Rating: 0
Group Four—Below Acceptable Quality: *NOT RECOMMENDED*

PUBLISHER

Hammond Inc., Maplewood, N.J. 07040, but it may also appear under imprint of other publishers.

PUBLISHING HISTORY AND REVISION PROGRAM

This title was first used for a Hammond atlas in 1951, but it applied to the older series of Hammond atlases, which was completely replaced by their New Perspective series in 1966. The present work, which was first copyrighted in March 1967, is, for all practical purposes, the *Citation World Atlas* (q.v.) with some additional material.

EDITORS, CARTOGRAPHERS, AND CONTRIBUTORS

No individuals are named, although a list of sources and acknowledgments is printed in the prefatory pages. The atlas is compiled, edited, and produced by the cartographic and research staff of Hammond Inc.

HOME SALE AND RETAIL PRICE

According to the publishers, available in one edition only, at $25.00. This is in a simulated leather ("Classics") binding. It is not available through regular trade channels and is primarily a premium and subscription item, which may be published under a number of other imprints, and possibly at different prices. In 1964, for example, it was distributed as the *Grolier International Atlas*. To all intents and purposes, it is identical to the *Citation World Atlas* (less than half the price but contains 36 more pages).

PURPOSE AND AGE SUITABILITY

As indicated above, this atlas is designed for premium and subscription sales to homes for general family use, and will almost certainly be encountered in combination deals with encyclopedias and other subscription reference books. Age suitability is from the age of 12 through general adult use.

SIZE AND NUMBER OF PAGES

Single-page size is 12½ by 9½ in. The atlas is comprised of 396 pages, made up of xii prefatory pages, and 384 consecutively numbered pages. The first 360 pages are identical to those in the *Citation World Atlas*, but the *Classics* edition includes a further 36-page section on the Universe, Earth and Man.

TOTAL MAP PAGES AND TYPES OF MAPS

The 320 pages of maps, indexes, political, social, and economic data, are identical to the same 320 pages in the *Ambassador, Medallion, Hallmark,*

Citation, and *Standard* world atlases, all of which are published by Hammond Inc. Full details of these will be found under the entry for the *Ambassador World Atlas*.

SCALE
See full details under the *Ambassador World Atlas* entry.

BALANCE
See full details under the *Ambassador World Atlas* entry.

INDEXING
Fully detailed in the *Citation World Atlas* entry.

SCOPE, CONTENTS, AND ARRANGEMENT
Identical to the *Citation World Atlas* up to page 360, and to the *Standard World Atlas* up to page 332. The only difference in the *Classics* edition is the additional provision of an illustrated section on the Universe, Earth and Man.

SUMMARY
The *Hammond World Atlas—Classics Edition* is identical, with the exception of 36 pages, to the *Citation World Atlas*, and is basically the same as the *Ambassador*, *Medallion*, and *Hallmark* world atlases. Its cost, however, in relation, is out of all proportion. The *Classics* edition, for $25.00, offers only a very little more than the *Citation*, which costs far less at $10.95. Although costing practically the same, it offers far less than the *Medallion World Atlas*, which contains 672 pages! The simulated leather binding and the relatively superfluous section on the Universe, Earth and Man certainly do not justify the high cost of this atlas which, even with the well-executed Hammond maps, is still a mediocre work at best. It is not recommended.

CRITICAL REVIEWS AND INFORMATIVE ARTICLES
None recorded under this title. See the entries for the other Hammond atlases.

OTHER SOURCES OF INFORMATION
None list this title. See entries for the several other Hammond atlases.

SCHOOL AND LIBRARY ATLAS OF THE WORLD

Merit Rating: 0
Group Four—Below Acceptable Quality: *NOT RECOMMENDED*

PUBLISHER

School and Library Publishing Co., 110 North Sacramento St., Sycamore, Ill. 60178.

PUBLISHING HISTORY AND REVISION PROGRAM

First published under this title in 1953, but a great deal of the material is derived from the same publisher's *Commercial and Library Atlas of the World*, which was published in 1950. The publishers claim that the atlas is revised continuously and this would seem to be supported by the inclusion of all the most recent census figures (including the U.S. census of 1970), and by the copyright date of 1971 for the edition examined.

EDITORS, CARTOGRAPHERS, AND CONTRIBUTORS

Listed as editor in chief is Professor Fred W. Foster, Department of Geography, University of Illinois, assisted by the editorial and map department of the Geographical Publishing Company. Also listed on the title page are ten special contributors, all of whom are professors of geography at various universities in the United States (with one from Canada). Their contributions, however, are apparently restricted to the special-reference text sections.

HOME SALE AND RETAIL PRICES

The last recorded prices are $39.50 to business establishments and private individuals, and $29.50 to schools, libraries, and educational institutions. The atlas can be purchased for personal use, but its sales are normally to the educational field.

PURPOSE AND AGE SUITABILITY

Designed primarily for business use, and for use by students attending senior high school from the age of 15, through the college and university level. Large and unwieldy, it is an impractical atlas for home use.

SIZE AND NUMBER OF PAGES

An unusually large atlas, it measures a 22 by 16 in. single-page size. The map areas are considerably smaller due to the wide margins, and there are frequently several maps on one page. There is a total of 350 pages. A truly substantial volume, with heavy calendered paper, it weighs approximately 16 lbs.

TOTAL MAP PAGES AND TYPES OF MAPS

Of the 126 map pages, 76 are comprised of two-color political maps of the world. The other 50 (some of which are in black and white) are all allocated to the United States. The main series of maps is political only, and the maps are dully colored in yellow, with blue boundary lines on a white background. On some of the maps, however, high ground is shown by the use of hachures. Also provided are a fewer number of special-topic, distribution, and resource maps. The methods of projection employed are not shown, and scale is shown only in a bar scale of miles (not kilometers). The usual natural fractional scale is not given, except for a few special maps, which makes comparison difficult. As the maps are basically political, heights are not given, and elevations are indicated only by indeterminate hachures. Neither locator nor comparative area maps are provided, and the only legend of symbols is to differentiate between county seats and state capitals. Railways and rivers are shown, but not roads. Some maps are drawn with the north to the top of the page, the usual method, but on others north is to the left or side of the page. The maps, overall, are dull, unimaginative, poorly printed, and lacking in detail.

SCALE

Except for some of the specially prepared thematic maps, which give the natural scale, its equivalent in miles per inch, and a scale bar in miles and kilometers, the only map measurements are by a scale bar in miles. Obviously, however, the scales at which the maps are drawn do vary quite widely. The 50 states of the United States, for example, each occupy one full page in most cases, while some others spill over into two pages, and yet others are mapped two states to a page. Much the same criticism applies to Canada, but important European countries such as France, Spain, and Portugal are allocated only one half of a page. Yet a further example of the variation in scale is the provision of only one page for the whole of China, the same space allocated to the relatively small state of New Jersey.

BALANCE

Heavily weighted towards (a) the United States, (b) Canada, and (c) the western hemisphere generally. Of the 126 pages of maps, no less than 61 deal exclusively with the United States. Canada with eight pages, Central America with two pages, and South America with six pages, make a total of 77 pages for the Americas alone. For Europe there are only 11 pages, for Asia eight, and for Africa four. Surprisingly, Australasia is allocated nine pages. Overall, the atlas is seriously imbalanced in its coverage.

INDEXING

The publishers claim a comprehensive indexing system of some 140,000 entries, but these, unfortunately, are spread throughout the atlas in a multiplicity of indexes, and their value is thus negated. The only general index is the 14-page section at the end of the atlas which lists and locates some 17,000 cities outside the western hemisphere, and locates these by the grid letter-number method. The United States is quite comprehensively indexed, with an alphabetical list of places for each state, and these are accompanied by the 1970 census population figures and gazetteer-type information. Similar indexes are provided for the provinces of Canada, but without population figures. Additional indexes are provided for Mexico and for each of the South American countries. The atlas would be greatly improved if all these separate indexes were consolidated.

SCOPE, CONTENTS, AND ARRANGEMENT

Divided into five main sections: (1) prefatory material and world information tables; (2) United States Information Tables; (3) atlas section: 182 pages of maps and text, including special purpose maps; (4) reference section: 115 pages of geographic and other information, some of which is non-atlas material; (5) index to cities outside the western hemisphere.

Pages i–xii include: prefatory material and world information tables, including a master gazetteer of the world by major political divisions; an alphabetical list of world cities with over 100,000 population; airline distances; a list of cities of more than one million population; a table of outlying possessions, territories, and associated states of Britain, France, The Netherlands, Portugal, Spain, the U.S.S.R., and the United States; world geographic comparisons; a list of the members of the United Nations; and similar information.

Pages xii–xxiv and pages 1–16 contain: United States information tables containing the 1970 census figures; a table of the 50 largest U.S. cities since 1850; figures on population of the individual states from earliest times; geographic and climatic data for states and major cities in the United States; lists of principal U.S. rivers, mountains, and other physical features; tables of Army posts, Air Force bases, and major Navy installations; airline distances between cities in the United States; and a list of recreational areas in the United States, with maps of the National Park System.

Pages 17–196 make up the main map section, comprised of : (1) political maps for each of the 50 states, in alphabetical order, and accompanied by tables of counties and classified indexes of some 100,000 cities, towns, and villages; (2) physical maps for each of the individual countries of the world; (3) political maps for each of the individual countries, each with its own index of cities; (4) a collection of historical, pictorial, and other special-purpose maps, and maps of the North and South Polar regions.

Pages 197–311 comprise the reference section and contain a wide variety of lists, tables, text, and photographs providing information about all the various states and countries of the world, including vital data on climate, vegetation, surface, soils, drainage, population, sources of income, agriculture and exploitation activities, industry, commerce, and transportation. Pages 308–311 include a discussion on the solar system, a description of the atom bomb, and a list of U.S. colleges and universities.

Pages 312–325 contain the index to cities outside the western hemisphere, with about 17,000 entries. Page 326 is a black and white world map of the voyages of famous explorers.

SUMMARY

More than half of the *School and Library Atlas of the World* is comprised of a mass of statistical and text material, much of which, although unusual, interesting, and useful, is not within the function of a geographic reference tool. In itself, the reference section is good and would, outside this context, be quite useful. As an atlas per se, however, this is a poor work, with nearly all the maps below modern standards of acceptability, varying in both quality and format. A few, especially the special world maps, are in quite pleasing, well-printed, pastel shades, but the majority are gaudy and harsh. The maps in the main series are dull, unattractive, poorly detailed, and too often badly printed. None of them show scale other than on a simple bar scale of miles per inch, and none show the methods of projection used. Because of this, comparison of areas is difficult, and the scale varies widely from large for some of the states of the United States to very small for some important countries of Europe, Asia, and Africa. The total number of index entries claimed by the publisher (140,000) is high, but as these are broken up into an inconvenient multiplicity of separate and inconsistent indexes throughout the atlas, their value is diminished. The use of good but heavy calendered paper, the awkward format, and considerable weight, are other less desirable features. The poor quality of the maps, the overemphasis on coverage of the western hemisphere, the inconvenient arrangement of the contents, and the inadequate indexing, do not commend this atlas for purchase in school, library, office, or home, especially in view of the ready availability of more comprehensive, cartographically superior, more attractive, and less expensive general atlases. Large special and university libraries may perhaps consider it because of the useful statistical and other data.

CRITICAL REVIEWS AND INFORMATIVE ARTICLES

Subscription Books Bulletin, April 1955. The article is dated, but still pertinent.

OTHER SOURCES OF INFORMATION

Shores. *Instructional Materials.* 1960.

Part III: STATISTICAL TABLES

MERIT RATING CHART

Listed below are the 38 largest general-purpose world atlases which retail at $7.50 or more in their regular trade editions (but with one or two special exceptions) which comply in varying degrees with the criteria for reference atlases established by professional librarians, cartographers, and educators. With some exceptions, chiefly those atlases with low and zero ratings, the titles below are currently approved by the Reference and Subscription Books Committee of the American Library Association, are listed as desirable purchases in the various H. W. Wilson library catalogs, and appear on the approved lists issued by several state and local education authorities. Each atlas has been allocated a numbered merit rating based on (a) its frequency of inclusion in standard reference book selection guides and bibliographies, (b) where too new to be included in such standard guides, the degree of its compliance with professionally acceptable evaluative criteria, and (c) its cost in relation to other similar and equally rated works. Where two or more atlases are equally rated, they are listed in the order of cost ruling at the time of going to press. Where such basic criteria are not yet available for recently published atlases, or for atlases which have been extensively revised in recent years, the compiler has applied an interim rating based on the standard professional evaluative procedures formulated by one or more of the above-cited authorities.

The maximum quality rating is 25, irrespective of price. The 38 atlases listed below have been divided into four groups. The atlases considered to be of superior quality are listed in GROUP ONE. Atlases considered to be above average in quality but not superior works are listed in GROUP TWO. Works which were judged to be fair in quality, content, and price are listed in GROUP THREE. Titles listed in GROUP FOUR were considered to be of an inferior nature either in quality or because they were exorbitant in cost in relation to quality. Atlases in this group are not recommended for purchase.

Several of the titles listed are also available in more expensive bindings. Such additional expense is rarely justifiable and, if taken into account as a rating factor, would tend to reduce the merit rating of such titles. Conversely, some atlases are available at a discount when purchased in combination with other works such as encyclopedias which, if taken into account, could favorably influence the ratings.

A number of atlases, especially those in the lower price ranges, adopt the practice of arranging their indexes in a broken or nonalphabetical order, usually by indexing the countries, states, or provinces separately, adjacent to the respective maps. Some of these atlases consolidate these separate indexes into one general comprehensive index, but others do not. Thus, the notation "no index" found in the tables indicates lack of an overall, consolidated index. One or two atlases also supplement their main index by providing an additional updating supplement or a separate index for a specific region.

MERIT RATING	TITLE AND COMMENT	REGULAR RETAIL PRICE ($)	SUGGESTED AGE SUITABILITY	NUMBER OF PAGES	SINGLE PAGE SIZE (in.)	INDEX ENTRIES
GROUP ONE: TOP QUALITY ATLASES						
25	THE TIMES ATLAS OF THE WORLD (p. 33) The world's best atlas. Superb maps with wealth of detail. Massive index. New edition 1972.	65.00	15–Advanced	556	18 × 11½	200,000
23	BRITANNICA ATLAS, also COMPTON ATLAS (p. 42) Excellent. Same as *International* except for 40 pages of thematic maps. Well detailed.	35.00	15–Advanced	575	14¾ × 11	160,000
23	THE INTERNATIONAL ATLAS (p. 38) Best atlas ever produced in U.S. International cooperation. Thorough index. Well balanced.	35.00	15–Advanced	558	14¾ × 11	160,000
21	NEW YORK TIMES WORLD ATLAS, also TIMES CONCISE ATLAS OF THE WORLD (p. 45) Superb maps based on *Times Atlas*. Brand new 1972. Wealth of detail. Great value.	25–30.00	12–College	272	14¾ × 10¾	95,000
GROUP TWO: ATLASES RATED ABOVE AVERAGE IN QUALITY						
19	NATIONAL GEOGRAPHIC ATLAS OF THE WORLD (p. 49) Wealth of detail. Comprehensive coverage, but political maps only. Wide variation in scales.	24.50	15–Advanced	331	19 × 12½	139,000
18	PERGAMON WORLD ATLAS (p. 54) Polish origin. Excellent maps, fine index, but becoming dated in vital areas.	49.50	15–Advanced	524	16 × 12	140,000
17	McGRAW-HILL INTERNATIONAL ATLAS (p. 58) German origin. Superb maps, fine index, but last published 1964. Badly dated in parts.	59.50	15–Advanced	544	16 × 12	150,000 plus 25,000
16	UNIVERSAL REFERENCE ATLAS (p. 62) (Provisional rating)	17.50 (est.)	12–College	300	13½ × 9½	90,000 (est.)

To be published in 1973. Well-detailed maps. Good index. Based on *Pergamon World Atlas.*

MERIT RATING	TITLE AND COMMENT	REGULAR RETAIL PRICE ($)	SUGGESTED AGE SUITABILITY	NUMBER OF PAGES	SINGLE PAGE SIZE (in.)	INDEX ENTRIES
15	THE OXFORD ATLAS, also CANADIAN OXFORD ATLAS (p. 64) Excellent well-detailed maps. Adequate index. Could have been more comprehensive.	16.50	15–Advanced	214	15½ × 10½	50,000
15	ATLAS OF THE EARTH, also CAXTON ATLAS OF THE EARTH (p. 68) Good well-detailed maps. Adequate index. Allied to 144-page encyclopedia of the environment.	35.00	12–Family	446	14½ × 10½	65,000
14	ALDINE UNIVERSITY ATLAS (p. 72) Small inexpensive atlas for school and college use. Fine maps. Good index. Great value.	8.50	10–18	318	11½ × 9½	50,000
13	GOODE'S WORLD ATLAS (p. 75) Basic school and college atlas on all approved lists. Beautiful maps. Index rather short.	10.95	10–18	327	11½ × 9¼	35,000
12	UNIVERSITY ATLAS (PHILIP'S) (p. 78) Identical to *Library Atlas* except for omission of 32 pages thematic maps. British.	7.50	10–18	312	11½ × 9½	50,000
12	LIBRARY ATLAS (PHILIP'S) (p. 78) Good medium-sized British atlas. Good thematic maps. Adequate index. Similar to *Aldine.*	8.50	10–18	344	11½ × 9½	50,000
12	PANORAMIC WORLD ATLAS (HAMMOND) (p. 82) Useful and attractive atlas with three-dimensional relief maps. Limited index.	8.95	12–College	205	12½ × 9½	25,000

		Price	Age	Pages	Size	Index
11	WORLD BOOK ATLAS (p. 84) — Fine series of thematic maps and explanations of atlas skills, but maps lack detail.	31.20	10–18	424	14 × 11¼	82,000
10	COSMOPOLITAN WORLD ATLAS (p. 89) — Popular U.S. atlas. Emphasizes United States. Good index but maps somewhat lacking in detail.	19.95	12–College	428	14 × 11¼	82,000
9	AMBASSADOR WORLD ATLAS (p. 93) — Fine index but maps small and lack detail. Confusing mixture of scales. Emphasizes United States.	14.95	12–College	496	12½ × 9½	110,000

GROUP THREE: ATLASES RATED AVERAGE QUALITY

		Price	Age	Pages	Size	Index
8	ODYSSEY WORLD ATLAS (p. 99) — Good series of maps and fine index, but dated in vital areas. Being phased out of existence.	9.95	12–College	318	13¼ × 10	105,000
8	PHYSICAL WORLD ATLAS, also EDINBURGH WORLD ATLAS and ADVANCED ATLAS OF MODERN GEOGRAPHY (p. 102) — Good intermediate atlas from makers of *Times* atlases. Limited index. Sold under various titles.	14.95	12–College	165	15 × 10	24,000+
7	CONCISE OXFORD ATLAS (p. 106) — Small format, reduced 20% from *Oxford Atlas*. Good maps. Adequate index. British emphasis.	8.00	12–College	288	10 × 7½	40,000
7	READER'S DIGEST GREAT WORLD ATLAS (p. 109) — Encyclopedic atlas. Much text and illus. Some good maps, but inconveniently indexed.	17.00	12–Family	232	15½ × 10¾	80,000 (broken)
6	MEDALLION WORLD ATLAS (p. 93) — Well arranged. Fine index. Maps small, lack detail. Emphasis on United States (See *Ambassador.*)	24.95	12–College	672	12½ × 9½	110,000

MERIT RATING	TITLE AND COMMENT	REGULAR RETAIL PRICE ($)	SUGGESTED AGE SUITABILITY	NUMBER OF PAGES	SINGLE PAGE SIZE (in.)	INDEX ENTRIES
6	THE WORLD ATLAS (p. 112) Superb maps but confusing use of place names. Some wrong locations. Index published separately. Expensive.	76.50 ($85.00)	15–Advanced	250	19 × 13	Separate
5	PREMIER WORLD ATLAS (p. 114) Identical to *Cosmopolitan World Atlas* except for omission of 107 pages text, city plans.	14.95	12–Family	336	14 × 11¼	82,000
4	WORLDMASTER ATLAS (p. 118) Identical to first 247 pages of *Family Edition World Atlas* (below). Maps lack detail.	6.95	12–Family	247	12½ × 10	30,000
4	FAMILY EDITION WORLD ATLAS (RAND McNALLY) (p. 118) Reduced version of the *Cosmopolitan* and *Premier* atlases, but shorter index.	9.95	12–Family	328	12½ × 10	30,000
4	CITATION WORLD ATLAS (p. 122) Identical to *Ambassador World Atlas* except for much shorter index. Same shortcomings.	10.95	12–College	360	12½ × 9½	25,000
3	CRAM MODERN WORLD ATLAS (p. 125) Identical to *Citation World Atlas* but with 48 pages additional material. Same faults.	12.50	12–College	408	12½ × 9½	25,000
3	HALLMARK WORLD ATLAS (p. 93) Overly expensive 2-volume deluxe edition of *Medallion World Atlas*. Padded cushion covers.	39.95	12–College	672	12½ × 9½	110,000

GROUP FOUR: ATLASES RATED BELOW ACCEPTABLE STANDARDS; NOT RECOMMENDED

I	THE FABER ATLAS (p. 128)	8.50	12–College	204	12¼ × 8¾	20,000
	Fair quality maps but limited index. British made. Emphasis on Europe.					
1	HAMMOND CONTEMPORARY WORLD ATLAS (p. 130)	12.50	12–Family	288	11 × 8	no index
	Published by Doubleday but made by Hammond. Emphasizes United States. Maps lack detail. No general index.					
0	ADVANCED REFERENCE ATLAS (p. 133)	7.50	12–Family	180	12½ × 9½	no index
	Comprised of four separate works: Bible, History, etc. Poor maps. No general index.					
0	INTERNATIONAL WORLD ATLAS (HAMMOND) (p. 122)	6.95	12–Family	200	12½ × 9½	no index
	Identical to first 200 pages of *Citation World Atlas*, omitting maps of United States. No general index.					
0	ILLUSTRATED ENCYCLOPEDIA LIBRARY WORLD ATLAS also HAMMOND ILLUSTRATED FAMILY WORLD ATLAS (p. 135)	11.72	12–Family	376 2 v.	12¼ × 9¼	42,000 (broken)
	Subscription item in 2 volumes. Poorly detailed maps. Inconveniently indexed.					
0	STANDARD WORLD ATLAS (p. 138)	12.50	12–Family	332	12½ × 9½	no index
	Identical to first 332 pages of *Citation World Atlas*. Maps lack detail. No general index.					
0	HAMMOND WORLD ATLAS—CLASSICS EDITION (p. 140)	25.00	12–Family	396	12½ × 9½	25,000
	Practically identical to *Citation World Atlas* but more than twice the cost. Overpriced.					
0	SCHOOL AND LIBRARY ATLAS OF THE WORLD (p. 141)	39.50	15–Special	350	22 × 16	140,000 (broken)
	Wealth of statistical data but very poor maps. Awkwardly arranged. No general index.					

SUGGESTED AGE SUITABILITY CHART

An explanation of the categories into which this chart has been divided has already been given in the section on "Choosing and Using an Atlas." A further word of caution is advisable. Because of the variations in ability among children at each age level, and the overlapping of age groups, the figures given should be regarded as approximations only, indicating the most likely ages at which maximum usefulness is achieved. Most publishers will claim a wider age range than here suggested, but such claims are usually rather ambitious and perhaps wishful thinking, and their validity

should be carefully considered. Atlases vary widely in treatment and some of the advanced reference atlases can, in parts at least, be used by students in the upper elementary grades. Conversely, even those smaller atlases which are designed for students at a lower beginning level will contain geographic material of both interest and advantage to much older users.

Titles marked with an asterisk (*) are the best buys in their respective groups.

SUGGESTED BEGINNING AGE	SUGGESTED MAXIMUM USEFULNESS	TITLE	MERIT RATING
ELEMENTARY, SECONDARY, AND HIGH SCHOOL ATLASES			
10	18	ALDINE UNIVERSITY ATLAS*	14
10	18	GOODE'S WORLD ATLAS	13
10	18	LIBRARY ATLAS	12
10	18	UNIVERSITY ATLAS	12
10	18	WORLD BOOK ATLAS	11
INTERMEDIATE SCHOOL AND COLLEGE ATLASES			
12	College	AMBASSADOR WORLD ATLAS	9
12	College	CITATION WORLD ATLAS	4
12	College	CONCISE OXFORD ATLAS	7
12	College	COSMOPOLITAN WORLD ATLAS	10
12	College	CRAM MODERN WORLD ATLAS	3
12	College	PHYSICAL WORLD ATLAS (also known as the EDINBURGH WORLD ATLAS and ADVANCED ATLAS OF MODERN GEOGRAPHY)	8
12	College	THE FABER ATLAS	1

12	College	NEW YORK TIMES WORLD ATLAS* (also known as THE TIMES CONCISE ATLAS OF THE WORLD)	21
12	College	ODYSSEY WORLD ATLAS	8
12	College	PANORAMIC WORLD ATLAS	12
12	College	UNIVERSAL REFERENCE ATLAS (to be published 1973)	16 (prov.)

GENERAL PURPOSE HOME, ENCYCLOPEDIC, AND DESK ATLASES

12	Family use	ATLAS OF THE EARTH* (CAXTON ATLAS OF THE EARTH)	15
12	Family use	ADVANCED REFERENCE ATLAS	0
12	Family use	FAMILY EDITION WORLD ATLAS	4
12	Family use	HALLMARK WORLD ATLAS	3
12	Family use	HAMMOND CONTEMPORARY WORLD ATLAS	1
12	Family use	HAMMOND WORLD ATLAS–CLASSICS EDITION	0
12	Family use	ILLUSTRATED ENCYCLOPEDIA LIBRARY WORLD ATLAS (also known as HAMMOND ILLUSTRATED FAMILY WORLD ATLAS)	0
12	Family use	INTERNATIONAL WORLD ATLAS (Hammond)	0
12	Family use	MEDALLION WORLD ATLAS	6
12	Family use	PREMIER WORLD ATLAS	5
12	Family use	READER'S DIGEST GREAT WORLD ATLAS	7
12	Family use	STANDARD WORLD ATLAS	0
12	Family use	WORLDMASTER ATLAS	4

ADVANCED REFERENCE AND SPECIALIZED ATLASES

15	University/Advanced	BRITANNICA ATLAS (also known as COMPTON ATLAS)	23
15	University/Advanced	THE INTERNATIONAL ATLAS	23
15	University/Advanced	McGRAW-HILL INTERNATIONAL ATLAS	17
15	University/Advanced	NATIONAL GEOGRAPHIC ATLAS OF THE WORLD	19
15	University/Advanced	OXFORD ATLAS (also known as CANADIAN OXFORD ATLAS)	15
15	University/Advanced	PERGAMON WORLD ATLAS	18
15	Specialized use	SCHOOL AND LIBRARY ATLAS OF THE WORLD	0
15	University/Advanced	THE WORLD ATLAS	6
15	University/Advanced	THE TIMES ATLAS OF THE WORLD*	25

ATLASES IN ORDER OF COST

The prices quoted are the lowest at which atlases can be purchased for general home or office use in a regular hardcover edition. In some instances atlases are sold in a range of deluxe bindings at increasingly higher costs. These may improve the outward appearance but add nothing to the quality of the atlas per se. Details of such alternative bindings will be found in the individual analyses for each title. Note that state and local taxes, where applicable, should be added to the costs shown and also, where applicable, the cost of postage and packing.

TITLE	MERIT RATING	REGULAR RETAIL PRICE ($)	NUMBER OF PAGES	SINGLE PAGE SIZE (in.)	INDEX ENTRIES	MAP PAGES
OVER $30.00						
THE WORLD ATLAS	6	76.50	250	19 × 13	no index	250
THE TIMES ATLAS OF THE WORLD	25	65.00	556	18 × 11½	200,000	244
McGRAW-HILL INTERNATIONAL ATLAS	17	59.50	544	16 × 12	150,000 +	252
PERGAMON WORLD ATLAS	18	49.50	524	16 × 12	140,000	380[a]
HALLMARK WORLD ATLAS	3	39.95	672	12½ × 9½	110,000	320[a]
SCHOOL AND LIBRARY ATLAS OF THE WORLD	0	39.50	350	22 × 16	140,000[b]	126
ATLAS OF THE EARTH (CAXTON ATLAS OF THE EARTH)	15	35.00 (est.)	446	14½ × 10½	65,000	176
BRITANNICA ATLAS (COMPTON ATLAS)	23	35.00	575	14¾ × 11	160,000	280
THE INTERNATIONAL ATLAS	23	35.00	558	14¾ × 11	160,000	261
WORLD BOOK ATLAS	11	31.20	424	14 × 11¼	82,000	167
FROM $15.00 to $30.00						
NEW YORK TIMES WORLD ATLAS (TIMES CONCISE ATLAS)	21	25.00–30.00 (est.)	272	14¾ × 10¾	95,000	144
HAMMOND WORLD ATLAS: CLASSICS EDITION	0	25.00	396	12½ × 9½	25,000	320[a]
MEDALLION WORLD ATLAS	6	24.95	672	12½ × 9½	110,000	320[a]
NATIONAL GEOGRAPHIC ATLAS OF THE WORLD	19	24.50	331	19 × 12½	139,000	140
COSMOPOLITAN WORLD ATLAS	10	19.95	428	14 × 11¼	82,000	172
UNIVERSAL REFERENCE ATLAS (to be published 1973)	16 (prov.)	17.50 (est.)	300	13½ × 9½	90,000 (est.)	176

READER'S DIGEST GREAT WORLD ATLAS	7	17.00	232	15½ × 10¾	80,000[b]	90
OXFORD ATLAS (CANADIAN OXFORD ATLAS)	15	16.50	214	15½ × 10½	50,000	134
FROM $10.00 to $15.00						
AMBASSADOR WORLD ATLAS	9	14.95	496	12½ × 9½	110,000	320[a]
PHYSICAL WORLD ATLAS (EDINBURGH WORLD ATLAS, (ADVANCED ATLAS OF MODERN GEOGRAPHY)	8	14.95	165	15 × 10	26,000	106
PREMIER WORLD ATLAS	5	14.95	336	14 × 11¼	82,000	150
CRAM MODERN WORLD ATLAS	3	12.50	408	12½ × 9½	25,000	358[a]
HAMMOND CONTEMPORARY WORLD ATLAS	1	12.50	288	11 × 8	no index	250[a]
STANDARD WORLD ATLAS	0	12.50	332	12½ × 9½	no index	320[a]
ILLUSTRATED ENCYCLOPEDIA LIBRARY WORLD ATLAS (HAMMOND ILLUSTRATED FAMILY WORLD ATLAS)	0	11.72	376 (2 v.)	12¼ × 9¼	42,000[b]	207
CITATION WORLD ATLAS	4	10.95	360	12½ × 9½	25,000	320[a]
GOODE'S WORLD ATLAS	13	10.95	327	11¼ × 9½	35,000	184
LESS THAN $10.00						
FAMILY EDITION WORLD ATLAS	4	9.95	328	12½ × 10	30,000	103
ODYSSEY WORLD ATLAS	8	9.95	318	13¼ × 10	105,000	169
PANORAMIC WORLD ATLAS	12	8.95	205	12½ × 9½	25,000	147
ALDINE UNIVERSITY ATLAS	14	8.50	318	11½ × 9½	50,000	192
THE FABER ATLAS	1	8.50	204	12¼ × 8¾	20,000	152
LIBRARY ATLAS	12	8.50	344	11½ × 9½	50,000	208
CONCISE OXFORD ATLAS	7	8.00	288	10 × 7½	40,000	120
ADVANCED REFERENCE ATLAS	0	7.50	180	12½ × 9½	no index	160[a]
UNIVERSITY ATLAS	12	7.50	312	11½ × 9½	50,000	208
INTERNATIONAL WORLD ATLAS (Hammond)	0	6.95	200	12½ × 9½	no index	160[a]
WORLDMASTER ATLAS	4	6.95	247	12½ × 10	30,000	103

[a] Map pages combined with text pages.
[b] Broken index arrangement, not in one complete sequence. Note also that the following atlases contain separate indexes for each country, state or province: *Hammond Contemporary World Atlas; Standard World Atlas; Advanced Reference Atlas; International World Atlas.* These do not have an overall general index. The following atlases provide, in addition to a general index, separate indexes for countries, states, and provinces: *Hallmark World Atlas; Hammond World Atlas: Classics Edition; Medallion World Atlas; Ambassador World Atlas; Cram Modern World Atlas; Citation World Atlas.*

ATLASES IN ORDER OF SIZE: SINGLE-PAGE SIZE

The sizes given in this table are for single-page sizes only, with no allowance made for margins. Many atlases, however, contain maps spread over two facing pages for an actual map size of approximately double the width measurement, and some also contain folding maps which open out to approximately three times the single-page width. In some instances the map pages also contain text material, indexes, etc., which reduces the actual map size.

TITLE	MERIT RATING	SINGLE PAGE SIZE (in.)	TOTAL PAGES	TOTAL MAP PAGES	INDEX ENTRIES
LARGE FORMAT ATLAS (18 in. or more in height)					
SCHOOL AND LIBRARY ATLAS OF THE WORLD	0	22 × 16	350	126	140,000[a]
THE WORLD ATLAS	6	19 × 13	250	250	no index
NATIONAL GEOGRAPHIC ATLAS OF THE WORLD	19	19 × 12½	331	140	139,000
THE TIMES ATLAS OF THE WORLD	25	18 × 11½	556	244[b]	200,000
INTERMEDIATE FORMAT ATLASES (13–16 in. in height)					
McGRAW-HILL INTERNATIONAL ATLAS	17	16 × 12	544	252	150,000 +
PERGAMON WORLD ATLAS	18	16 × 12	524	380[c]	140,000
READER'S DIGEST GREAT WORLD ATLAS	7	15½ × 10¾	232	90	80,000[a]
OXFORD ATLAS (CANADIAN OXFORD ATLAS)	15	15½ × 10½	214	134	50,000
PHYSICAL WORLD ATLAS (EDINBURGH WORLD ATLAS: ADVANCED ATLAS OF MODERN GEOGRAPHY)	8	15 × 10	165	106	24,000 +
BRITANNICA ATLAS (COMPTON ATLAS)	23	14¾ × 11	575	280	160,000
THE INTERNATIONAL ATLAS	23	14¾ × 11	558	261	160,000
NEW YORK TIMES ATLAS OF THE WORLD (TIMES CONCISE ATLAS OF THE WORLD)	21	14¾ × 10¾	272	144	95,000
ATLAS OF THE EARTH (CAXTON ATLAS OF THE EARTH)	15	14½ × 10½	446	176	65,000
COSMOPOLITAN WORLD ATLAS	10	14 × 11¼	428	172	82,000
PREMIER WORLD ATLAS	5	14 × 11¼	336	150	82,000
WORLD BOOK ATLAS	11	14 × 11¼	424	167	82,000

UNIVERSAL REFERENCE ATLAS (to be published 1973)	16 (prov.)	13½ × 9½	300	176	90,000 (est.)
ODYSSEY WORLD ATLAS	8	13¼ × 10	318	169	105,000

SMALLER INTERMEDIATE FORMAT ATLASES (12–12½ in. in height)

FAMILY EDITION WORLD ATLAS	4	12½ × 10	328	103	30,000
WORLDMASTER ATLAS	4	12½ × 10	247	103	30,000
ADVANCED REFERENCE ATLAS	0	12½ × 9½	180	160 (mixed)	no index
AMBASSADOR WORLD ATLAS	9	12½ × 9½	496	320[d]	110,000
CITATION WORLD ATLAS	4	12½ × 9½	360	320[d]	25,000
CRAM MODERN WORLD ATLAS	3	12½ × 9½	408	320[d]	25,000
HALLMARK WORLD ATLAS	3	12½ × 9½	672 (2 v.)	320[d]	110,000
HAMMOND WORLD ATLAS: CLASSICS EDITION	0	12½ × 9½	396	320[d]	25,000
INTERNATIONAL WORLD ATLAS (Hammond)	0	12½ × 9½	200	160[d]	no index
MEDALLION WORLD ATLAS	6	12½ × 9½	672	320[d]	110,000
PANORAMIC WORLD ATLAS	12	12½ × 9½	205	147	25,000
STANDARD WORLD ATLAS	0	12½ × 9½	332	320[d]	no index
ILLUSTRATED ENCYCLOPEDIA LIBRARY WORLD ATLAS (HAMMOND ILLUSTRATED FAMILY WORLD ATLAS)	0	12¼ × 9¼	376 (2 v.)	207	42,000[a]
THE FABER ATLAS	1	12¼ × 8¾	204	152	20,000

COMPACT FORMAT SCHOOL AND DESK ATLASES (less than 12 in. in height)

ALDINE UNIVERSITY ATLAS	14	11½ × 9½	318	192	50,000
LIBRARY ATLAS	12	11½ × 9½	344	208	50,000
UNIVERSITY ATLAS	12	11½ × 9½	312	208	50,000
GOODE'S WORLD ATLAS	13	11¼ × 9½	327	184	35,000
HAMMOND CONTEMPORARY WORLD ATLAS	1	11 × 8	288	250[d]	no index
CONCISE OXFORD ATLAS	7	10 × 7½	288	120	40,000

a Broken index arrangement, not in one sequence.
b All maps spread over two pages for actual map size of 18 × 22.
c Includes fold-out maps and text pages.
d Individual indexes included on map pages.

ATLASES IN ORDER OF SIZE: INDEX ENTRIES

TITLE	MERIT RATING	INDEX ENTRIES	INDEX PAGES
COMPREHENSIVE (more than 100,000 entries)			
THE TIMES ATLAS OF THE WORLD	25	200,000	272
McGRAW-HILL INTERNATIONAL ATLAS	17	175,000[a]	240
BRITANNICA ATLAS (COMPTON ATLAS)	23	160,000	223
THE INTERNATIONAL ATLAS	23	160,000	195
PERGAMON WORLD ATLAS	18	140,000	150
NATIONAL GEOGRAPHIC ATLAS OF THE WORLD	19	139,000	148
AMBASSADOR WORLD ATLAS	9	110,000[b]	142
HALLMARK WORLD ATLAS	3	110,000[b]	142
MEDALLION WORLD ATLAS	6	110,000[b]	142
ODYSSEY WORLD ATLAS	8	105,000	128
INTERMEDIATE COMPREHENSIVE (50,000–100,000 entries)			
NEW YORK TIMES WORLD ATLAS (TIMES CONCISE ATLAS OF THE WORLD)	21	95,000	88
UNIVERSAL REFERENCE ATLAS (to be published 1973)	16 (prov.)	90,000 (est.)	–
COSMOPOLITAN WORLD ATLAS	10	82,000	100
PREMIER WORLD ATLAS	5	82,000	100
WORLD BOOK ATLAS	11	82,000	110
ATLAS OF THE EARTH (CAXTON ATLAS OF THE EARTH)	15	65,000	110
ALDINE UNIVERSITY ATLAS	14	50,000	102
LIBRARY ATLAS	12	50,000	110
UNIVERSITY ATLAS	12	50,000	110
OXFORD ATLAS (CANADIAN OXFORD ATLAS)	15	50,000	90
ABRIDGED (25,000–50,000 entries)			
CONCISE OXFORD ATLAS	7	40,000	168
GOODE'S WORLD ATLAS	13	35,000	123
FAMILY EDITION WORLD ATLAS	4	30,000	96
WORLDMASTER ATLAS	4	30,000	96

PHYSICAL WORLD ATLAS (EDINBURGH WORLD ATLAS: ADVANCED ATLAS OF MODERN GEOGRAPHY)	8	26,000[c]	51
CITATION WORLD ATLAS	4	25,000[b]	24
CRAM MODERN WORLD ATLAS	3	25,000[b]	24
HAMMOND WORLD ATLAS: CLASSICS EDITION	0	25,000[b]	24
PANORAMIC WORLD ATLAS	12	25,000	44
SMALL (less than 25,000 entries)			
THE FABER ATLAS	1	20,000	44
ATLASES WITH BROKEN INDEX ARRANGEMENTS AND ESTIMATED TOTAL ENTRIES			
SCHOOL AND LIBRARY ATLAS OF THE WORLD	0	140,000	
STANDARD WORLD ATLAS	0	90,000	
HAMMOND CONTEMPORARY WORLD ATLAS	1	80,000	
READER'S DIGEST GREAT WORLD ATLAS	7	80,000	
ILLUSTRATED ENCYCLOPEDIA LIBRARY WORLD ATLAS (HAMMOND ILLUSTRATED FAMILY WORLD ATLAS)	0	42,000	
INTERNATIONAL WORLD ATLAS (Hammond)	0	42,000	
ADVANCED REFERENCE ATLAS	0	25,000	
THE WORLD ATLAS	6	separated[d]	

[a] This atlas contains a main index of 150,000 entries and a supplementary index of 25,000 entries.

[b] These atlases, in addition to a main general index, contain a multiplicity of separate indexes for countries, states, and provinces totalling approximately 90,000 entries.

[c] This atlas contains a main index of 24,000 entries and a supplementary index of 2,000 entries.

[d] At present the only index available to the contents of this atlas is published separately.

APPENDIX A

ATLASES RETAILING AT LESS THAN $7.50 OR £2.50

BARTHOLOMEW'S INTERMEDIATE SCHOOL ATLAS

Published by Oliver and Boyd, Edinburgh, but actually prepared and printed by John Bartholomew and Son Limited. A popular school atlas, it contains 48 pages of maps, most of them in full color. It has been in existence for many years, and in 1970 was published in a fifteenth edition, when it retailed at 43 pence. A brief index is provided. A good school atlas but too limited for general reference use.

BARTHOLOMEW'S MINI ATLAS

Sometimes known as the *Bartholomew Pocket Mini Atlas*. A very small prayer-book-sized atlas, measuring only 5¾ by 4 in. The latest edition is dated 1971. Priced at 50 pence (about $1.30), it is comprised of 128 pages of colored maps, including five world thematic maps. Although the maps are very small, the world is mapped in quite good detail. Forty-four pages are allocated to the United States, eight to Canada, and eight to the British Isles. Apart from the one relief map of the world, all the maps are political. A bar scale is provided for each map, but not the representative fraction. Projections employed are not identified. Because of the very small scale at which the maps are drawn, detail is limited, but all show major rivers, and the larger-scale maps show railroads also. There is no index, but a brief 32-page gazetteer lists all major countries, states, provinces, cities, and physical features. Containing 164 pages in all, it is well printed and up-to-date, and is a useful little work for quick identification or casual use.

BARTHOLOMEW'S NEW COMPARATIVE ATLAS

Similar to but larger than *Bartholomew's Intermediate School Atlas*, this is also published under the imprint of Oliver and Boyd, although prepared and printed by John Bartholomew and Son Limited. The last recorded edition was in 1964, when it retailed at 60 pence. It is comprised of 120 pages and contains 83 maps, 80 of which are colored.

BLOND WORLD ATLAS

A Canadian work, published in Toronto by Holt, Rinehart, and Winston of Canada Limited, and in England by Blond Educational, Leicester. It was first published in 1969 as the *Holt World Atlas*. It retails in Britain at £2.00 (about $5.00). Measuring 13 by 10 in., it contains 160 pages, divided into nine pages of world maps, 69 pages for the continents, 36 for Canada (an exceptionally high proportion), and 16 for the United States, supplemented by eight pages of resource maps and eight pages of statistics. It is a somewhat unusual atlas, specifically designed, according to the publishers, for use in secondary and high schools. The maps are all in vivid, sometimes garish, colors. A considerable number of these are thematic maps showing economic development, population density, precipitation, ethnology, temperature, land use, geology, vegetation, soil, growth periods, etc. For such special uses it has merit, but as a general world atlas, offering only physical maps on a very small scale and showing little detail, it will have little appeal. There is a considerable emphasis on Canada, which lessens its usefulness elsewhere.

COLLINS CHILDREN'S ATLAS

A small and simple atlas for children published by Wm. Collins, London. The last-known recorded edition is 1967, when it retailed at 52½ pence. It contains 54 colored plates of maps.

COLLINS CLEAR SCHOOL ATLAS

Published in 1971 by Wm. Collins, London. A small but useful work, it retails at 20 pence, for which it provides, in board covers, 16 pages of statistics and index, and 48 pages of four-color maps dealing with physical, political, climatic, and economic features, and also with vegetation and population. Comprised of 64 pages in all, it measures 8¾ by 7 in.

COLLINS GRAPHIC ATLAS

One of the larger atlases published by Wm. Collins, London, but still small by most standards, the 1972 edition contains 136 pages and measures 10¾ by 8½ in., retailing at 90 pence. Sixty-four of the pages contain colored, up-to-date maps. There are eight pages of half-tone illustrations, and a further 64 pages of additional maps, statistics, and an index. It is cased in a three-color varnished jacket.

COLLINS-LONGMAN ATLAS ADVANCED

One of the best atlases available at this price (£2.50), it was first published in 1968. Eminent cartographers throughout the world have here attempted to combine international scholarship with the most modern cartographic techniques, and the result is a geographic reference work of considerable merit, which will be useful to teachers and students as well as in the home and office. The large-scale general maps are basically physical and combine hill shading with layer tints and contours to show the configuration of the land with exceptional clarity. Settlements are selected according to local importance, and insets of urban areas at a scale of 1:1,000,000 are frequently included. There is an exceptionally good range of thematic maps covering a wide range of topics, and the 72 pages of text matter include a quite full index of about 30,000 entries. It is a better atlas than several costing much more. Recommended.

COLLINS-LONGMAN ATLAS ONE

This is an entirely new atlas for the youngest children, published jointly by Wm. Collins and Longmans, London. Measuring 10½ by 8¼ in., it retails at only 30 pence, and is the first in a series of such atlases (see below). First published in 1968, it will be useful for the introduction of elementary grade children to the use of atlases. Of the 28 pages of maps, eight are allocated to the British Isles, four for the rest of Europe, but only two pages each for Africa, Asia, Australasia, North America, and South America. Each map of the continents has a facing page of informative full-color photos. Additional useful material includes a map of the Holy Land, very simple explanations of scale and mapwork, and a short descriptive index. Recommended.

COLLINS-LONGMAN ATLAS TWO

A more advanced version of the *Collins-Longman Atlas One*, this edition is retailed at 40 pence. The second edition, published in 1966, contains 64 pages, 57 of which are in full color. It is described as a multipurpose atlas, containing basic historical and scripture maps as well as a full geographic coverage, combining simplicity with comprehensiveness. The contents are colorful, meaningful, and visually exciting. There is an emphasis on the British Isles, with the maps and accompanying text and illustrations developing outwards from Britain to western Europe and then to the continents of the world. It measures 10½ by 8¼ in.

COLLINS-LONGMAN ATLAS FOUR

The most advanced in the series (*Atlas Three* is not yet available), and in the same format of 10½ by 8¼ in., this larger work was designed for 'O' level and fifth form pupils (ages 15–18). The 1969 edition is arranged continent by continent but, as with the more elementary editions, emphasizes coverage of the British Isles, which are allocated 21 pages. Each section contains large-scale maps, political maps, maps of land cover, relief and structure, climate, and economic topics. There are 112 pages of maps and 48 pages of text, including a quite full index. It is very reasonably priced at 82 pence.

COLLINS-LONGMAN STUDY ATLAS

Comprised of 152 pages, and measuring 11¼ by 8⅝ in., this small atlas retails in two editions, the regular trade edition (with color jacket) at £1.00 and another edition, bound in black Brymor, and without a color jacket, at 70 pence. Now in its seventeenth (1970) edition, it contains 64 pages of six-color maps, 26 color photographs, and a considerable amount of preliminary matter and statistics, concluded with a 16-page index of some 6,000 entries. It was planned, compiled, drawn, and produced under the direction of a Joint Advisory Board.

COLLINS-LONGMAN VISIBLE REGIONS ATLAS

Similar to but smaller than the *Collins-Longman Study Atlas* (see above), this smaller edition is comprised of 96 pages, in the same format of 11¼ by

8⅝ in. The 1970 edition has the same 64 pages of six-color maps and 26 color photographs, but a reduced amount of supplementary data and a shortened index. It costs 50 pence in board covers, and 45 pence in limp covers.

COLLINS POCKET ATLAS

A small, topical world atlas whose 1972 edition contains 96 pages of four-color physical and political maps, and 16 pages of two-color social and economic maps, special Press Headline maps. Making up the total of 160 pages is data about the various countries of the world and a fairly full index. In limp covers it retails at 35 pence, and at 40 pence in a cased edition. It appears to be identical to the *Fontana Pocket Atlas of the World.*

COLLINS WORLD ATLAS

New in 1970, this one of the more important of the Collins range of atlases. Containing 160 pages, it measures 10½ by 8¼ in., and retails at £1.50 in a hardcover edition with full-color laminated wrappers. It is attractive to look at and contains several new ideas in cartographic presentation. A small but useful reference atlas of the world, at a modest cost it provides medium-scale maps of the world, supplemented by other maps giving details of political divisions, land cover, relief and structure, climate and economic tables, and an index. It bears a marked resemblance to the *Collins-Longman Atlas Four* (q.v.).

COLLINS WORLD WIDE ATLAS

Although measuring 10½ by 8¼ in., this is a very small atlas of only 48 pages, retailing at 25 pence. It contains 40 pages of maps in full color and a brief index. It is derived from the larger Collins atlases described previously.

CRAM'S STUDENT QUICK REFERENCE ATLAS OF THE WORLD

First published by the Geo. F. Cram Company in 1950, this is now in a 1972 edition. Measuring 12½ by 9½ in., with limp paper covers, it contains 27 rather gaudily colored political maps of the major areas of the world. Scale generally is small and is shown on the maps only as a bar distance scale in miles. Rivers are shown, but not highways or railroads. Relief is absent in most cases, but where elevations are shown, it is by means of hachures. There is no indication of the methods of projection employed. A three-page index lists some 1,500 major places and gives the degrees of latitude and longitude for these. The inside covers are used to provide a brief index to the contents, the dimensions of the earth, and some world facts.

DAILY TELEGRAPH WORLD ATLAS

Published under the imprint of the London *Daily Telegraph* in 1968, but actually produced by Wm. Collins and Sons. Edited by D. L. Barker, with a space supplement by A. R. Michaelis. Measuring 10½ by 7½ in., it contains 144 pages, of which 80 are comprised of six color physical maps, 16 pages of a two-color supplement of exploration of space, a fairly full index of 20,000 entries, and a good amount of world statistics. The maps are good and combine clarity with maximum coverage of the world. The space supplement is interesting, and illustrates the most exciting achievements up to 1968. The usual trade edition is in soft covers at £1.05, but a hard-cased library edition is also available at £1.50.

DENOYER'S STUDENT ATLAS

First published by the Denoyer-Geppert Company, Chicago, in 1949, its latest edition is dated 1971. Designed primarily for school use, it retails at $1.50. Measuring 12½ by 9½ in., it is comprised of 88 pages, of which 48 contain political-physical maps, and a variety of special thematic maps. It is mapped by regions and is quite well balanced, but the map coloring is on the dark side and the quality of the printing is low. A ten-page index lists some 4,500 places, with degrees of latitude and longitude.

DIMENSION 3 ATLAS

First published in 1969 by Johnston and Bacon, London. Retailing at 80 pence, it is comprised of 72 pages in hard covers. Designed for school use, it is intended to cover the first four years of a secondary course. A feature is the three-dimensional effect achieved in the portrayal of land relief. Each country or continental map is presented in three forms: physical, political, and economic. Thematic maps, an exploration map, and diagrams of the solar system are also included, plus three pages of world statistics and a simple index. Place names on the maps have been kept to a minimum.

FIRST BOOK ATLAS

Published by Franklin Watts (a division of Grolier Inc.) but actually made by Hammond Inc. First published in 1960 and recopyrighted in 1968, it retails at $3.75. Designed specifically for children in the elementary grades, it measures 8½ by 7¼ in. and is comprised of 96 pages, 60 of which contain Hammond political maps of the world, showing the political boundaries, capitals, major cities, important rivers, seas, and other major physical features, but detail is otherwise limited. One third of the contents is devoted to the United States, supplemented by plans of the leading cities and national parks. A quite useful, simplified atlas at a reasonable cost, it is listed in the twelfth edition (1971) of the *Children's Catalog*. Recommended.

FIRST SCHOOL ATLAS

A small British atlas, published by Johnston and Bacon, London in 1970. Similar in some ways to the *Dimension 3 Atlas*, it succeeds *My First Atlas*, which is reputed to have sold more than one million copies. Designed for the elementary grades, it develops the pupil's knowledge of reading maps by leading him through a series of carefully graded maps and colored aerial photographs. The elementary maps are accompanied by four pages of color illustrations depicting contrasting landscapes, peoples, ways of life, modes of transport, products and industries, and topics for further discussion and study. Attractive and eye-catching, it will appeal to and motivate the younger child. It retails at 45 pence in limp paper covers.

GINN WORLD ATLAS

A popular elementary school atlas, published by Ginn and Co., but distributed by A. J. Nystrom and Co., Chicago. Retailing at $1.32, it is edited by the well-known cartographer, Richard Edes Harrison. First published in 1957, it measures 10½ by 7½ in. and contains 62 pages in a limp-cover edition. There are 30 political-physical maps in full color, and a brief index of some 3,000 entries.

HAMLYN'S NEW RELIEF WORLD ATLAS

Published in London by the Hamlyn Group in 1967, edited by S. Carpenter, this is a good value at £1.50. It claims to be the first atlas to use the technique of shadow relief, but similar maps have been published earlier in the *Reader's Digest Great World Atlas*. There are 205 pages in all, of which 144 are devoted to maps, including 34 well-colored regional maps, 32 quite large-scale detailed maps, plus relief maps of the ocean floors. It is reasonably well balanced, with particularly good coverage of the Balkan states, and the Suez and Panama Canals. The atlas begins with a conventional section on map projections and an interesting section on space exploration. Following these sections are relief and vegetation maps for all the continents, and smaller thematic maps depicting climate, historical features, soil, land use, etc. The most important areas of the world are drawn on larger scales, but colored in a somewhat flat ochre and blue only. A good clear, well-printed atlas, made more useful by the provision of a well-compiled index of 25,000 entries, it comes in a format of 12 by 8½ in. It was favorably reviewed in the *Geographical Journal,* December 1967, p. 582, and is described also in Walford's *Guide to Reference Material* and Lock's *Modern Maps and Atlases.* This atlas is a very good value at a low cost. Highly recommended.

HAMMOND ATLAS OF THE WORLD

Published by W. H. Sadlier, Inc., New York, but actually produced by Hammond Inc. First published in 1955, it is revised annually. A small atlas, costing only $.25, it is designed for use in schools. In paper covers, it measures 10½ by 7½ in.

HAMMOND COMPARATIVE WORLD ATLAS

Published by Hammond Inc. As with other 1971 Hammond atlases, it now measures 12½ by 9½ in. A small paperback atlas, it contains only 48 pages, and retails at $1.25 in a paper cover edition. It provides a series of comparative maps for each continent, showing the political and physical features, vegetation, population, and temperature and rainfall. It also includes land types in pictures, and world distribution and resource maps. A brief index lists only major cities and physical features, but this is supplemented by a gazetteer-index which lists countries and political divisions, giving for each the area, population, and capital. There is a surprising number of maps, 81 in all, but all, of course, on a quite small scale.

HAMMOND GLOBEMASTER WORLD ATLAS

Subtitled *A Two-in-One Atlas for Home and Travel,* this is a relatively small 105-page atlas in two parts, published by Hammond Inc. at $2.95 for the 1971 edition. Measuring 11 by 8½ in., its first part contains 48 pages of colored maps, a two-page gazetteer of countries, states, and colonial possessions, a page of geographic comparisons, a two-page index (about 800 entries), and a page of geographic terms. The main series of maps is political, but accompanying these maps on facing or accompanying pages are smaller physical maps, some thematic maps, and brief information and color flags of the principal countries. Part 2 is comprised of a 51-page road atlas of the United States, Canada, and Mexico. The usual arrangement is state by state or province by province. Included are inset maps of cities, indexes of cities and towns, a small locator map, a small relief map, travel highlights, and tourist areas of interest. Concluding the second part is a map of National Parks and Monuments, and a highway mileage distance table. The end papers are used for lists of oceans and seas, great ship canals, principal lakes and inland seas, elements of the solar system, and dimensions of the earth. The atlas presents quite a useful combination. Note that the first part can be purchased separately as the *Hammond Headline World Atlas.* It was reviewed in the *American Reference Books Annual,* 1972, p. 195.

HAMMOND HEADLINE WORLD ATLAS

An inexpensive soft-cover 52-page atlas, published by Hammond Inc. and retailing at $1.00. It is designed mainly for multiple classroom and desk use. Measuring 11 by 8½ in., it contains 48 pages of colored maps. The main series consists of the well-known Hammond political maps, accompanied by smaller topographic maps and thematic maps, together with brief data on each country, including national flags in color. The first 17 pages are devoted to North, Central, and South America. Only 12 pages are allocated to Europe (including the Soviet Union), and the remainder of the world is dealt with in only 18 pages. Pages 1–48 of this atlas are identical to the first 48 pages in the *Hammond Globemaster Atlas* (see above), as also are the two-page gazetteer-index of the world, and the end papers, but the general index is omitted. It was reviewed in the *American Reference Books Annual,* 1970, p. 98.

HAMMOND ILLUSTRATED ATLAS FOR YOUNG AMERICA

This is an excellent atlas for children who are beginning to study maps. First published by Hammond in 1957, it measures 10 by 7 in. and is comprised of 96 pages, retailing at $4.50. In addition to the 30 full-color political, physical, and pictorial maps, it provides a great deal of very useful text material, such as the explanations of methods of projection, what scale means, what a map does, the different kinds of maps, how to use a map, and reading maps. The index is brief, however, with only some 300 entries, and there is an emphasis on the United States, which is quite fully mapped. There are no maps of individual countries, however, only larger regions. It is, nonetheless, excellent as an introduction to the use of more advanced reference atlases. It is listed in the *Children's Catalog*, 12th ed. 1971. A review appeared in the *Library Journal*, January 15, 1967. Recommended.

LIFE ATLAS OF THE WORLD

Not to be confused with the much larger and much more expensive *Life Pictorial Atlas of the World* (long since out of print), this useful small atlas was produced by Rand McNally for Time-Life Books, as an integral volume of the *Life World Library* series. First published in 1960, it contains 160 pages, measures 10¾ by 8¼ in., and retails at $4.95, but it is being phased out and will not be available after 1973. It contains 81 color maps of the countries of the world (the United States is mapped by regions), and a group of special thematic world maps dealing with such features as climate, economics, and population. An additional feature of note is the section providing useful statistics on countries and major cities of the world. The 63-page index, containing some 25,000 entries, is very good for an atlas of this size. It is listed in the *Junior High School Library Catalog*, 2nd ed. 1970; the *Senior High School Library Catalog*, 9th ed. 1967; and the *Public Library Catalog*, 5th ed. 1968. It is recommended, but note that it is being phased out of print.

LITTLE OXFORD ATLAS

One of the smallest of the well-known series of Oxford atlases, this 70-page work comes in a 10 by 7½ in. format, and retails in the United States at $2.00 and in Britain at 75 pence. Prepared by the cartographic department of the Clarendon Press, it is published by the Oxford University Press, New York and London. Derived directly from the series of larger Oxford atlases, it was first published in 1962, and was reissued with revisions in 1970. It contains 66 pages of the well-executed Oxford physical-political maps.

NELSON CONCISE WORLD ATLAS

Edited by J. Wreford Watson, this was published in 1961 by Thomas Nelson and Sons, London. Well planned, it is comprised of 80 pages, and retails at 75 pence. Six introductory plates are given to astronomical geography and the structure of the earth. There are 48 pages of physical maps of outstanding clarity, which use effective layer coloring and hill shading for relief representation. There is an emphasis on the British Isles which, in addition to maps, is fully treated with photographs, diagrams, and text. The *Nelson School Atlas* is practically identical, but less durably bound. The *Nelson Junior Atlas* is a shorter version of 56 pages.

NEW GROSSET WORLD ATLAS

A small but relatively expensive pocket-sized atlas, published in 1968 by Grosset and Dunlap, New York. Retailing at $2.50, it contains 80 full-page maps in seven colors, a gazetteer of 10,000 place names, and a mass of statistics on 211 countries and areas of the world.

THE OXFORD HOME ATLAS OF THE WORLD

First published in London in 1955 by the Oxford University Press. A second edition appeared shortly after, and a third edition, issued in 1960, has been reprinted at frequent intervals with revisions. Basically, it is an abridgment of the larger *Oxford Atlas* and the *Concise Oxford Atlas*, and it is also sold in school text edition as the *Oxford School Atlas* at the much lower price of 70 pence as opposed to £1.50 for the trade edition. Prepared by the cartographic department of the Clarendon Press, it is edited by D. P. Bickmore and F. C. Couzens. Measuring a convenient 10 by 7½ in., it is suitable for home use by students from the age of 12. In the United States it retails at $5.00.

The maps, contained in 114 pages, are basically physical, but with a considerable amount of political information and good detail also. These are supplemented by a series of thematic world maps dealing with vegetation, rainfall, soils, temperature, air routes, land uses, population, etc., and some historical maps. Most maps are spread over two facing pages and, as these are bled to the edges of the pages, are reasonably large in scale. A useful feature is the provision of inset maps and tables of statistical data as insets. Relief is shown on the pleasantly colored maps by a fine series of layer tints and hill shading. Two indexes are provided: one for the British Isles of about 4.000 entries, and another for the rest of the world, with approximately 8,000 entries. Usefully, these also include physical features and locate names with the correct degrees of latitude and longitude.

North American users will be irritated by the considerable emphasis on the British Isles and Europe in this 144-page atlas, 35 pages being allocated to these areas, as against 21 for both North and South America. Practically identical to the *Oxford Home Atlas* are the *Canadian Oxford School Atlas*, the *Canadian Oxford Desk Atlas*, and of course, the *Oxford School Atlas*. The Canadian editions, however, have been adapted to emphasize the sections on Canada and the United States at the expense of the British Isles. The editor of the Canadian editions is given as E. G. Pleva, with the assistance of Spencer Inch, although the atlases are actually produced in Britain. In the Canadian works, the first of the two separate indexes refers to the expanded Canadian section. Derived directly from the *Oxford Home Atlas* and its variants are the *Oxford Shorter School Atlas*, the *Oxford Junior Atlas*, and the *Canadian Oxford Junior Atlas*.

PERGAMON GENERAL WORLD ATLAS

Not to be confused with the much larger and quite different *Pergamon World Atlas* (q.v.) from the same publisher, the Pergamon Press Limited, Oxford, London, New York, and elsewhere. Published once only, in 1966, this is a small to medium-sized atlas of 130 pages, retailing now at 65 pence (it used to be more expensive at £1.05). Better than most in this price range, it contains 87 pages of maps of all types and a 40-page gazetteer. Measuring 10¾ by 8½ in., and using the end papers for additional special maps and diagrams, it was produced by the cartographic department of the Pergamon

Press under the general editorship of Stanley Knight, F.R.G.S. A detailed list of contents precedes the atlas section proper and specifies the scales used on each map. These are given again on the map pages, both as a representative fraction and as a bar distance scale in miles and kilometers. The maps, which are in two styles—human and physical—are exceptionally well detailed and well produced, in six pleasing colors. A notable feature is the provision of a legend of symbols and copious informative notes on each map page. Another feature worthy of note is the abundance of thematic maps (more than 90 counted) on both world and regional bases. There is an emphasis on Britain (18 pages), which is mapped at a scale of 1:1,000,000. The United States, conversely, is poorly scaled at 1:15,000,000. The index or gazetteer section is divided into two parts for (a) Great Britain, with about 7,000 entries, and (b) the rest of the world, with about 12,500 entries. The correct degrees of latitude and longitude are given for each entry. This is an attractive, well-printed atlas, and a good buy at its present low price. Further information about it will be found in Lock's *Modern Maps and Atlases* and Walford's *Guide to Reference Material.*

PHILIP'S COMMERCIAL COURSE ATLAS and PHILIP'S NEW SCHOOL ATLAS

Two small atlases published by George Philip and Son Limited, London, and edited by Harold Fullard. The 1970 *Commercial Course Atlas* retails at 78 pence and the *New School Atlas* at 58 pence. The works are identical except that the *Commercial Course Atlas* provides an extra 24-page economic section dealing with world distribution of resources and production. Maps are mainly physical, many of which are spread over two facing pages for special study. Hill shading appears on the continental maps. Climate graphs, a variety of thematic maps, and a 23-page index of some 13,000 entries make this a useful and inexpensive atlas for classroom use.

PHILIP'S ELEMENTARY ATLAS

Another of the several small school atlases published by George Philip and Son Limited, London. With limp covers, this small title is comprised of 64 pages, 40 of which are allocated to maps, and it retails at 38 pence. Designed for the 9–16 age group, it is a mainly physical world atlas, although some political maps are also included. It includes details of major countries and cities and 12 pages of climate graphs, vegetation and economic maps, and a number of thematic maps. A fairly substantial index completes the atlas. Edited by Harold Fullard, it was in its 104th edition in 1967.

PHILIP'S FIRST VENTURE ATLAS

A small limp-cover atlas of only 24 pages, the 1971 edition retails at 21 pence. It contains full-color maps with hill shading, which are augmented by small insets and color photographs. A useful feature is the provision of questions on each page to develop the most important points. Designed for the under-nine age group, it is published by George Philip and Son Limited,

London. A special British Isles edition is also available, with an additional eight pages providing a section of regional maps of the British Isles. This retails at 26 pence.

PHILIP'S MODERN HOME ATLAS

Edited by Harold Fullard and also published by George Philip and Son, this is a small general reference, handily illustrated atlas for limited general use. Comprised of 95 pages, it provides 41 pages of colored physical-political maps and a good 24-page index. Last published in 1968, it retailed then at 52½ pence. A brief mention of it is made in Lock's *Modern Maps and Atlases.*

PHILIP'S MODERN SCHOOL ATLAS

A larger school atlas designed for the 9–16 age group, this is published in a hardcover edition of 144 pages, at 80 pence. There are 100 pages of political and physical maps, and these are supplemented by special maps showing climate, vegetation, geology, land use, and population, eight pages of climate graphs, and an index of some 18,000 entries. A popular school atlas, it was in its 68th edition in 1971. As with all atlases published by George Philip and Son, it is edited by Harold Fullard.

PHILIP'S POCKET ATLAS OF THE WORLD

A very small prayer-book-sized atlas of 124 pages, this contains 96 pages of colored political maps and a 24-page index. Of necessity, the maps are cluttered and the print is very small, but the quality is high. The 1971 edition retails at 65 pence, which is rather expensive for an atlas of this size and purpose.

PHILIP'S PRACTICAL ATLAS

One of the better small atlases published by George Philip and Son Limited, and edited by Harold Fullard. Hardbound, it retails at £1.50 (about $4.00). It was first published in 1960, and was in its fourth edition by 1969, with a new impression in 1971. The 80 pages of full-color maps are all political, except for a couple of special world maps. Most maps are spread over two facing pages for maximum coverage of approximately 11 by 16 in. (atlas measures 11 by 8½ in.). It has a number of good features, including a well-detailed list of contents which shows the scale for every map, several useful inset maps, and good detail. Scales are shown on every map in both numerical fractions and miles per inch (unusual in a British atlas), and on a bar distance scale in miles and kilometers. A quite good index of some 38,000 entries is provided, and a good feature of this is the provision of the exact degrees of latitude and longitude for each named place or feature. It contains 182 pages in all, and is a good value at this low price.

PHILIP'S PRIMARY ATLAS

A very small and very simple atlas designed for the under-nine age group. In limp covers, the 1971 edition contains only 16 pages and retails for 18 pence. With simple bold coloring and a minimum of detail on each map, this would be useful as an introductory atlas for the younger pupils in primary schools.

PHILIP'S RECORD ATLAS

One of the larger Philips atlases, this useful political reference atlas is identical in several respects to the publisher's *Library Atlas* (q.v.), but is in a smaller format of 11 by 8½ in. Retailing at £2.25, it offers 266 pages, of which 128 are political maps of the world with good detail. Perhaps its best feature is the 130-page index of some 60,000 entries. A good, cheap atlas for locating places and for following world affairs. Mention of it is made in Walford's *Guide to Reference Material* and Lock's *Modern Maps and Atlases.*

PHILIP'S SECONDARY SCHOOL ATLAS

Very similar to the same publisher's *Elementary Atlas*, this small school atlas is also comprised of 66 pages, of which 40 are color pages of mainly physical maps, supplemented by 16 pages of thematic maps, climate graphs, information about the moon, and details of principal countries and cities of the world. Now in its 101st edition, it is designed for the 9–16 age group of students, and retails in a limp-cover edition at 38 pence, which includes a fairly comprehensive index.

PHILIP'S VENTURE ATLAS

A more advanced version of the same publisher's *First Venture Atlas*, this larger work is designed for the 9–16 age group. Edited by Harold Fullard, the 1971 edition is comprised of 50 pages, of which 42 are allocated to maps, and, like the *Secondary School Atlas,* retails at 38 pence. Both the hill-shaded physical maps and the political and thematic maps are printed in bold colors, with legible type. Color is also used quite extensively for the material on the solar system, the moon, and the seasons, and to a lesser extent in the combined gazetteer and index.

PHILIP'S VISUAL ATLAS

Last in the series of small atlases published by George Philip and Son Limited, London, this 1967 publication contains 56 pages and retails at 32 pence. It is a world atlas with both political and physical maps in 47 pages, including thematic maps of the British Isles. There is also a useful map-reading section and a nine-page index. It, like several other Philip atlases, is designed to meet the map reference needs of the 9–16 age group.

RAND McNALLY ANSWER ATLAS

Published in 1968 by Rand McNally, it retails at $2.95. Hardbound, it contains 72 pages in a format measuring 11 by 9 in. It is comprised almost entirely of double page spreads of the continents and the major land areas of the world. Preceding each major section is a global relief view of the continent or area following, and this is followed by medium-scale political maps, with elevations shown by hill shading. Highways and rivers are shown and, on some maps, railroads. Each map page carries interesting and informative notes. Maps of the United States and Canada are at a scale of 1:12,000,000 (where 1 inch equals 190 miles), with most other areas at a scale of 1:16,000,000 (1 inch equalling 250 miles). Scale is shown on every map in three ways: (a) as a numerical fraction, (b) in miles to the inch, and (c) on a bar distance scale in both miles and kilometers. The projections employed are well identified. This is not an atlas for reference, but a useful small work for following world affairs, and for motivating younger users and teaching the uses of an atlas. The most unusual feature is the provision of a series of questions on each region designed to stir interest. Other useful data such as a list of principal cities, and a list of geographic comparisons, for example, are included. Completing the work is a small but useful seven-page index of some 2,500 entries, which locates places by the exact degrees of latitude and longitude. Recommended.

RAND McNALLY CLASSROOM ATLAS

First published in 1960 and now in its sixth edition (1970), this is a small but very handy paperback atlas, prepared and published by the cartographic staff of Rand McNally. Retailing at $1.40 and measuring 10 by 7½ in., it is comprised of 84 pages, plus the utilization of the four-page stiffer cover. Seventy-three of the numbered pages contain a wide variety of physical, political, and thematic maps. The maps for Canada and the United States take up 22 pages and outweigh considerably the rest of the world, which is mapped by continents only. On the political maps, scale is shown by fractions, by miles per inch, and by a bar scale, but on the physical and other maps it is shown by a bar scale only. Projections employed are identified only on the political maps. Useful are the several pages of thematic maps of the world and the continents, showing climate, population, natural vegetation, rainfall, and similar information. The 11 pages of text provide useful data on geographic comparisons; a world political information table (showing area, population, population per square mile, form of government, largest and capital cities, etc.); and geographic and historical facts about the United States. A limited index of some 2,000 entries locates places by a simple letter-number grid system. Designed for individual student use in elementary grades and junior high schools as well as for group classroom use, this is an excellent small atlas at a low price, especially where interest in North America is the first consideration.

RAND McNALLY NEWS ATLAS OF THE WORLD

An unusually large (14 by 11 in.) and interesting paperback atlas first published in 1970 by Rand McNally, retailing at $1.95. It is comprised of 96 pages, made up as follows: List of Contents (but scale for each map is not given); a Quick Find Index to Major Map References; a map of the moon, with photos and text; eight pages of world thematic maps and text on population distribution, transportation, natural forests, etc. (drawn from the material in *The International Atlas*); two-page physical maps of the world, the Pacific and Indian Oceans, the Atlantic Ocean, Antarctica, Europe and Africa, Asia, Australasia, Oceania, North America, South America, and a list of map symbols; and these are followed by a political map of the world and political maps of regions, with hill shading to show elevations. A noteworthy feature is the inclusion of large-scale inset maps of important regions and metropolitan areas. A scale bar in both miles and kilometers is provided on the political maps as also is a 40,000 square-mile diagram for comparative purposes. Detail is quite good and railroads (but not highways) are shown along with a number of other cultural and natural features. A world political information table, world facts and comparisons, and a list of abbreviations precedes the 13-page index of some 5,000 entries which, usefully, give the exact degrees of latitude and longitude for each place and feature. This is a useful, inexpensive, quick-reference atlas with good maps of most areas of the world. Further information will be found in the review of this work which was published in the *American Reference Books Annual*, 1971, p. 70.

RAND McNALLY ONE DOLLAR FIFTY WORLD ATLAS

Formerly the *Rand McNally One Dollar World Atlas*, this is one of the several small atlases produced by Rand McNally. Unlike others in this price range, the 1972 edition is hardbound, although containing only 28 pages, 27 of which are comprised of the well-known *Cosmo* series of political maps with some physical features, such as the showing of elevations by hachures. Most maps are on one page (the atlas measures 12 by 9 in.) but a few maps, principally those of the continents, are spread over two pages, with largerscale insets of metropolitan areas and important regions. A scale bar is given for each map in miles and kilometers, and the projections employed are identified. Within such a limited compass, the maps are obviously on a small scale but are still quite well detailed. There is no index, however, which limits its usefulness. The two inside covers are utilized to provide (a) world geographic facts and comparisons and (b) a list of the principal cities of the world and their populations.

RAND McNALLY POCKET WORLD ATLAS

Measuring only 6 by 4 in., this is the smallest atlas (physically) in the Rand McNally range. Despite its small format, however, it provides a great deal of geographic and political information in its 316 pages. First published in 1970, it retails at $1.50, and is a good value at this low cost. The first 21 pages are extracts from "Patterns and Imprints of Mankind," an excellent essay contained in the highly rated *The International Atlas*. Following this is a map of the moon, an explanation of scale, the index reference system, and a list of map symbols. These in turn are followed by 178 pages of maps of the world, reduced from the well-known *Cosmo* series, all of which are political. There is a map for each of the states of the United States and for each Canadian province. Detail is good, but the print and scale are so small that the maps are often difficult to read. A scale bar in both miles and kilometers is provided for each map and the projections employed are clearly identified. A feature is the inclusion of larger-scale maps as insets for metropolitan areas and important regions. The scale, of course, is extremely small even on the insets. Pages 204–220 are comprised of text material, providing a world political information table, geographic facts and comparisons, largest metropolitan areas and cities, geographic facts about the United States, general information about each U.S. state, and historical facts about the United States. A 96-page section indexes the contents with about 30,000 entries (including population figures). A useful small atlas with a wealth of geographic information.

RAND McNALLY REGIONAL ATLAS

First published under this title by Rand McNally in 1953, this small (11 by 9 in.) but exceptionally useful atlas is now in its fourth edition (1971). Retailing at $2.95, its 64 pages (plus two inside covers) are abridged from the excellent *Goode's World Atlas* (q.v.) edited by Professor Edward B. Espenshade, Jr. Fifty of the 64 pages contain 14 pages of thematic maps and 36 pages of the Goode-originated physical-political maps in full color, most of which are spread over two facing pages for maximum visual effect. Every map gives the scale as a fraction, its equivalent scale in miles per inch, a bar distance scale in both miles and kilometers, the projection used, and a key to the color relief shading. Relief is shown by contour lines, a much-improved series of layer tints, and shaded hill rendering. Most of the maps are drawn at the small but still useful scale of 1:16,000,000, and detail is good, with rivers, railroads, and boundaries clearly shown (but not highways). The excellent series of well-balanced physical-political maps are preceded by a list of principal countries and regions of the world, a detailed list of contents, which also indicates the scale at which each map is drawn, and nine thematic maps of the world and the United States, showing climate, population, economies, minerals, physiography, etc. A 12-page index of some 5,000 entries concludes the atlas, which usefully gives the latitude and longitude for each named place. This is an excellent atlas for group and individual use in schools. Recommended.

SCHOLASTIC-HAMMOND WORLD ATLAS

Made by Hammond Inc., but published by Scholastic Book Services, this small atlas was first published in 1959. It has been reissued frequently since then with revisions. Retailing at $.60, it is comprised of 64 pages, in a format of 9¼ by 6¼ in. It is designed mainly for elementary classroom use, for those beginning to study maps and atlases, and contains as much text as it does maps. The maps are a mixture of political, physical, and pictorial, but are very limited in detail. A very small index of only 300 entries identifies only major places, but is useful as an instructional device.

SCHOLASTIC WORLD ATLAS or COLORPRINT SCHOLASTIC WORLD ATLAS

Apparently first published in 1967 by the American Map Co., this is a small but useful paper-covered atlas which retails at $.89. Measuring 12½ by 9½ in., it is comprised of 48 pages, of which 35 are full-color political maps of the world. These are preceded by a diagram of the solar system and a table of contents and followed by a seven-page glossary of geographic terms and an index of about 2,500 entries. The index, as well as locating places, provides brief information about countries and populations of major cities. Concluding the atlas is a table of geographic comparisons, a polar projection map of the world, and (an unusual feature) a 250-year calendar for the period 1800–2050. The projections employed on each map are identified and a scale bar in both miles and kilometers is provided, although not, as in most small atlases, the representative fraction. All the maps are political and there are no relief features. Detail is limited and only rivers are shown. Except for the world sea route maps, no lines of communication are provided, even on the larger-scale metropolitan area insets. A review of this title appeared in the December 1967 issue of the *Consumer Bulletin*, p. 34. Useful, and a worthwhile acquisition at this price, the *Colorprint Scholastic World Atlas* provides quick, accurate but limited answers to modern geographic questions.

STUDENTS POLITICAL ATLAS OF THE WORLD

First published by Rand McNally in 1964 and revised in 1968, this does not appear in the current catalog of the publisher and may now be out of print. It was designed for use in junior and senior high schools and retailed in 1968 at $1.00. It portrays in 39 pages of maps and nine pages of supporting data, the political areas of the world, with relief shown by shaded relief rendering. The maps are based on those contained in the highly rated *Goode's World Atlas*. All major cities, towns, and features are located in an index of some 3,500 entries.

TEACH YOURSELF ATLAS OF THE WORLD

A useful British work, edited by Harold Fullard, Cartographic Director of George Philip and Son Limited, London. First published in 1964, it is comprised of 192 pages and retails at 62½ pence. Not so much an atlas as an explanation of how atlases are made and used, it is useful for self-study and as an introduction to the use of atlases and maps.

VISUAL-RELIEF ATLAS OF WORLD CONTINENTS

Published by the Denoyer-Geppert Co., Chicago, this was first published in 1963, and recopyrighted in 1966, when it retailed at $1.00. It is apparently available on subscription only. It is designed for use in elementary, junior, and senior high schools. Measuring 11 by 8½ in., all of its maps are spread over two facing map pages for a maximum coverage of 11 by 17 in. It is comprised of only 32 pages, 20 of which contain physical maps of the continents, with elevations shown by contour layer coloring and relief shading. A brief index is provided, but political and cultural detail is virtually nonexistent.

WHEATON ATLAS FOR THE MIDDLE SCHOOL

Edited by L. R. Hawkes, and produced by the cartographic department of the Pergamon Press under their Wheaton imprint in 1968, this small British paperback atlas measures 10½ by 8½ in. and contains 54 pages, including the two inside covers. Retailing at 45 pence, it is designed to meet the atlas reference needs of students from the age of 9 through 13, and includes photographs, diagrams, and explanatory notes as well as conventional maps. Useful features are the explanation of the conventions used in map making and the page notes, which can provide starting points for a number of geographic projects. More than half of the atlas is devoted to coverage of the British Isles, which limits its usefulness in the North American market. An unusual and attractive atlas cum textbook, it is a useful tool for classroom use. Most of the maps are physical, in a variety of rich colors, but some political maps and a good selection of thematic maps are also provided.

WHEATON-PERGAMON SECONDARY SCHOOL ATLAS

A relatively new atlas designed for use in secondary schools in Great Britain, with special features which make it particularly suitable for syllabuses there. The 1966 edition retails at 45 pence; its general editor is Stanley Knight, F.R.G.S., Cartographic Director of the Pergamon Press. Of its 100 pages, 67 are allocated to maps and 32 pages to an index gazetteer. All maps are in six colors. Special emphasis is placed on the British Isles, which are allocated ten pages, containing maps at a scale of 1:1,000,000, and more than 7,000 names on a land-use background. Special-topic maps are included such as physical, weather forecasting areas, climate, and geology.

WHEATON PRIMARY ATLAS

First published in 1971, this is another in the series of Wheaton atlases published by the Pergamon Press. Like the *Atlas for the Middle School*, it is edited by L. R. Hawkes, with G. R. Evans also listed as a consultant editor. Comprised of 36 pages, plus the utilization of the inside covers, it is designed for use by younger children in British schools, with most of the atlas devoted to a coverage of the British Isles. It is useful as an introduction to the use of more advanced atlases, and there are good explanations of scale, finding direction, and similar things. Lavishly illustrated, it is an interesting and useful work for the elementary grades.

WORLD IN REVIEW

A unique and useful work produced jointly by the *New York Times* and Rand McNally, and first published in 1972. This is not so much an atlas as an attempt to present the background of situations rather than geographic facts, but it does so in combination with a series of maps and map charts. Edited by Lester Markel, the text, which comprises by far the greater part of the work, is written by correspondents of the *New York Times* from all parts of the world. The accompanying maps are largely the work of Rand McNally and are drawn from their series of *Cosmo* political-physical maps. Retailing at $4.95, it is divided into four principal sections: Part 1, which describes the general background of world affairs; Part 2, which describes the ambitions, successes, and failures of the "Big Three" powers (The United States, Russia, and China); Part 3, which measures the impact of the

"Big Three" on other nations and surveys their special problems; and Part 4, entitled the "World Background," which presents statistics, geography, and basic elements of the world picture. It is, in effect, a useful work of reference for understanding current events as they happen. It is not, and is not intended to be, a general reference atlas per se.

THE WORLD: ITS GEOGRAPHY IN MAPS

Published by the Denoyer-Geppert Co., Chicago. It was first published in 1965 and recopyrighted in 1967. Edited by Clarence B. Odell, it is apparently available on subscription only, at $3.25 in hard cover edition, and $2.00 in a paper-cover format. Measuring 11 by 8½ in., it is designed for use in the upper elementary grades and high schools. It is comprised of 97 pages, of which 43 are full-color, physical-political and visual-relief maps of countries and regions of the world, most of which are spread over two facing pages. The maps are interspersed with useful explanatory text, and there is a fairly comprehensive index. Also included are eight thematic maps on population, pressure and winds, climates, soils, vegetation, occupations, and world relationships. A useful work, it provides a great deal of useful reference data. The visual-relief maps are particularly effective, producing a three-dimensional effect.

WORLD PATTERNS: THE ALDINE COLLEGE ATLAS

First published in 1971 by the Aldine Publishing Co., but actually produced and printed in Great Britain by George Philip and Son Limited, London. In effect, it is an abridged edition of the excellent *Aldine University Atlas* (q.v.), with the same editors and cartographic staff. Retailing at $3.95, it is comprised of 128 pages, all of which are a selection of the maps contained in the *Aldine University Atlas*, but it contains only 96 pages of maps as against the 192 pages in the larger work. The main series of maps consists of the superb physical medium-scale maps of the more important regions of the world, supplemented by a considerable number of world and regional thematic maps dealing with a wide range of topics. Scale is shown on every map by a numerical fraction and by a bar scale in miles and kilometers. A color key to the layer coloring is provided in the margin area of each map page. Detail is excellent, with principal highways shown in red and railroads in black. Also shown are such important features as airports, canals, tunnels, rivers, and other natural features. The 27-page index lists some 13,000 places, each located by its exact degrees of latitude and longitude. A fine explanation of scale is provided inside the back cover, and an excellent explanation of map projections inside the front cover. There is some emphasis on the United States, but the entire world is covered in reasonably large scale. This is an excellent alternative to the larger *Aldine University Atlas* where cost is a determining factor.

APPENDIX B

DISCONTINUED ATLASES

While up-to-dateness is an important factor in choosing any reference book, there are several reasons the reader may seek information on a discontinued atlas. He may already own one, or the low price of a used atlas may be a strong consideration. He may be interested in comparing a current atlas with an older one, to see what recent changes have been incorporated. Moreover, there is always a possibility that a discontinued atlas will be reissued, with or without major revisions. In all such cases, the reader will find here a convenient reference source.

AMERICAN OXFORD ATLAS

Published by the Oxford University Press Inc., New York, in 1951 at $10.00. It was virtually identical to the *Oxford Atlas* (q.v.) except for the addition of some material of particular American interest. It contained 120 pages of maps in six colors, with an additional 24 pages of maps on the western hemisphere, and a 100-page gazetteer. The physical maps emphasized regions of the world rather than individual countries, and it was a useful medium-sized reference atlas. The editors were the same as for the *Oxford Atlas*. It was listed in the 4th ed. 1958 of the *Standard Catalog for Public Libraries* and was also mentioned briefly in the 1966 edition of Barton's *Reference Books*. Although technically out of print in this edition, it is still available in almost the same contents as the *Oxford Atlas* and the *Canadian Oxford Atlas*.

CASSELL'S NEW ATLAS OF THE WORLD

Subtitled *the world in physical, political and economic maps, with statistics and index*. A British atlas, it was published in London by the well-known firm of Cassell and Co., and was one of a long line of good atlases published by them since their first *Universal Atlas* in 1891. The cartography was by the equally well-known firm of George Philip and Son Limited, who publish several atlases under their own imprint. Surprisingly, despite its high quality, the *Cassell's New Atlas* was published once only, in 1961. It was edited by an eminent cartographer, Dr. Harold Fullard, and retailed in Britain in two editions, a cloth at £5.50 (now £5.25) and a half leather at £8.40. It was comprised of 262 pages in a format of 13½ by 9½ in., including 96 pages of regional political maps in four colors, 32 pages in six colors, 18 pages of introductory material, and an index gazetteer of almost 70,000 entries in 104 pages. Of the 130 map plates, 30 contained special maps dealing with world economic and commodity distribution maps. Statistical data was shown by bar diagrams, a method still found in other atlases from George Philip and Son Limited. Quite an expensive atlas for its time, it was considered especially useful for commercial use. For a European atlas, it allocated more space than usual to North America, the United States alone being allocated five double pages, with good coverage at a scale of 1:2,500,000. More information will be found in Walford's *Guide to Reference Material* and Lock's *Modern Maps and Atlases.*

CAXTON WORLD ATLAS

Not to be confused with the quite different new *Caxton Atlas of the Earth,* although made by the same cartographic firm of George Philip and Son Limited. Edited by William Gordon East, it was published only once, in 1960, by the British subscription book publishing firm, the Caxton Publishing Co. (now a subsidiary of International Learning Systems Corporation). It retailed in Britain at the then high cost of £13.75, and was also available in the United States (through International Publications Service, 18 East 33rd St., New York, N.Y. 10016) at $37.50. Measuring 16 by 12 in., it was comprised of 562 pages, but it was much more than an atlas, being in fact two works in one, a profusely illustrated geography textbook combined with the atlas. It also had two separate indexes, one for the test material (4,500 entries) and one for the atlas (60,000 entries). The 773 illustrations included 32 color plates. The 104 pages of physical maps were of various scales and sizes, with inset sketch maps, but these were too small and generalized to be of any real value. It was reviewed in the *Geographical Journal,* September 1960, and further information about it can be found in Walford's *Guide to Reference Material* and Lock's *Modern Maps and Atlases.*

CHILDREN'S PICTURE ATLAS OF THE WORLD

Published by Golden Press, Inc., a division of the Western Publishing Co., New York, who are also the publishers of the *Odyssey World Atlas.* The *Children's Picture Atlas* was designed to meet the map needs of younger children from the ages of about ten through junior high school, not so much as an atlas per se but as an introduction to the use of maps. It was first published in 1960 as the *Golden Picture Atlas of the World,* and under this title was available in either a three-volume or a six-volume edition. Except for the format and the quality of the paper, the 1966 edition of the *Children's Picture Atlas* was identical to the older title. Containing 544 pages in all, it retailed in the United States at $4.95 and in the United Kingdom, until very recently, at £1.25 (under the imprint of Paul Hamlyn). Measuring 10 by 7¼ in., it contained some 1,000 color photos and maps. Of these, 130 were full-color political, physical, and thematic maps in a simple presentation for younger children. A simple but reasonably adequate index of 3,500 entries appeared in the last 20 pages of the text. Because of its lively, informative, and interesting illustrations and explanatory text, it was a popular, reasonably priced elementary atlas, which was recommended as an introduction to the use of more advanced works. The publishers have no plan to revise the work, which is rather a pity. A review appeared in the *Library Journal,* January 15, 1967.

CITIZEN'S ATLAS OF THE WORLD

A very fine world atlas for many years, the *Citizen's Atlas of the World* was one of the best and biggest produced by the well-known cartographic publishing firm of John Bartholomew and Son, Edinburgh (makers of the famous *Times Atlas of the World*). The tenth edition, published in March 1952, was the last. This was retailed in Great Britain at £6.30 and in the United States, through Frederick Warne and Co., at $35.00. Measuring 14½ by 10 in., it contained 200 pages of excellent maps which, except for the layer-tinted small maps of the continents, were political in character, the only physical elevations indicated being the heights of the principal mountains and ranges. Introductory pages were occupied by maps showing the world's climate, its land uses, population density, air routes, time zones, and similar data. An excellent index of 95,000 entries located any place included on the maps. Designed primarily to show both national and international settlements and boundaries, this was one of the best reference atlases ever published in Britain. Brief mentions of it are contained in Walford's *Guide to Reference Material* and in the 4th ed. 1958 of the *Standard Catalog for Public Libraries.*

COLLIER'S WORLD ATLAS AND GAZETTEER

This once very useful atlas was first published in 1953 by P. F. Collier, Inc. (now a division of Crowell-Collier-Macmillan), and was usually sold by them as a subscription item in a package deal with their *Collier's Encyclopedia.* It was also available separately in two editions at $12.50 for the standard, and $17.50 for a deluxe edition. Measuring 14 by 10½ in., it was comprised of 472 pages, of which 120 were multicolor physical-political maps specially developed by Rand McNally. These maps were substantially the same as those used in the *Cosmopolitan World Atlas* and other atlases published by Rand McNally. Collier's improved on these, however, by using the map margins for lists of cities and population figures. Additionally, *Collier's World Atlas* included other special material, such as a chapter on the geography of the world, profiles of the 50 states of the United States, and various statistical tables and charts. An excellent 266-page index gazetteer of some 75,000 entries was particularly useful, in that it provided population figures and information (often quite full) on the more important cities, including geographic, historical, economic, and touristic facts. An unusual but useful supplement provided hunting and fishing data for the United States and Canada. Useful also were the plans of the business centers of 50 large cities of the United States. *Collier's World Atlas* continued in existence until 1957, the last-known date of printing. It was held in sufficiently high esteem to be listed in the *Junior High School Library Catalog* (1965); the *Standard Catalog for Public Libraries* (4th ed. 1958); and the *High School Libraries Catalog* (8th ed. 1962). More information about it will be found in Lock's *Modern Maps and Atlases* and Winchell's *Guide to Reference Books,* 8th ed. 1967.

THE COLUMBUS ATLAS

This was made in Britain by the well-known firm of John Bartholomew and Son, Edinburgh (see the *Citizen's Atlas of the World*). The *Columbus Atlas* was first published under this specific title in August 1953 but it was, in fact, a relatively minor revision of an earlier atlas, first published in 1948, known as the *Regional Atlas of the World*. It retailed in Britain at £2.25 and in the United States, for which it was designed, at about $12.50. The *Columbus* differed from the *Regional* only in that the order and balance of the maps was altered. In the *Regional* edition there were 20 pages on the Americas and 15 on the British Isles. In the revised *Columbus* edition, this was altered to 27 pages for the Americas and only seven for the British Isles. Relatively small in format, 11 by 8 in., the atlas was comprised of 305 pages, of which 160 were devoted to full-color physical maps of the world, using the famed Bartholomew layer tints for relief, and a reasonably comprehensive index-gazetteer of approximately 50,000 entries. This, unlike other British atlases, included population figures. A briefer description will be found in the first edition of Walford's *Guide to Reference Material*.

THE COMPACT ATLAS OF THE WORLD

Yet another atlas from the famed Bartholomew range, but this was a very small pocket-sized work, measuring only 6¾ by 4½ in. It was distributed in the United States by Frederick Warne and Co., where it retailed at $2.50. The last-known edition was the fourth (1957). It was then comprised of 180 pages, 128 of which contained small and rather cluttered political maps, and a series of thematic or special-purpose maps dealing with climate, temperature, rainfall, vegetation, races of mankind, population, languages, and world economy. An introductory section of 16 pages provided informative data on areas, populations, and other statistics for the various countries of the world, and tables of geographic comparisons. The 32-page index was restricted to only 4,000 place names, which severely restricted its reference usefulness. An abridged edition, omitting the 16 introductory pages, was also issued as the *Pocket World Atlas*. For more information, see Lock's *Modern Maps and Atlases*.

CRAM'S UNRIVALLED ATLAS

Published by the George F. Cram Co., Indianapolis. The last edition to be published was the 64th in 1952, when it was being sold at the very considerable price of $25.00. A large atlas, measuring 15½ by 11 in., its 300 pages contained 120 colored political maps, more than half of which were devoted to the United States alone. More than just an atlas, it also included a 74-page history section and the story of the United Nations. Among its more unusual features were maps by ancient geographers, and historical maps tracing the development of world civilization from 3,000 B.C. Two indexes were provided, one for the United States, and the other for the rest of the world. It was a poor and crude atlas, however, with crowded maps showing little or no relief (only mountain heights), and awkwardly arranged indexes which gave the latitude and longitude of places, but not the map page number! Further information will be found in Shores' *Instructional Materials* and *Whyte's Atlas Guide*. A full evaluation was published in the *Subscription Books Bulletin* for January 1954.

CURTIS-DOUBLEDAY WORLD ATLAS

Published by Doubleday and Co., New York, but actually made by Hammond, Inc. Sold in two editions, a plain standard edition at $15.00 and a thumb-indexed one at $17.00. Designed for general home and family use, it was published once only, in 1962. In a small format, 12 by 8 in., it was comprised of 408 pages (in five separate paginations), of which 162 were maps of all types: 106 colored political maps of the world, eight political maps of Canada, 32 pages of the Bible lands, and 16 pages of historical maps of the world. Three separate indexes were provided: one for the United States, one for Canada, and another for the rest of the world. A great deal of the material was encyclopedic in character, and of little or no reference value. Short lived, it was a poor atlas at a high cost. A review appeared in the *Wilson Library Bulletin*, June 1963.

GEOGRAPHIA WORLD ATLAS

Also known as the *Geographia Atlas of the World*, this was a small paperback atlas of only 40 pages. Directed by Alexander Goss, it was first published in 1960, with further editions in 1962 and 1963. In a format of 14 by 10 in., 32 of the pages contained colored political maps, and the remaining eight were comprised of black and white special-topic maps.

GOLDEN BOOK PICTURE ATLAS OF THE WORLD

Published once only, in 1960, by Golden Press, Inc. Designed for children aged from about 8 to 11, it was retailed in a standard six-volume edition for $14.95. It was also available through supermarkets on the "book a week" plan for $5.88 in flimsier covers. It measured 10 by 7 in. and contained 577 pages. This included some 100 pages of maps, with 130 full-color political, physical, and special-purpose maps which were prepared by Map Projects, Inc., New York, together with some reproduced from the *Westerman Bildkarten Lexicon*. It was a colorful and quite well produced work, distinguished by its quantity of illustrative material, numbering more than 1,000 color photographs, and including features on animals, climate, people, and transportation. More an illustrated geography than an atlas, it was suitable for continuous reading and browsing by children. Reviews appeared in the *Wilson Library Bulletin*, March 1961; the *Library Journal*, January 15, 1961; and *Commonweal*, November 18, 1960. In 1966 it was reissued in a one-volume format as the *Children's Picture Atlas of the World* (q.v.).

GRAPHIC ATLAS OF THE WORLD

This is similar in several respects to other atlases in the fine series which have been produced in Britain by John Bartholomew and Son Limited, over a period of years. Relatively small in format, measuring 10½ by 7½ in., it was designed for the home bookshelf and desk use rather than for detailed reference. The last recorded edition is the eleventh, which was published in 1960. It was then comprised of 184 pages, which included 96 plates of colored political maps for the individual countries and regions of the world, with additional physical maps for the continents. An 84-page index-gazetteer contained approximately 30,000 entries, adequate for an atlas of this size and purpose. Containing a great deal of interesting and informative material, it was distributed in the United States at $4.50. Some further information about it is contained in Lock's *Modern Maps and Atlases.*

HAMMOND COMPLETE WORLD ATLAS

This was one of several titles published by C. S. Hammond and Co. (now Hammond, Inc.) in the 1950s. First published in 1950, it went through several printings before its last recorded issue in 1961, when it was retailing at $5.95. In 1959 it was also published as the *Replogle Comprehensive Atlas,* by special arrangement with Replogle Globes, Chicago. In several respects it was very similar to other Hammond atlases of the time, particularly the *Library World Atlas* and the *Classics* edition of the *Hammond World Atlas.* A small atlas, it measured only 9 by 6 in., but contained 400 pages which, in addition to a full range of maps (all of them political), included a descriptive gazetteer of the world, with black and white maps and color illustrations, air line distance tables, an illustrated geography of the world, and the flags of the leading nations. A then unique, but not entirely convenient feature of the atlas was the provision of indexes on the back of each map. It was listed in the 1959–1963 supplement to the *Standard Catalog for Public Libraries,* and mention of it was also made in Shore's *Instructional Materials.*

HAMMOND DIPLOMAT WORLD ATLAS

One of the older atlases, first published in 1961, by C. S. Hammond and Co., and derived directly from the similar but larger *Hammond Ambassador World Atlas* (not the same work as current title). Nearly all of the older Hammond atlases, including this work, went out of print when Hammond introduced their new range of New Perspective atlases in 1966, although, in some instances, the titles were retained. The *Diplomat,* which was designed for high school students and as a general family reference atlas, retailed at $9.95. It was comprised of 276 consecutively numbered pages, 159 of which contained multicolored political maps of the world and a variety of special-topic maps for larger areas, showing climate, vegetation, population, temperature, etc., together with inset maps of the most important metropolitan areas. Some relief features were shown, principally by hill shading. Two indexes were provided, one for the United States, arranged in order of states, and one for the rest of the world, both of which provided population statistics. The maps were good although limited in detail, but the indexes, in two inconvenient sections, nullified its better features. A more detailed evaluation will be found in the *Booklist and Subscription Books Bulletin,* November 1, 1962.

HAMMOND-DOUBLEDAY NEW ILLUSTRATED WORLD ATLAS & GAZETTEER

As far as could be ascertained, this small atlas was published once only, in 1957, under the imprint of Doubleday and Co. New York, although actually produced by C. S. Hammond and Co. It retailed at that time for the quite reasonable cost of $3.50, although it was comprised of only 128 quarto-sized pages. Only one quarter of the work—consisting of 32 pages—contained maps, which were political only, with limited detail, and small and crowded. The remainder of the work was encyclopedic in nature and contained a great deal of gazetteer-type information. Designed more for general home use than for reference work, it was reviewed in the *Wilson Library Bulletin,* June 1958, and was listed in the 1958–1969 supplement to the *Standard Catalog for High School Libraries.*

HAMMOND FAMILY REFERENCE WORLD ATLAS

Another title published under the imprint of Doubleday and Co., New York, or Hanover House, although actually made by C. S. Hammond and Co. This was apparently available only through a book club subscription at the reasonable cost of $5.95 First published in 1956, a new printing appeared each year thereafter until the last recorded edition in 1966. A very small atlas, it measured only 9½ by 6½ in., and was comprised of 256 pages. Most maps, however, were spread over two facing pages. The main series of maps (184 pages) was political only, but these were supplemented by 11 pages of special thematic maps in black and white, and physical maps of the continents, the United States, and Canada. More than half the atlas was given over to coverage of the United States and Canada. A very limited index of only 3,000 entries was provided, which included population statistics. Designed for general family use, it was a poorly produced work. Further information will be found in *Whyte's Atlas Guide.*

HAMMOND FAMILY WORLD ATLAS

Yet another instance of an atlas produced by C. S. Hammond and Co. being published by another publisher, in this instance the Standard Reference Works Publishing Co. (This company has since been absorbed into the Funk and Wagnalls Co., and no longer publishes an atlas.) Rather an obscure work, it was sold only through book clubs or as part of a set of other books as a subscription item. It was first published under this title in 1963 and revised editions appeared from time to time, the last of which was recorded in 1967, when it retailed at $9.96 ($4.98 per volume). In two volumes, it measured 12¼ by 9¼ in., and was comprised of 376 pages, 192 in the first volume, and 184 in the second. The first volume, which dealt with the world generally, contained 86 pages of multicolored political maps, supplemented by a number of black and white resource-relief maps of the continents, a historical atlas of world civilization, and an atlas of the Bible lands. Volume 2 was given over almost entirely to the United States and Canada. There were two index-gazetteers, both small and inconveniently arranged. The first, a world index, was arranged between pages 57 and 88 of volume 1 and listed approximately 12,000 places, with population statistics. The second, which was for the United States only, was contained in volume 2 between pages 194 and 225, and listed some 30,000 cities, towns, and villages in the United States. A poor work by any standards, it is no longer available under this title, but may well have been adapted to become the *Illustrated Encyclopedia Library World Atlas* (q.v.) It is believed to have been issued also, in earlier years, as the *Sears Family World Atlas.*

HAMMOND LIBRARY WORLD ATLAS

One of many atlases published by C. S. Hammond and Co. over the years, this small but useful title went out of production when Hammond launched their new series of New Perspective world atlases in 1966. The *Library World Atlas* was first published in 1953 and was reprinted frequently until about 1963, at which time it retailed at $6.95. Measuring 12½ by 9½ in., it was designed mainly for the upper elementary and junior high school grades and for general family use. It was comprised of 336 pages in all, of which 115 contained multicolored political maps, and a scattering of black and white relief, distribution, resource, and other thematic maps. No less than three separate indexes were provided: (1) for the United States, (2) for Canada, and (3) for the rest of the world, this latter containing some 50,000 alphabetically arranged entries. Both the U.S. and Canadian indexes were arranged by states and provinces, and, as with the main index, provided population statistics. All of the material in the *Library World Atlas* was also contained in the *Classics* edition of the *Hammond World Atlas* except Sections B (The Bible Lands) and C (A Historical Atlas of the World). Pages 1–192 were also identical to the same pages in the *Hammond Universal Atlas.* A detailed evaluation was published in the *Subscription Books Bulletin,* October 1950 (earlier than the original publication date stated by the publishers). It was also described in *Whyte's Atlas Guide,* and was listed in the 1957 edition of the *Standard Catalog for High School Libraries.*

HAMMOND MODERN WORLD ATLAS AND GAZETTEER

A very small atlas in the Hammond series, consisting of only 40 pages, which contained 49 maps and a brief gazetteer of the world. First published in 1953, further editions were issued in 1960 and 1965, when it retailed at $.69. Measuring 12½ by 9½ in., it has been out of print for several years in the United States, but was listed as being available in Britain in 1971, at the sterling price of 37½p. It was apparently designed for overseas use.

HAMMOND NEW ERA WORLD ATLAS

First published by C. S. Hammond and Co. in 1959, a new copyright was registered in 1964, but it was reported to be out of print by 1967. However, a work of this same title was listed as being available in Britain in 1971, through the British distributors of Hammond atlases. Measuring 12½ by 9½ in., the original American edition contained 176 pages and retailed at $7.95.

Designed more for popular family use than for reference purposes, it was derived directly from the old series of Hammond atlases (pre-1966), and was sometimes offered as a premium through other publishers or distributors. It contained 86 pages of maps, of which 44 were multicolored political maps of the world. Fifteen pages were allocated to a historical atlas, and the remainder to thematic, special-purpose, and distribution maps. Apart from six pages of black and white resource relief maps of the continents, physical features were not represented. A small index-gazetteer of some 12,000 entries provided population statistics.

HAMMOND NEW INTERNATIONAL WORLD ATLAS

First published in 1956, a revised edition appeared in 1963 when this, another of the many titles published by C. S. Hammond and Co., retailed at $2.95. Unlike other pre-1966 Hammond atlases, the coverage of North America was scanty, as it was designed specifically for sale overseas. Measuring 12¼ by 9¼ in., it was comprised of 112 pages: 100 pages containing 42 colored political maps of the world, 46 pages of historical maps, and 12 pages of black and white resource, distribution, and relief maps of the continents. There was no index as such, although the prefatory material listed some 1,000 cities of the world, with population statistics. It was superseded in 1966 by the *Hammond International World Atlas*, a much larger work.

HAMMOND NEW PRACTICAL WORLD ATLAS

One of the smallest atlases ever produced by C. S. Hammond and Co., although this particular version appeared under the imprint of Hanover House (a division of Doubleday and Co.). Only one edition was recorded, in 1956, which was retailed then at $2.95. Measuring 12½ by 10 in., it contained 43 pages of political maps of the world, and 48 maps of the United States, all in eight colors, and a small number of three-dimensional land-tone maps. Heavily emphasizing the United States, it provided three separate indexes: (1) for the United States only, with population statistics; (2) an alphabetical list of the principal cities of the world, again with population figures; and (3) an index gazetteer of all major political units, giving area, population, capital city, and related material.

HAMMOND NEW SUPREME WORLD ATLAS

A quite useful smaller desk atlas in its time, it was first published by Doubleday in 1952, revised and enlarged in 1962, and recopyrighted again in 1965. It was then replaced by the new series of Hammond atlases in 1966. Much of the material was identical to that in several other Hammond atlases. Measuring 12½ by 9½ in., its 192 pages contained 107 pages of colored political maps of the world, and six black and white relief maps. The index-gazetteer contained 12,500 entries, with population statistics for inhabited places. By 1965 it was retailing at $4.50. A separate map was published for each of the 50 states of the United States. It was considered of sufficient merit to be listed in the *Standard Catalog for Public Libraries*, 4th ed. 1958, 1965 supplement, and the *Senior High School Library Catalog*, 9th ed. 1967.

HAMMOND NEW WORLD ATLAS

Little is known about this rather nebulous title. It appears to have been first published in 1947, under the imprint of the Garden City Publishing Co. (a division of Doubleday and Co.). It was then comprised of 344 pages, and retailed at $16.75, which was very expensive for that time. A detailed evaluation of this atlas was published in the *Subscription Books Bulletin*, April 1948. In addition to the usual collection of political maps, it contained a section on the races of mankind, an illustrated gazetteer of the world, and an illustrated gazetteer of the United States. In 1962 a work with exactly the same title, and also manufactured by Hammond, was published under the imprint of the Educational Book Club, Des Moines. This was only slightly shorter, with 328 pages, and appears to be the same work, although it was identical in content to the older pre-1966 edition of the *Standard World Atlas* by Hammond. The earlier 1947 edition was listed in Winchell's *Guide to Reference Books*.

HAMMOND PACESETTER WORLD ATLAS

Although first published as recently as 1967, this small softcover world atlas is now out of print. Although measuring 12½ by 9½ in., it contained only 38 pages, 32 of which were full-color political maps of the world, with inset maps of the larger metropolitan areas. Derived directly from the New Perspective series of Hammond atlases, it was designed for general use, such as following news events, and retailed at only $1.00. A two-page index of some 300 entries was the only locating aid. The world gazetteer gave area, population, and capital city of each major political division, and indicated membership of the United Nations. A four-page color supplement on "Our Family of Planets," and end papers with statistical and comparative world data were additional materials.

HAMMOND UNIVERSAL WORLD ATLAS

Another of the pre-1966 series of Hammond atlases which have been superseded by the new series started in 1966. First published under this title in 1942, it continued in existence until about 1962, at which time it was retailing at $4.95. Measuring 12½ by 9½ in., it contained 192 pages, numbered consecutively (rare in Hammond atlases), of which 107 pages were allocated to the provision of political maps in full color. Also included were gazetteers, resource-relief maps of the continents, world social and economic tables, airline distances and other miscellanea. A 20,000-entry index concluded the work. It was, in actual fact, a shortened version of the *Hammond Library Atlas*, being an exact facsimile of the first 192 pages of that atlas. It was listed as an atlas of merit in the 1963 supplement to the eighth edition (1962) of the *Standard Catalog for High School Libraries*.

HAMMOND WORLD WIDE ATLAS

Probably published once only, in 1963, this small atlas, although produced by Hammond, was published under the imprint of the New York Herald Tribune, and was designed to accompany news events. Costing only $.39, it measured 10 by 7 in., and was comprised of 32 pages, most of which were small-scale political maps of the world. In 1971 it was still being sold in the United Kingdom at 20p sterling.

HEYDEN NEW WORLD ATLAS

A quite large and quite expensive world atlas which has only recently gone out of print. Measuring 11½ by 9 in., it was comprised of 270 pages, of which 140 were colored maps of the world in a relatively large scale, accompanied by a 100-page index of some 50,000 entries. Published by Heyden and Son Limited, Alderton Crescent, London NW4 3XX, it retailed in Britain at £4.50 and in the United States, through the British Book Center, New York, at $17.50. As far as can be ascertained, it was published once only, in 1970, but was reported in 1972 as going out of print "shortly."

INTERNATIONAL STANDARD ATLAS OF THE WORLD

Produced by Consolidated Book Publishers, Chicago, a division of Book Production Industries, Inc. (now Books and Processing, Inc.), and distributed also at one time by Grosset and Dunlap, although the atlas per se was manufactured by Rand McNally and Co. It was first published in 1947 as the *International Standard Encyclopedic World Atlas and Gazetteer* and was probably sold only as a subscription item with an encyclopedia package deal. The last recorded edition was that of 1961, when it retailed in a trade edition at $13.95. Measuring 14 by 10 in., it was quite a large work of 448 pages, but many of these included a great deal of geographic and miscellaneous encyclopedic information. Anthony M. Kronbauer was listed as the chief editor, with Dianne Fox and Karl Hudgins as associate editors.

KIPLINGER-HAMMOND FORECAST ATLAS OF THE WORLD

Published jointly by the Kiplinger Washington Editors, Inc., and C. S. Hammond and Co., and apparently published once only in 1961–1962. The text material was supplied by Kiplinger, and the maps by Hammond, drawn from their series of pre–1966 atlases. Only pages K1–K160 were original, and were specially compiled by the Kiplinger Washington Editors. These consisted of forecasts of business and economic conditions, population growth, employment, new products, consumer spending, etc., with projections for 10–15 years ahead from the 1961–1962 date of compilation. This special section also contained a useful listing of bibliographies and sources of further information but, as no index was provided, this useful information was not easily located. At the time of its first publication it was retailing at the rather high cost of $16.95.

LIFE PICTORIAL ATLAS OF THE WORLD

A specially compiled and much discussed atlas, published by Time-Life Books Inc., and the result of collaboration between the editors of *Life* and the cartographic staff of Rand McNally and Co., who created the maps. Published once only, in 1961, it retailed for several years in two editions, a regular Sturdite binding at $30.00 and a deluxe boxed edition at $35.00. Measuring 14 by 10½ in., it was a bulky work of 600 pages, but only 200 of these were allocated to maps. A further 150 pages contained an interesting collection of color photographs selected from the files of *Life*, and a series of three-dimensional diagrams. The basic series of reference maps consisted of the special terrain and political maps originally developed by the editors of *World Book Encyclopedia* and the cartographic staff of Rand McNally, and were of good quality, although somewhat limited in communications detail. A comprehensive index of some 75,000 entries included prominent geographic features and provided population statistics for inhabited places. It was quite an impressive atlas, handsomely produced and printed, and one which contained a great deal of interesting, illustrative material of excellent quality, and a great deal of explanatory text. The maps, in themselves, were of good quality, but the text and illustrative material, interesting though it was, was not considered to be of any real reference value and, as such, the work was overpriced in comparison to similarly sized world atlases. A detailed evaluation of the work was published in the *Subscription Books Bulletin* for April 1, 1962, and some additional information can be gained from Lock's *Modern Maps and Atlases*, and in particular from Katz's *Introduction to Reference Work*, where it is described as "in attempting to be everything, the *Life Pictorial Atlas* fails to be much of anything."

MERRILL SCHOOL ATLAS

Published in 1964 by the Charles E. Merrill Publishing Co., but actually British in origin, with the maps made by Thomas Nelson and Sons. Designed for use in school, it retailed at $4.50. Edited by Paul Francis Griffin, with Janus J. Klawe as cartographer, it consisted of 100 pages measuring 11 by 8½ in. Eighty-five of the pages contained good, well-colored physical-political maps, and a good variety of special-purpose thematic and distribution maps. Coverage was reasonably uniform, but at a small scale over broad regions, although the section dealing with the United States was larger than usual in an atlas of this size and purpose.

NEW HAMMOND-DELL WORLD ATLAS

A very small pocket-sized world atlas, measuring only 7 by 5 in., with very small-scale maps. First published in 1964, it was made by C. S. Hammond and Co., but published under the imprint of Bantam Books. For $.75, it was comprised of 272 pages of small, colored political maps and some useful statistical information. It appears to be identical in content to the *New Hammond World Atlas*, which is also published under the imprint of Bantam Books, but which is priced slightly higher at $.85.

NEW HOME REFERENCE WORLD ATLAS AND GAZETTEER

A small two-volume atlas, measuring only 9½ by 7 in., which was originally published in 1960 by the now defunct World Scope Publishing Co. as part of their "World Scope Family Library." When the company ceased operations in 1963, distribution of the atlas was continued by the Gache Publishing Co., New York, which reissued the atlas in 1964 in a deluxe edition. No editions have been recorded since and the work, which was made to specifications by the then C. S. Hammond and Co. (now Hammond, Inc.), is believed to be out of print, although it may possibly have been adapted to become, more recently, the *Illustrated Encyclopedia Library World Atlas* (q.v.). It bears some resemblance also to the old *Hammond Family World Atlas* (q.v.). No retail price was ever quoted and it was undoubtedly sold on a subscription basis at a considerable cost. It was a poor atlas by any standards.

NEWNES INTERNATIONAL WORLD ATLAS

First published in Britain in 1967 and subtitled the *New Perspective Edition*, this is apparently identical to the *Hammond International World Atlas* (New Perspective Edition), which was published in the United States in 1966 at $5.95 and which is still in existence. This British edition is published by George Newnes (a member of the Hamlyn Group), London. Priced at £2.25, it measured 12½ by 9½ in. and contained exactly 200 pages. Earlier, in 1964 there was also a *Newnes World Atlas*, which was in the same general format and also priced at £2.25, but which contained 260 pages, and was probably a quite different work.

NEW RAND McNALLY POCKET WORLD ATLAS

A very small pocket atlas measuring only 7 by 5 in., this was published by Pocket Books, Inc., in 1961, although actually made by Rand McNally and Co. Comprised of 295 pages, it retailed at $.75 in a paperback edition. The maps, though good, were very small, with barely readable type and a crowded appearance. It has since been replaced by the original publisher's own *Rand McNally Pocket World Atlas*, although this is twice the price at $1.50.

OUR WORLD IN SPACE ATLAS

A relatively small atlas of only 50 pages, measuring 12 by 9 in. in a paperback edition. It was made and published by Hammond in one edition, and in another edition under the imprint of W. B. Saunders and Co., Philadelphia, at $2.75. An abbreviated atlas with a few small-scale maps, it also included material on the exploration of space occurring at that time, and a good explanation of map projections and the understanding of maps.

PHILIP'S STANDARD REFERENCE ATLAS

Once a quite useful large reference atlas, but no edition has been recorded since 1956. It was then edited by the late George Goodall and Harold Fullard, the present editorial director of all Philips' atlases. It was published in London by George Philip and Son Limited, who retailed it in two editions at £5.77½p. and £7.87½p., which was expensive in those days. It was comprised of 120 pages of mainly political maps and included many large-scale insets. A good index of some 100,000 entries was contained in the 103-page index section. Further information can be found in the first edition of Walford's *Guide to Reference Material* and Lock's *Modern Maps and Atlases.*

PHILIP'S WHITEHALL ATLAS

Unlike several other atlases emanating from the well-known British cartographic publishers, George Philip and Son Limited, this title originated in Amsterdam, where it was first published by the equally well-known Dutch firm, Elsevier, as the *Atlas van de Westerse Beschaving.* It was adapted for use in English-speaking countries by Harold Fullard, the cartographic editor, and was first published in London by a subsidiary of George Philip and Son Limited (Stanford), in 1960, with a second revised edition in 1962, the last recorded. It retailed at that time in Britain at £3.15 and in the United States, through Barnes and Noble, at $12.50. The main series of reference maps (pages 1–121) is political in character. These maps were supplemented by 14 pages of physical maps and 15 pages of economic and resource thematic maps. An index of some 50,000 entries, with geographic coordinates, readily located all but the most obscure places. Particularly good were the special-topic maps covering such topics as geology, earthquakes and volcano zones, climate, ethnography, vegetation, and soil and land uses. It usefully supplemented larger atlases, although its format, 11 by 8¾ in., was on the small side. Fuller information will be found in Walford's *Guide to Reference Material*, 2nd ed. 1966–1970.

PRENTICE-HALL WORLD ATLAS

Yet another instance of a European-made atlas being adapted for use in the English-speaking countries, the *Prentice-Hall World Atlas* was first published in 1958, with a second edition, revised and enlarged, in 1968. Although printed under the imprint of Prentice-Hall Inc., Englewood Cliffs, N.J., it was originally prepared in the Geographisches Institut und Verlag, Vienna, under the direction of Dr. Hugo Eckelt, and was reedited to conform with American map reference requirements by Joseph Earl Williams, Professor of Geography at Stanford University. Designed primarily for school use, it retailed in a text edition at $6.95 and in a trade edition for home use at $9.25. Measuring 12½ by 8½ in., it was comprised of 145 pages divided into three main sections. The first portrayed the systematic geography of the world in physical-political maps, the second contained world economic maps, and the third a further series of physical maps of the continents. The index was rather limited, with only 17,724 entries, but they did give the exact degrees of latitude and longitude. The atlas was favorably reviewed in the *Library Journal*, April 15, 1962, and the *Wilson Library Bulletin*, January 1962. Further information about it will be found in Lock's

Modern Maps and Atlases, Walford's *Guide to Reference Material*, and *Whyte's Atlas Guide*.

RAND McNALLY ATLAS FOR THE HOME

A small but attractive atlas measuring 10½ by 7½ in., and comprised of 252 pages. Produced by Rand McNally but actually published under the imprint of Doubleday and Co., who retailed it at $5.95. It was first published in 1965, but no further editions have been recorded and it was reported out of print by 1968. In addition to the 136 pages of political-physical maps, there were several relief maps, historical maps of the Ancient World, Classical Greece, Europe and the Crusader States, Asia at the death of Kublai Khan, Europe in 1810 and 1815, and the partition of Africa. Supplementing the full-color maps were 85 pages of black and white maps and photographs. There was also a great deal of statistical information and a large section devoted to places of interest in the United States. More for reading and browsing than for straight reference work, it was a popular atlas for home use. In several respects it was very similar to the *Rand McNally Reader's World Atlas*, which was only a little larger.

RAND McNALLY ATLAS OF NATIONS

A very small paperback atlas consisting of only 32 pages, nearly all of which consisted of colored political maps. Measuring 13½ by 10 in., the maps were on a reasonably large scale. It was apparently published once only, in 1964, when it retailed at $.69. A work which was very similar to it, but with an additional 18 pages, was the *Rand McNally Atlas of the World*, published in 1961.

RAND McNALLY COLLEGIATE WORLD ATLAS

Once one of the major atlases in the Rand McNally range, the *Collegiate World Atlas* was first published in 1951, and revised editions appeared in 1955, 1961, 1964, and 1967, when it was subtitled the *unabridged desk edition*, and retailed in three editions, at $7.95, $9.95 (thumb indexed), and at $12.50 in a so-called deluxe edition. Measuring 10½ by 7½ in., it contained 416 pages of maps, text, and photos, including 178 pages of political-physical maps drawn directly from the well-known Rand McNally *Cosmo* series. Also included were several historical and special-purpose maps. Although in a relatively small desk format, most of the maps were spread over double pages for an actual map size of 15 by 10½ in., providing detail in reasonable depth. Fairly well indexed, with some 25,000 entries, it contained a great deal of up-to-date factual information about the world generally and the United States particularly. In the last-recorded edition in 1967, a new section on the solar system, global views of the Earth from space, and new text and illustrations on places of interest were included. A very odd inclusion was a special section on colleges in the United States. A useful quick-reference atlas in its day, it was accorded a detailed evaluation in the eighth edition of Winchell's *Guide to Reference Books,* and in Lock's

Modern Maps and Atlases, where it was described as probably the most useful of the Rand McNally series.

RAND McNALLY CONTEMPORARY WORLD ATLAS

A relatively small atlas of 96 folio pages, published by Rand McNally in 1957 and priced then at $2.95, although, according to the publishers, it was not a regular trade item. Designed specially for the International Geophysical Year (1957–1958), it contained relief maps of the continents, full-color political maps of the world and the United States, various miscellaneous information and, of greater interest, a special map of Antarctica, showing the sites of areas to which various nations sent teams of explorers and scientists for the IGY. A useful and inexpensive small atlas, it was listed in the 1958–1960 supplement to the *Standard Catalog for High School Libraries*.

RAND McNALLY CONTINENTAL WORLD ATLAS

A general-purpose home and desk atlas, appropriately subtitled *Quick Reference Edition*, this was a small atlas particularly suitable for use where detailed information was not a prime requirement. First published by Rand McNally in 1965, a new copyright was issued in 1967, but no further printings have been recorded. Measuring 10½ by 6¾ in., it contained 324 pages, and retailed at $5.95 in a red Holliston Sturdite binding. There were 178 pages of maps, including the basic series of *Cosmo* political-physical maps, and a number of thematic and special-purpose maps, such as a reproduction of the "Vinland" map. It was reasonably well indexed with some 25,000 entries, which included population statistics. For its intended purpose it was quite a useful and inexpensive work, especially for information on the United States.

RAND McNALLY CURRENT EVENTS ATLAS or RAND McNALLY $1.00 WORLD ATLAS

First published in 1967, this very limited atlas of only 32 pages replaced the older *Rand McNally Atlas of Nations* (q.v.). Compiled and published by Rand McNally, the *Current Events Atlas* was published in a paperback edition at $.69 and in a laminated board cover (as the *Rand McNally $1.00 World Atlas*) at $1.00. Designed for very general home and desk use, it measured 12¼ by 9¼ in. and was comprised of only 32 pages, 28 of which were allocated to the *Cosmo* series of political-physical maps. A further two pages were given over to tabular and statistical material, but no index was provided. Maps were arranged by broad areas rather than by individual countries.

RAND McNALLY GEOGRAPHICAL WORLD ATLAS

This was a handsomely produced atlas with the map material drawn directly from the excellent *Goode's World Atlas*, also published by Rand McNally. In a handy 11 by 9 in. format, it was well arranged and well balanced on a uniform scale. First published in 1964, its 96 pages contained 75 pages of maps, mostly of a political nature, but with a good rendering of physical features. With a small but accurate index of some 5,000 entries, this was an excellent atlas for general informational purposes, and particularly as an introduction to the use of more comprehensive atlases.

RAND McNALLY ILLUSTRATED ATLAS OF TODAY'S WORLD

More than just an atlas, this was an illustrated geography and gazetteer of the world, containing a great deal of geographic and encyclopedic information. It was designed primarily for sale through supermarkets and similar retail outlets on the "book-a-week" plan and would have had some appeal for home users. In 12 slim volumes, it contained a total of 1,079 pages and a profusion of colored maps and colored illustrations. It was apparently published once only in 1962 and by 1965 was reported out of stock by the publishers, and unlikely to be reprinted.

RAND McNALLY INTERNATIONAL WORLD ATLAS

Not to be confused with the same publisher's *The International Atlas* published in 1969, although the earlier title, in its day, was for several years one of Rand McNally's major atlases, retailing at $11.95. It has since then been replaced by the *Premier World Atlas* (q.v.) in this size and price range. The *International World Atlas* was first published in 1961, but was actually an abridgment of the *Cosmopolitan* and *Collegiate* world atlases of that period, omitting only the special-purpose, distribution, and resource maps; the section on world history; part of the section on world geographic facts, figures, and information; and all of the section illustrating places of interest in the United States. Measuring 14 by 11¼ in., it was comprised of 312 pages (in three sections of 16, 172, and 124 pages). Of these, 136 contained detailed *Cosmo* political-physical maps of every country, every U.S. state, and every Canadian province, in addition to a series of special thematic maps. The index, containing 80,000 entries (with 1960 population statistics) was identical to that in the larger *Cosmopolitan* atlas. It has been incorrectly described as a successor to the *Rand McNally Cosmopolitan World Atlas*, but it was in fact simply a scaled-down version of the parent atlas, pages 1-125 and 1a-124a being identical. No further editions are known to have been published since 1961. A good medium-sized atlas in its day, it was listed in the 1965 edition of the *Junior High School Library Catalog*, the 1963 supplement to the *Standard Catalog for High School Libraries*, and the 1959-1963 edition of the *Standard Catalog for Public Libraries*. A brief mention of it is made in Lock's *Modern Maps and Atlases*, and in an earlier edition of Winchell's *Guide to Reference Books*.

RAND McNALLY PICTORIAL WORLD ATLAS

One of the more recent, smaller, abridged atlases published by Rand McNally, this atlas was first published in 1967, when it retailed at $4.95, although some of the maps were revised from the same publisher's *Geographical World Atlas*, also out of print. Designed for students from the upper elementary grades through high school, its 160 pages contained 76 pages of maps (35 of which were double page spreads). Most of the maps were political in character, with some relief shown by hill shading, but also provided were nine special-purpose and thematic maps, 56 pages of text and photographs, 15 pages of preliminary and tabular material, and a 15-page index of some 5,000 entries. The section of maps on the United States is especially good, drawn as they were from the excellent physical-political maps contained in the highly rated *Goode's World Atlas*. The thematic maps showed surface and air transportation routes, world languages, races and religions, vegetation, climate, and landforms. It provided a good overview of the world and its political structure in clear, easy-to-read maps, interesting color photos, and informative text. A good review of the atlas was printed in the *Saturday Review*, dated May 18, 1968, and it is still listed in the second edition (1970) of the *Junior High School Library Catalog*.

RAND McNALLY POPULAR WORLD ATLAS

First published by Rand McNally in 1958 and apparently never reprinted, this was a quarto-sized, 180-page atlas of colored political maps, nicely produced, in a handy format for desk use. An index of approximately 8,000 entries readily located all principal towns and cities. Retailing in two editions, a hardcover at $3.50 and a limp-cover for $1.95, it was replaced in 1964 by the similar but superior *Worldmaster Atlas* (q.v.).

RAND McNALLY READER'S WORLD ATLAS

Yet another in the older series of Rand McNally atlases, this was first published in 1951 and was a direct abridgment of the same company's *Collegiate World Atlas*, with this smaller version containing 116 fewer pages. Retailing at $4.95, new copyrights were registered in 1955 and in 1962, which was the last recorded edition. Measuring 10 by 7½ in., it was a conveniently sized desk atlas of 300 pages, 178 of which contained the *Cosmo* series of political-physical maps and a series of thematic maps. Pages 1–180 (including the 178 pages of maps) were identical to the corresponding pages in the *Collegiate*, as was also the 25,000-entry index.

RAND McNALLY STANDARD WORLD ATLAS

First published in 1951 by Rand McNally, this was a good, compact atlas of 400 pages, retailing at $6.95 in its last-known edition in 1956. It included such unusual features as world political information, keys to railroad abbreviations, selected world and United States information, and a glossary of geographic terms, in addition to a wide range of political, physical, and special-purpose maps. It was listed in the fourth edition (1958) of the *Standard Catalog for Public Libraries* and again, although still at the same price, in the fifth edition (1968), where the atlas is described as being frequently revised with slightly variant titles. There is nothing in the current Rand McNally catalog, however, to suggest that the work is still in existence.

RAND McNALLY WORLD PORTRAIT ATLAS

Published once only in 1963, and based on the manufacturer's well-established *Cosmo* series of maps, this fairly large (14 by 10½ in.), 93-page general atlas contained 80 pages of colored political maps and an informative variety of relief and special-purpose thematic maps, the scope of which extended to races, religions, languages, governments, populations, climates, and flora and fauna. Pleasing in its overall appearance, the maps were reasonably large and clear, although somewhat advanced. The text, however, was of a relatively elementary nature. A considerable disadvantage was the lack of an index.

REPLOGLE COMPREHENSIVE WORLD ATLAS

Although published under the imprint of Replogle Globes, Chicago, this atlas was made by Hammond, Inc., and was identical in every respect to the *Hammond Complete World Atlas* (q.v.). A small desk-type atlas, it measured only 9 by 6 in. and contained 400 pages. Retail price of this edition is not known, but as the *Complete* world atlas it was sold at $5.95. The only recorded edition was that of 1959.

SEARS FAMILY WORLD ATLAS

The only recorded edition of this atlas was in 1961, when it was being sold through Sears Roebuck at an undisclosed price. Comprised of 324 pages, it was apparently identical in content to an older edition of the *Hammond World Atlas: Classics Edition*, but not including two of the more unimportant sections.

SIMMONS-BOARDMAN WORLD ATLAS

Long out of print, this was a small atlas for schools which retailed in a trade edition at $2.95. Although published under the imprint of Simmons-Boardman, it is believed to have been made by the famous British cartographic publishing firm of John Bartholomew and Son Limited, the makers of the universally acclaimed *Times Atlas of the World.*

VAN NOSTRAND ATLAS OF THE WORLD

Apparently published once only in 1961 by the scientific publishing firm of Van Nostrand, Princeton, N.J. (now Van Nostrand-Reinhold). Very small in format, measuring only 8 by 5 in., it contained 240 pages and retailed at that time at $1.25. It is listed as still in print, however, in the 1971 edition of *British Books in Print* at 37½p. It contained short encyclopedic-type articles on the countries of the world; tables of geographic facts and statistics; a useful section on map projections; and 60 pages of small-scale maps. The index was better, but still limited with only 13,000 entries. The publisher's claim that this was a comprehensive source of geographic and statistical information was somewhat overstating its limited merits.

WORLD AND SPACE AGE ATLAS

A special subscription item, published under the imprint of the Educational Book Club, Des Moines, and available only to members at a special membership price, this was in fact made for the publishers by Rand McNally and Co. First noted under this title in 1964, it bore a marked resemblance to the *Rand McNally World Atlas—Family Edition* of the same period. It measured 12½ by 9½ in., and was comprised of 323 pages. Although reported out of print in 1965, it or a successor may still be offered through the Educational Book Club.

APPENDIX C

SCALE CONVERSION CHART

All maps are drawn to a given scale. This is or should be represented on the map by a representative fraction which indicates the number of times the map page should be multiplied to correspond with the area which it covers. Thus, a map of the state of New York which is drawn at a scale of 1:300,000 means simply that the map is exactly one three hundred thousandth the size of the state of New York. The trained cartographer can easily visualize this, but it can be quite a mystery still to the lay user. Some atlas publishers, and this is a commendable practice, also provide the equivalent miles-per-inch scale along with the numerical fraction, far more easily comprehended by those unversed in cartographic techniques. For ease of use when such equivalents are not provided, the following list of map scales and their equivalent in miles per inch (approximately in some instances) is provided.

REPRESENTATIVE FRACTION	MILES PER INCH (APPROX.)	REPRESENTATIVE FRACTION	MILES PER INCH (APPROX.)
1:50,000	¾	1:550,000	8¾
1:63,360	1 (exactly)	1:570,240	9
1:75,000	1¼	1:575,000	9¼
1:100,000	1½	1:600,000	9½
1:125,000	1¾	1:625,000	9¾
1:126,720	2 (exactly)	1:633,600	10
1:150,000	2½	1:650,000	10½
1:175,000	2¾	1:675,000	10¾
1:190,080	3	1:700,000	11¼
1:200,000	3¼	1:725,000	11½
1:225,000	3½	1:750,000	12
1:250,000	3¾	1:775,000	12½
1:253,440	4	1:800,000	12¾
1:275,000	4½	1:825,000	13¼
1:300,000	4¾	1:850,000	13½
1:316,800	5	1:875,000	14
1:325,000	5¼	1:900,000	14½
1:350,000	5½	1:925,000	14¾
1:375,000	5¾	1:950,000	15¼
1:380,160	6	1:975,000	15½
1:400,000	6½	1:1,000,000 (1:1M)	16
1:425,000	6¾	1:1,100,000	17½
1:450,000	7¼	1:1,200,000	19¼
1:475,000	7½	1:1,300,000	20¾
1:500,000	7¾	1:1,400,000	22½
1:506,880	8	1:1,500,000 (1:1½M)	24
1:525,000	8½	1:1,600,000	25½

REPRESENTATIVE FRACTION	MILES PER INCH (APPROX.)	REPRESENTATIVE FRACTION	MILES PER INCH (APPROX.)
1:1,700,000	27¼	1:19,000,000	300
1:1,800,000	28¾	1:19,500,000	308
1:1,900,000	30½	1:20,000,000	316
1:2,000,000 (1:2M)	32	1:21,000,000	332
1:2,250,000	36	1:22,000,000	348
1:2,500,000	39	1:23,000,000	364
1:2,750,000	44	1:24,000,000	380
1:3,000,000 (1:3M)	47	1:25,000,000	396
1:3,250,000	51	1:26,000,000	412
1:3,500,000	55	1:27,000,000	428
1:3,750,000	59	1:28,000,000	444
1:4,000,000 (1:4M)	63	1:29,000,000	460
1:4,250,000	67	1:30,000,000	476
1:4,500,000	71	1:31,000,000	492
1:4,750,000	75	1:32,000,000	508
1:5,000,000 (1:5M)	79	1:33,000,000	524
1:5,500,000	88	1:34,000,000	540
1:6,000,000	95	1:35,000,000	555
1:6,500,000	103	1:36,000,000	569
1:7,000,000	111	1:37,000,000	584
1:7,500,000	119	1:38,000,000	600
1:8,000,000	127	1:39,000,000	617
1:8,500,000	135	1:40,000,000	632
1:9,000,000	143	1:41,000,000	648
1:9,500,000	150	1:42,000,000	664
1:10,000,000 (1:10M)	158	1:43,000,000	680
1:10,500,000	166	1:44,000,000	696
1:11,000,000	174	1:45,000,000	712
1:11,500,000	182	1:46,000,000	727
1:12,000,000	190	1:47,000,000	742
1:12,500,000	198	1:48,000,000	760
1:13,000,000	206	1:49,000,000	786
1:13,500,000	214	1:50,000,000	802
1:14,000,000	222	1:55,000,000	882
1:14,500,000	230	1:60,000,000	962
1:15,000,000	237	1:65,000,000	1,042
1:15,500,000	245	1:70,000,000	1,122
1:16,000,000	253	1:75,000,000	1,200
1:16,500,000	261	1:80,000,000	1,280
1:17,000,000	268	1:85,000,000	1,360
1:17,500,000	276	1:90,000,000	1,440
1:18,000,000	284	1:95,000,000	1,520
1:18,500,000	292	1:100,000,000	1,600

APPENDIX D

DIRECTORY OF ATLAS PUBLISHERS

Aldine Atherton, Inc.
529 South Wabash Ave.
Chicago, Ill. 60605

American Map Co.
3 West 61st St.
New York, N.Y. 10023

Bantam Books, Inc.
666 Fifth Ave.
New York, N.Y. 10019

John Bartholomew and Sons Ltd.
The Geographical Institute
12 Duncan St.
Edinburgh 9, Scotland

Blond Educational Ltd.
56 Doughty St.
London WC1N 2LS, England

Bobley Publishing Corp.
Glen Cove
Long Island, N.Y. 11542

British Book Center
996 Lexington Ave.
New York, N.Y. 10021

Cassell and Co. Ltd.
35 Red Lion Square
London WC1R 4SJ, England

P. F. Collier, Inc.
866 Third Ave.
New York, N.Y. 10022

William Collins Sons and Co. Ltd.
14 St. James's Place
London SW1, England

F. E. Compton Co.
425 North Michigan Ave.
Chicago, Ill. 60611

Consolidated Book Publishers
1727 South Indiana Ave.
Chicago, Ill. 60616

George F. Cram Co., Inc.
301 La Salle St. South
Indianapolis, Ind. 46206

Daily Telegraph
135 Fleet St.
London EC4 TA, England

Denoyer-Geppert Co.
5235 Ravenswood Ave.
Chicago, Ill. 60640

Doubleday and Co., Inc.
277 Park Ave.
New York, N.Y. 10017

Elsevier Publishing Co.
P. O. Box 211
Amsterdam, Netherlands

Encyclopaedia Britannica, Inc.
425 North Michigan Ave.
Chicago, Ill. 60611

Faber and Faber Ltd.
3 Queen Square
London WC1N 3AU, England

Field Enterprises Educational Corp.
510 Merchandise Mart Plaza
Chicago, Ill. 60654

Garden City Publishing Co.
Garden City, N.Y. 11530

Geographia Ltd.
178–202 Great Portland St.
London W1TA, England

Ginn and Co.
Statler Building
Back Bay P. O. 191
Boston, Mass. 02117

Golden Press
850 Third Ave.
New York, N.Y. 10022

Grossett and Dunlap
51 Madison Ave.
New York, N.Y. 10010

The Hamlyn Publishing Group Ltd.
Hamlyn House
42 The Centre
Feltham, Middlesex, England

Hammond, Inc.
Maplewood, N.J. 07040

Heyden and Son Ltd.
Alderton Crescent
London NW4 3XX, England

Holt, Rinehart, and Winston of
   Canada, Ltd.
55 Horner Ave.
Toronto 530, Ontario

Houghton Mifflin Co.
2 Park St.
Boston, Mass. 02107

International Learning Systems
   Corp., Ltd.
72–90 Worship St.
London EC2, England

Johnston and Bacon
18 High St., Wimbledon
London SW19, England

Kiplinger Washington Editors, Inc.
1729 H St., N.W.
Washington, D.C. 20006

Longman Group Ltd.
Longman House, Burnt Mill
Harlow, Essex, England

Macdonald and Co. Ltd.
49 Poland St.
London W1, England

McGraw-Hill Book Co.
1221 Ave. of the Americas
New York, N.Y. 10020

Charles E. Merrill Publishing Co.
1300 Alum Creek Drive
Columbus, Ohio 43216

The National Geographic Society
17th and M Sts.
Washington, D.C. 20036

Thomas Nelson and Sons Ltd.
36 Park St.
London W1, England

New York Times Co. (Book Division)
229 West 43rd St.
New York, N.Y. 10036

George Newnes
Tower House, Southampton St.
London WC2, England

A. J. Nystrom and Co.
3333 Elston Ave.
Chicago, Ill. 60618

Oliver and Boyd Ltd.
Tweeddale Court
14 High St.
Edinburgh EH1 1YL, Scotland

Oxford University Press, Inc.
417 Fifth Ave.
New York, N.Y. 10016

Oxford University Press, Inc.
70 Wynford Drive
Don Mills, Toronto, Ontario

Oxford University Press, Inc.
Ely House
37 Dover St.
London W1X 4AH, England

Pergamon Press, Inc.
Maxwell House, Fairview Park
Elmsford, N.Y. 10523

Pergamon Press Ltd.
Headington Hill Hall
Oxford OX3 OBW, England

George Philip and Son Ltd.
12–14 Long Acre
London WC2E 9LP, England

Prentice-Hall, Inc.
Englewood Cliffs, N.J. 07632

Purnell Library Service
850 Seventh Ave.
New York, N.Y. 10019

Quadrangle Books
12 East Delaware Place
Chicago, Ill. 60611

Reader's Digest Association
380 Madison Ave.
New York, N.Y. 10017

Reader's Digest Association Ltd.
7–10 Old Bailey
London, England

Replogle Globes
1901 North Narragansett Ave.
Chicago, Ill. 60639

Rand McNally and Co.
P. O. Box 7600
Chicago, Ill. 60680

W. H. Sadlier, Inc.
11 Park Place
New York, N.Y. 10007

W. B. Saunders and Co.
218 West Washington Square
Philadelphia, Pa. 19105

Scholastic Book Services
50 West 44th St.
New York, N.Y. 10036

School and Library Publishing Co.
110 North Sacramento St.
Sycamore, Ill. 60178

Simmons-Boardman
350 Broadway
New York, N.Y. 10013

Telborg Book Corporation
P. O. Box 545
Sag Harbor, N.Y. 11963

Time-Life Books
Time and Life Bldg.
Rockefeller Center
New York, N.Y. 10020

Times Newspapers Limited
Printing House Square
London EC4P 4DE, England

Van Nostrand Co. (now Van Nostrand-Reinhold Co.)
450 West 33rd St.
New York, N.Y. 10001

Franklin Watts, Inc.
575 Lexington Ave.
New York, N.Y. 10022

Western Publishing Co., Inc.
850 Third Ave.
New York, N.Y. 10022

TITLE INDEX